LYN REESE received her M.A. from Stanford University. An experienced resource teacher and researcher, she has also been Director of the Math-Science Sex Desegregation Project for the Novato Unified School District and has worked with the Women's Studies Program, Berkeley Unified School District. She is a coauthor of SOURCES OF STRENGTH: WOMEN AND CULTURE, and IN SEARCH OF OUR PAST: UNITS IN WOMEN'S HISTORY.

JEAN WILKINSON received her M.A. from the University of California, Berkeley. She brings over three decades of teaching experience to this anthology, including initiating and teaching a course in women's history at the junior high school level. She has worked with the Women's Studies Program, Berkeley Unified School District, and is a coauthor of IN SEARCH OF OUR PAST.

PHYLLIS SHEON KOPPELMAN received her M.A. from the University of California, Berkeley. She has been a teacher in both elementary and secondary school, has developed and taught women's studies courses in high school, and has worked with the Women's Studies Program, Berkeley Unified School District. A published poet, Ms. Koppelman is also the author of THE HOUSE THAT JILL AND JACK BUILT.

I'M ON MY
WAY RUNNING

Women Speak on
Coming of Age

LYN REESE
JEAN WILKINSON
PHYLLIS SHEON KOPPELMAN

 A DISCUS BOOK/PUBLISHED BY AVON BOOKS

I'M ON MY WAY RUNNING: *Women Speak on Coming of Age* is an original publication of Avon Books. This work has never before appeared in book form.

Front cover art: The Metropolitan Museum of Art, Robert Lehman Collection, 1975. Detail from Renoir's *Two Young Girls at the Piano.*

AVON BOOKS
A division of
The Hearst Corporation
1790 Broadway
New York, New York 10019

Copyright © 1983 by Phyllis Sheon Koppelman,
Lyn Reese, and Jean Wilkinson
Published by arrangement with the authors
Library of Congress Catalog Card Number: 82-90544
ISBN: 0-380-83022-1

First Discus Printing, April, 1983

DISCUS TRADEMARK REG. U.S. PAT. OFF. AND IN
OTHER COUNTRIES, MARCA REGISTRADA, HECHO EN
U.S.A.

Printed in the U.S.A

OP 10 9 8 7 6 5 4 3 2

I am on my way running,
I am on my way running,
Looking toward me is the edge of the world,
I am trying to reach it,
The edge of the world does not look far away,
To that I am on my way running.

> Traditional song for a young
> girl's puberty ceremony
> Translated by Frances Densmore
> Papago tribe

Many people have read the manuscript and made extensive comments or used selections in their classrooms. We especially wish to thank the following people:

Betty Bacon
Sonya Blackman
Mary Butler
Barbara Christian
Sarah Crome
Lucille Day
Meg Errington
Elizabeth Fishel
Susan Groves
Barbara Knox
Rita Maran
Betty McAfee

Karen Benveniste Nelson
Jayne Nelson
Moya O'Donnell
Paul Panish
Lisa Rubin
Kent Rush
Lin Salamo
Nancy Schimmel
Sarah Sheon
Florence Sloat
Pat Sumi
Linda Williams

To our children and grandchildren

Contents

CHAPTER TWO: *The Spring of Pleasure: Sexuality* 41

CHAPTER FOUR: *Sing Daughter Sing: Mothers and Daughters* 193

CHAPTER FIVE: *The Great Adventure: Taking Risks* 269

Acknowledgments　　351

Introduction

The passage from childhood to womanhood is a major turning point in a young girl's life. This is the time when she becomes acutely aware of the changes taking place in her body and the imminent pressure to assume the responsibilities of a woman in her culture. While birth, marriage, and motherhood are seen as important events in our society, adolescence has not been recognized in the same way. Too often it is viewed solely as a time of anxiety and crisis; the fact that it can also be a time of joy and vitality is overlooked.

To honor a girl's coming-of-age and to celebrate it as the springtime of life, we have collected prose and poetry from around the world. The writings are not meant to represent an entire culture or era, but to show the ethnic and historical universality of certain themes. They reveal concerns and emotions common to all women. There is a mix of drama, prose, and poetry, including first-person narratives, letters, diaries, and short stories. The voices are those of young women speaking of their immediate experience and of older women reflecting upon their own coming-of-age. Some writers, like Anne Frank, are famous; many, however, are ordinary women whose lives represent a diversity of experience.

Our title, *I'm On My Way Running*, comes from a Papago Indian puberty song. The Papago, from southwestern United States, recognize coming-of-age as a time of momentous change in a girl's life, and traditionally they have marked it with ceremonies and songs. The rituals guided a girl through the process of giving up her childhood in order to take on the greater responsibilities of an adult. While not all pre-industrial societies observed special rites, in many, puberty was the time when a girl was expected to assume her adult role and begin preparations for marriage. Her coming-of-age was brief, and she often married only a few months after her first body changes. Taught from childhood the skills she would need as an adult, she came of age in a world relatively unchanged from that of her mother.

In western, industrial societies, the transition from childhood to adulthood is longer and less formalized. It lasts from puberty to about eighteen or nineteen years of age. During these years of prolonged childhood there is no specific event that lets a girl know exactly when she becomes an adult. Sometime within this period she is expected to become independent of her parents and to begin functioning as an adult.

While girls today often have more options, they may find society's attitudes toward the changing roles of women contradictory and confusing. It is not surprising that adolescence has become a turbulent time in a girl's life. And this is why, in choosing the selections to be included in our book, we wanted to find dramatic personal accounts of coming-of-age that depict both the anxiety and the excitement of exploring new possibilities. We want our female students to discover that their concerns and experiences have been shared by girls everywhere, throughout the ages.

The five chapters in the book are organized around themes that emerged from the pieces themselves—body changes, stirrings of sexuality, preoccupation with appearance, mother-daughter relationships, and the yearning for adventure. The collection begins with the chapter entitled ''The Circle Dance,'' which focuses on first menstruation, the clearest sign of every girl's introduction into womanhood. The early selections in this chapter are from the puberty rituals of North American and African tribes in which the entire community celebrates a girl's first flow of blood. Other writings reveal the range of attitudes in cultures in which a girl's first menstruation has become mainly a private concern. The second chapter, ''The Spring of Pleasure,'' recognizes the impact of a girl's sexuality on her life during these years of physical change. The pieces in this chapter portray the first ventures into romance as well as the often contradictory lessons girls are taught regarding their sexuality.

Concern with appearance is the theme of the third

chapter, "The Wish." Some of the pieces depict the pleasures of growth and change, while others reveal the difficulties of striving to attain an ideal standard of beauty. The central theme of the fourth chapter, "Sing Daughter Sing," is the special bond between mother and daughter during the daughter's coming-of-age. Mutual as well as conflicting expectations are explored, as mothers through the centuries and in countries around the world try to guide their daughters into womanhood. In the final chapter, "The Great Adventure," heroines break away from traditional female roles and demonstrate their desire for adventure, their resistance to double standards, and their courage.

In this age each of us must mark the events important to his or her life in whatever way seems appropriate. We offer this collection as a way to rekindle memories, stimulate new insights, and open communication between mother and daughter, teacher and student, between sisters, and between friends. In celebrating this joyful time of life, *I'm On My Way Running* will link women, young and old, to the one experience we have all shared—the timeless rite of coming-of-age.

CHAPTER ONE

The Circle Dance: Onset of Puberty

Holding hands and singing, they formed a moving circle around Nomtaimet, dancing the old circle dance which had been the coming of age dance for girls since the beginning of time.

Myth
Wintu tribe, California

A girl's first menstruation is the clearest sign that she has begun her rite of passage into womanhood. The writings in this chapter reveal the profoundly different ways in which various societies regard menarche, and show how a young girl is affected by these attitudes. The first section, "And Then They Danced Me," includes writings from cultures that recognize a girl's first flow of blood as a milestone in her life to be celebrated by the entire community. These selections from North American and West African tribes describe a time in the tribe's past when every girl, at first menstruation, was guided through secret ceremonies by older women. This was the time to welcome the girl into the sisterhood and to instruct her carefully in the ways of sex, childbirth, household duties, and the arts of healing. After the girl's initiation, the community honored her with feasting, songs, and dances. Thus, a girl's biological maturation signaled an important change in her life, and was usually eagerly awaited.

In societies that considered the subject of menstruation taboo—whether because of its connection to sex and the female body or for other psychological or spiritual reasons—a girl's changes at puberty were usually kept hidden. In the second section, "There Once Was a Rite," women in Victorian England and in the twentieth century speak about their anxieties and lack of preparation arising from the fact that menstruation was considered a distasteful subject. When taboos taken out of their cultural context surround the onset of menstruation, it may be difficult for the family to prepare their daughter adequately and give her the support she needs.

In the concluding section, "Celebration," writings show that today special efforts are being made by family and friends to mark a girl's rite of passage. Some efforts are more formalized than others, as illustrated by "Coming of Age the Apache Way" and "On the Occasion of a Bat Mitzvah." Other acknowledgments are more private, as in "When you phoned home from California to tell me it had started," a poem written by a mother as a way to embrace her daughter at first menstruation.

When a girl feels honored, like Beryl in "Almost As If You Were Grown-up," she carries "something special inside," and can greet her coming of age with pride.

And Then They Danced Me

"Maiden Songs"

Maria Chona, as told to Ruth Underhill
Papago tribe, Arizona
Late 19th century

In the 1930s, anthropologist Ruth Underhill collected from Maria Chona the following description of her coming-of-age celebration, which is similar in many respects to others in North American Indian tribes. Most Native American cultures attributed magical powers to a woman's monthly flow because of its relation to her sexuality and reproductive function. At first menstruation a girl was considered to be in close touch with the powers of the spirits and was therefore watched particularly carefully, since improper behavior could seriously affect her character and bring harm to the group as a whole. It was thought that a mere glance from her could harm a man or unleash disasters such as floods or epidemics. Because of her power, she was subject to prescribed taboos and was placed in seclusion for a defined period of time to fast or to eat special foods. This was her time to be tested and to communicate with the spirits surrounding her. At the end of the seclusion there was a ceremony to present the transformed girl to her community, with dancing always an important part of this joyful celebration.

When I was nearly as tall as my mother, that thing happened to me which happens to all our women though I do not know if it does to the whites; I never saw any signs. It is called menses.

Girls are very dangerous at that time. If they touch a man's bow, or even look at it, that bow will not shoot any more. If they drink out of a man's bowl, it will make him sick. If they touch the man himself, he might fall down dead. My mother had told us this long ago and we knew what had happened in our village. . . .

Our mothers watch us, and so mine knew when it came to me. We always had the Little House ready, over behind our own house. It was made of some branches stuck in the ground and tied together at the top, with greasewood thrown over them to make it shady. There was no rain then, for it was winter, but it was cold in that little house. The door was just big enough to crawl through, like our house door, and there was room for you to lie down inside, but not to stand up. My mother made me a new bowl and drinking cup out of clay, and put them in that house. When my mother cooked food at the big house, she would come over and pour some in my bowl, but no meat and nothing with salt in it. My father sharpened a little stick for me to scratch my hair with, because if I touched it, it would fall out. I was so afraid to lose my nice long hair that I kept that stick in my mouth all the time. Even when I was asleep, I had it there.

It is a hard time for us girls, such as the men have when they are being purified. Only they give us more to eat, because we are women. And they do not let us sit and wait for dreams. That is because we are women, too. Women must work.

They chose my father's cousin to take care of me. She was the most industrious woman we had, always running with the carrying basket. That old woman would come for me in the dark when morning-stands-up. "Come," she said. "Let's go for water over across the mountain. Let's go for firewood."

So we would run, far, far across the flat land and up the mountain and bring the water back before daylight. I would leave it outside my father's house and not go in. Then that old woman would talk to me.

"Work hard. If you do not work hard now, you will be lazy all your life. Then no one will want to marry you. You will have to take some good-for-nothing man for a husband. But if you are industrious, we shall find you a good old man."

That is what we call our husbands: old man. But this woman did it out of modesty, too, so that I should not have young men in my mind. "When you have an old man," she said, "you will grind the corn for him and you will always have water there for him to drink. Never let him go without water. Never let him go without food. He will go to the house of someone else to eat and you will be disgraced."

I listened to her. Do you say that some girls might think of other things and not listen? But I wanted to be a good woman! And I have been. Ask anyone in our village if they ever saw me with idle hands. Or legs, either, when I was younger.

All the girls came around the Little House while that woman talked. They did not come near, because that would not be safe, and she would call to them, "Go away." But they sat and listened and when she was tired of talking, they laughed and sang with me. And we played a game with little stones and a ball. We pick up the stones in different ways with one hand while we catch the ball in the other. Oh, we have good times at the Little House, especially when that first month is over. But other women who were dangerous did not come; that would be too much. . . . My mother came in the dark of the morning with the water in a big new jar. The women had to run all day to get the water ready for me. I tried to get away, but my mother caught me and made me kneel down. Then she dipped a gourd in the jar and poured that cold water down over my forehead.

> Hail!
> I shall pour this over you.
> You will be one who endures the cold.
> You will think nothing of it.

It is true, I have never felt cold. . . . Then I could go back to our house, only still I had to use the stick for four days and I could not eat salt. And then they danced me. All that month they danced me, until the moon got back to the place where it had been at first. It is a big time when a girl comes of age; a happy time. All the people in the village knew that I had been to the Little House for the first time, so they come to our house and the singer for the maidens came first of all.

That singer was the Chief's Leg, the man I told you about. He knew all the songs, the ones that Elder Brother first sang when he used to go over the country, dancing all the maidens. That Leg was the man who danced every maiden in our village when she came of age. His wife danced opposite him. She was the one who was to get the hair that my mother had cut off. He had another wife, too, but not such a good dancer.

"Come out," said my father on that first night. "Now you must dance or the Leg will drag you out. He's mean."

I did not want to dance; I was sleepy and I had run so far. Always when I had heard the others singing those maiden songs, from far away, I had been wild to go. But now it was my turn and all I wanted to do was sleep. But Luis, the Leg, came into the house and took me by the arm. He always danced next to the maiden, with his arm over her shoulders and the rattle in his other hand. He and I were at one end of a long line of people and his wife at the end of a line opposite. There was first a boy and then a girl, all down the line, with their arms over each other's shoulder and the blankets held along at the back. I told you the boys always liked that dance.

Those were the songs they sang, with the rattle going in the night. We had no fire; we kept warm dancing. After every four songs Luis stopped, because his voice was hoarse. Then he let me go, and we girls went and sat together while the men smoked. How dark and cold it was then, with only one ember to light their cigarettes! . . . We stopped dancing in the dark of the morning and then my mother said, "Come and get firewood. Do you want to grow up a lazy woman?" So then I went out in the dark to pick up the dead branches and bring them back before I slept. It seemed I slept only an hour before they were saying, "Get up! Get water. Get wood. Grind the corn. If you sleep at this time you will be sleepy all your life."

Oh, I got thin in that time! We girls are like strips of yucca fiber after our coming of age is over. Always running, and mostly gruel and ash bread to eat, with no salt. And dancing every night from the time the sun sets until morning-stands-up. I used to go to sleep on Luis' arm and he pinched my nose to wake me.

Every night they came, the people who were not too sleepy from the night before. And always the young people came. Even Luis did not know songs enough for all that month and other men sang, too. It is a nice thing for a man to know maidens' songs. Every man likes to dance next to the maiden and to hold her on his arm. But Luis was an old man and his wife danced opposite. The wife always does.

At last the moon had come around again and they gave me a bath. It was over. I looked like half of myself. All my clothes were gone. All our dried corn and beans were eaten up. But I was grown up.

Poor little maiden!
In the evening you will clasp hands.
In the evening I arrive and hasten hither,
Hither I hasten and sing.
Songs follow one another in order.

The shining mocking bird
At evening could not sleep.
When the moon was in mid-sky
He ran to the maiden's dance.
At early dawn
High did he raise his song.

Traditional coming-of-age song
Papago tribe, Arizona

"Dance Mad"

Myth, as told to Theodora Kroeber
Wintu tribe, California

Once long ago a whole people went dance mad, dancing while the moons and seasons came and went, dancing all around the world. . . .

The occasion was a feast celebrating the initiation into full womanhood of Nomtaimet, the daughter of one of the village families. Nomtaimet's father and mother had neglected nothing of the customary observances and training belonging to this period in a girl's life. They knew that it is an important and indeed a dangerous time for her, and for others, too, if she does not learn to keep its prohibitions, to follow its complex ritual, and to behave with decorum.

When the long moons of learning and fasting and praying came to an end, her mother and her grandmother were more than satisfied with her behavior and her knowledge. They and her father, and her mother's and her father's brothers and sisters, made a feast in her honor, sending runners to invite the people from villages all up and down Swift Creek to come to feast and dance and sing with them. . . .

Nomtaimet emerged from her long seclusion pale, much changed, and very beautiful. The old as well as the young exclaimed at her beauty, while the old recalled that a girl is never so beautiful as at this time when she is newly returned to the world from her long initiation. She was carefully dressed for her great day. Her new buckskin skirt was elaborately ornamented with shells and beads. In her ears were enormous polished shell earrings and about her neck many strings of beads which half covered her breasts. Her hair, washed and shining, hung in two thick braids tied with mink. She carried rattles made from deer's hooves and a slender

11

willow staff given her by the young married women to
symbolize her coming of age.

The women who were not taken up with cooking or
caring for children gathered around Nomtaimet, admiring her. First one man and then another joined them until someone said, "We should dance—we are enough to
make a circle dance." Holding hands and singing, they
formed a moving circle around Nomtaimet, dancing the
old circle dance which had been the coming of age dance
for girls since the beginning of time. . . .

It was a great feast. For ten days and ten nights they
ate and sang and danced. At last the feasting was over.
The tenth night of singing and dancing came and went.
But the pale dawn of the eleventh day found all those
people still dancing. They kept right on dancing, all of
them. They went dance mad.

In a long line, singing as they went, they danced up
the trail leading out of the village to the east. Soon the
last house was left behind and they were dancing among
the hills they knew, the hills of home, up and over them
until they could no longer see their houses. Through bri-
ars and chaparral, over rocks and rough ground, up and
down hill, they danced on and on. . . . They were no
longer interested in hunting and gathering; they wished
only to dance and dance, and then to fish and cook and
eat more salmon. So now they danced close beside one
stream or another, wherever the salmon were best,
learning the names of the many different kinds of
salmon, their size and appearance and their favorite rivers. Dancing and fishing, they went farther and farther
downstream as the season drew on and the salmon
swam shorter distances upstream to spawn. . . .

The season of storms and cold, like the other seasons,
came and went, blown away by the big winds of the
awakening earth. And now the dancers turned inland,
away from the sea, dancing and half blown towards
home. They reached Swift Creek as the new clover was
making a green mat over the earth, just as it had done
when Nomtaimet first came out of her seclusion at the
beginning of the dance journey.

The dancers were home, and the dance madness was
no longer on them. It had lasted through all the moons

and seasons and had carried them all around the world. As long as she lived, Nomtaimet told her children, as her children's children tell even today, of the feast her father made for her, and of the dance madness that came after it.

Thou art a girl no more,
Thou art a girl no more;
The chief, the chief,
The chief, the chief,
  Honors thee
In the dance, in the dance,
In the long and double line
Of the dance,
  Dance, dance
  Dance, dance.

Traditional coming-of-age song
Wintu tribe, California

"The Fattening"

Anonymous, as told to Iris Andreski
Ibibio tribe, Nigeria
Early 20th century

In eastern Nigeria, to be sleek and fat was a sign of beauty and wealth. Therefore among many peoples a girl's initiation to womanhood included a custom called "the fattening" in which she went into seclusion and ate as many high-calorie foods as possible. Since seclusion meant that a girl was withdrawn from productive labor, the length of time of the fattening ritual depended upon the family's financial circumstances. Sometimes a mother-in-law or a prospective husband bore the cost of the ritual. When a young woman emerged from seclusion, a public celebration was held in her honor. Admired and treated as though she were a tribal chief, at that moment the young woman felt the power of her new beauty and status.

The most important thing that happened to me was the time I was put into the fattening room. Here I was made to eat and grow very fat. I was hidden in the house for two years without seeing my father and my proposed husband. It was the custom that before a girl was out from the fattening room, both the father and the proposed husband must pay a fat sum of money before they came to see her. On the last day, many native plays were staged and even the compound was crowded. I was asked to come and dance. Before I came out, I was well dressed with costly beads and with costly apparels. A handsome and strong young man was also dressed to carry me on his shoulders so that I might not be equal to those walking on the ground. It was an interesting thing as the man came out carrying me on his shoulders with my two legs across his neck, and he started dancing to the beating of the different drums. After dancing in the compound, the man still carried me to the market square

15

and danced the play round the market before going back to my father's compound. This was the day that I first counted my manillas up to an astonishing number of bunches. After all the functions had finished, I was again taken to my husband's house and before this time I was fully mature to be a woman. That was indeed a happy and the most interesting time in my life.

We play and dance for you
That you may remain with us,
That you may bear ten children,
That no bad thing may come upon you.
Let the elephant give you her womb
That you may bear ten children.
Long live the people of your village,
Long live your relatives and elders
Who celebrate this festival for you.

Puberty chant
Translated by R.S. Rattray
Ashanti tribe, Ghana

"They Danced and Did a Mock Aja Salute"

Buchi Emecheta
Ibo tribe, Nigeria, 1940s

The Bride Price describes the conflict between Aku-nna, whose aspirations have changed with the impact of western ideas, and her family, who maintain tribal customs. Aku-nna wishes to marry Chike, but he is forbidden her because he is the son of a former slave and her family is considering a betrothal to a man she dislikes. An Ibo custom is to begin marriage preparations at a girl's first menstruation, and knowing this Aku-nna has kept secret her first two flows. In spite of her dilemma, she has joined the other fifteen-year-old girls preparing for their special coming-of-age event, the aja *dance.*

The girls talked and dreamed about their outing dance. They worked and saved hard to buy their *jigida*, the red and black beads which they would wear above their bikini-like pants. Apart from these their tops would be bare, displaying the blue-coloured tattoes that went round their backs, then under their young breasts, and met at the heart. Their feet would also be bare, but small bells were to be tied round their ankles, so that when in the dance they jumped, or curtsied, or crawled in modesty, the bells would jingle in sympathy. It was to be the great moment of their lives and they knew it. In their old age, with clay pipes in their toothless mouths, they would turn to their grandchildren and say, "When we were young and our breasts were tight as tied ropes, we did the *aja* dance. It was the best dance in the whole land, and we did it."

In the afternoon of one Olie market day, about twelve of them decided to go for firewood. They had been to the stream that morning and had washed their clothes and bathed. Aku-nna had been claying the floor of her mother's hut, and welcomed the idea of a change. If she would have preferred to sit round and gossip with her friends, about their dance or about their men friends, she did not say, for she would rather follow the others than be left alone with her thoughts. She took her big cutlass and the ropes, and went with Obiajulu and Ogugua to fetch the rest. They felt safe and strong when there were many of them. They could tease old men on their way through their farms, they could sing, no enemy could terrify them; not that they had any enemies, but in Ibuza a young girl must be prepared for anything to happen. Some youth who had no money to pay for a bride might sneak out of the bush to cut a curl from a girl's head so that she would belong to him for life and never be able to return to her parents; because he had given her the everlasting haircut, he would be able to treat her as he liked, and no other man would ever touch her. It was to safeguard themselves against this that many girls cropped their hair very close; those who wanted long hair wore a headscarf most of the time. But when they were twelve strong, a man or boy who dared to attempt such a thing knew that he would be so mobbed that if he lived to go home to his mother she would not even recognise him.

When they reached the abandoned farm where they were to find the firewood, they scattered into the bush, agreeing to give each other a cat-call to indicate that they were ready to leave. With each piece of wood you had to pull, then shake it, and if it still did not come free when you pulled again you used your cutlass. Aku-nna had been trying hard for a long time with one piece of icheku wood, which looked deceptively dry on the surface but just would not give way. At this rate she would have to leave it and look for some other wood, or she would never be ready by the time the others started calling for them to go home.

With all her power, she gave another final push, and the wood broke and crashed to the ground, sending her crashing along in its wake. At the same moment she felt the needle-like pain in the back of her waist. This would be the third time, and she knew now what to expect. She still had not told her mother, but this time it would be

impossible to hide, for the others were bound to know.
All this passed through her mind as she lay there on the
dry twigs, looking at her hand that bled and knowing
that she was losing equally between her legs. Her
thoughts were in a turmoil of indecision about what to
do next. Her closeness with Chike had crystallised and
was now so established that she could not make a decision without wanting to know his opinion. But he was
not here on this farm. He might be miles away from
Ibuza for all she knew, judging by the distances he could
cover with the new autocycle he had just bought. She
came to the conclusion that there was no alternative
open to her but to let her mother know. She sensed what
this would mean; she would no longer be regarded as a
child who knew nothing, but as a young woman on the
verge of parenthood. It was not that she shrank from becoming an adult, but she was afraid of what her people
might force the future to hold for her. If only things
could go on being as they were now, with Chike seeing
her every market day at Asaba, and the two of them sitting by the river bank in the quiet place they had discovered for themselves, doing nothing, just talking and
talking, and he teaching her all the latest songs from a
record song book he had ordered from Lagos. Once or
twice he gave her a gentle caress but was careful to stop
himself from going too far, for to him she was something
apart, something pure that he did not want to pollute.
She was beginning to know this and to respond to his
unspoken wishes. She was beginning to realise too that
though Chike might talk endlessly in the classroom, because it was his job, when he was by himself or with her
he preferred silence. Sometimes they listened to the music of the river and the noises made by the leaves of the
nearby bushes, but in the main they simply listened to
their hearts. . . .

It was this very evening that he was due to come, and
now this was happening to Aku-nna on this farm before
she had had time to see him to prepare for their next
move. Her friends would certainly have to know about
her condition when it came to crossing the stream on the
way home. Would she have to be carried over it, or
would the god or whoever owned the river be reason-

able enough to forgive her crossing it even though she was unclean? After all, she had not known it was going to happen like this, on this farm, in this scorching heat. It was best to ask her friends' advice rather than to make a mistake and be condemned as an outcast leper for the rest of her life.

They must have missed her, for she could just make out a buzz of voices. Her cousin's sounded tearful, even at this distance, and quite agitated. They were still too far to hear her clearly if she shouted to them, so Aku-nna tried to get up and found that it was very painful, for she had actually knocked her back on the dry, hard earth, covered with sharp-edged weeds. Soon she recognised in the crackling noises of parched leaves the steps of someone approaching. The person obviously had a premonition that she was nearing where Aku-nna lay trapped in pain, for she called softly, as if in the presence of something holy.

"Aku. . . ."

"I'm here," she replied in a hoarse whisper. She was not badly hurt; what she lacked was the energy to confront the world of her people. The shock of being forced so suddenly to face up to this merged with the shock of her injury to such an extent that she could no longer tell which pain belonged to which, or which was worse. She thanked God now that the girl who had found her was her cousin Ogugua. She beckoned to her to sit down, and told her all.

Aku-nna was resigned to the fact that things would be different after that day, but she had not bargained for her cousin's instant reaction. Ogugua hugged her tightly with joy, laughing and telling her in her high voice that at last she was fully a woman. Before Aku-nna could stop her, she jumped up and screamed for the others to come—to bear witness that they had gone out to fetch firewood with a girl but that they would be returning home with a grown woman!

There were more crackling sounds around them and the others emerged, coal-black maidens with lightness in their step, like young goddesses let loose by a kind god. They were curious to find out what had kept Aku-nna down there among the twigs and dry cassava leaves;

they were curious to know why it was that Ogugua was so excited. They came, their necks craned like those of young giraffes looking for fruits in the tops of trees, and Ogugua told them the good news. For to her it was that; they had been wondering and worrying if Aku-nna would ever become a woman, and now she was happy, and she was sure her family would also be happy. The girls' laughter was like the sound of clear bells on a Christmas morning. They danced and did a mock *aja* salute, then, no longer in a hurry to go home, they all sat down and asked her with gentle but dignified concern how she felt and whether she could walk home. She said she could, for had not their spirit affected her own? They stayed there for a while, chatting away and talking lightly and unconcernedly, like all young girls in the spring of their lives, planning their marriages, looking forward to their coming *aja* dance, laughing and giggling out of sheer happiness.

It was decided that the god of the river would forgive Aku-nna this time, for how was a girl to know when and where she would become a woman? It was agreed, however, that she should walk through the shallow waters as quickly as possible, and not linger to bathe; and the very next day Ma Blackie would have to come and sacrifice a day-old chick to the stream. The whole episode sounded so elaborate that Aku-nna felt mean, knowing that she had hidden her two previous periods. Because her bunch of dry wood was so light the others promised to compensate by giving her mother some of theirs.

The sun was going down and they knew that by then most farmers would already have gone home. The less people they met the better. However on their trek back to the stream, chattering and once or twice bursting into song as they went, they came across no one. Obiajulu asked Aku-nna if she had any idea whom she was going to marry, and Aku-nna said that she did not know.

"But many men have asked for her," Ogugua confirmed, "and my father told them she was still a child. Not after today, though. . . ."

There Once Was
A Rite

First Menstruation

I had been waiting
waiting for what felt like lifetimes.
When the first girls stayed out of the ocean
a few days a month, wore shorts instead of a swimsuit
I watched them enviously.
I even stayed out once in a while, pretending.

At last, finding blood on my panties
I carried them to my mother, hoping
unsure, afraid—Mom, is this it?

She gave me Kotex and belt
showed me how to wear it.
Dot Lutz was there, smiling, saying when her Bonnie
got her period, she told her
when you have questions, come to me, ask me.
You can ask a mother anything.

I felt so strange when she said that.
Mom didn't say anything.

The three of us
standing in the bedroom
me, the woman-child, standing with the older women
and the feeling

23

there once was a feeling
that should be here,
there once was a rite, a communion.

I said, yes, I'll ask my mother
but we all, except maybe Dot,
knew it wasn't true.

Ellen Bass
California, 1970s

"Millicent's Condition"

Mary Loomis letter
Washington, D.C., 1893

Nineteenth-century medical thought emphasized abstinence from intellectual pursuits during menstruation since cerebral excitement was believed to cause an imbalance due to an over-supply of blood flowing toward the brain instead of downward. This Victorian grandmother advises her daughter to stop her work editing the poetry of Emily Dickinson in order to focus on the impending crisis of her granddaughter's first menstruation.

I must write you what has been troubling me for months—concerning Millicent's condition—When she was here—we all saw a great change in her spirits—She was so very sad—Of course we did not let her know we observed it—but tried to make her very happy—and cheerful. She is now thirteen years old and is not yet a woman! It is in our family to develop early in that respect—I was only eleven years old—and I remember as if it were yesterday—how fondly my Father walked the floor with me in his arms—when just before these periods—my head ached so that my eyes were bloodshot and I could not see the light. He would say in a voice of tender sympathy—"poor poor little child" and I did suffer! I was alone when Millicent's photograph came but when I first looked at the exceeding sorrow of her sensitive mouth—I cried most bitterly—for I read her feelings from that face and longed to take her away on a long trip—full of pleasure not where she would have excitement but to California or somewhere where she could feel the healing of Nature! Where she could forget herself! Oh you can never do a wiser thing than to *leave all your work*—and take that dear precious child away to Bermuda—or anywhere else—to give her a great change—and you will *always* be glad you did it! Do not delay! You need not let her see your motive—only say you both—need a change! For *months* before this change came *to you,* your Father, G'ma and I watched you daily. Especially just before the time the menses came—we planned walks in the Catholic grounds—Rock creek —Etc. Your father became your *companion*—talked in the liveliest manner—and kept your spirits even and happy —we saw to it that your studies did not depress you. You were so tenderly watched all through this dangerous crisis—that it came to you very naturally—and without any special sickness—Our great sorrow over our dear Eliza's death [Mary Loomis's sister]—made us very careful. She died at eighteen—and *slipped* away from us making no sign! She *loved* her books and studies so that she kept her distress away from us—until *too* late! She was never regular—and became more and more *irregular* until her death. When at last Dr. Wesselhoeft came he told us it was too late—and she lived only a few months— there was not *then* vitality enough to work on—

"Daphne Darling"

Daphne du Maurier
England, 1920s

One day, when I was twelve and a half, M called me into her morning room at Cannon Hall and told me to shut the door. She was sitting in her armchair, knitting.

"Daphne darling," she said gravely, "I want to speak to you."

"Yes?"

Already my heart thumped. It must be serious, when she had that voice. What had I done wrong? Had I broken something, or been rude to someone?

"Now that you are twelve," she went on, "you mustn't be surprised if something not very nice happens to you in a few weeks. You have had backaches recently, and this may be a sign."

"I haven't a backache now," I said quickly, momentarily relieved.

"No, perhaps not. But what I have to tell you is this. All girls, once they have turned twelve, begin to bleed for a few days every month. It can't be stopped. It's just something that happens. And it goes on happening, every month, until they are middle-aged, and then it stops."

I stared at her, dazed. To bleed, all my life, until I was old? Was it the same as the illness the poor little Tsarevitch Alexis had before he was murdered in a cellar with his parents and sisters?

She must have seen the expression on my face, for she continued. "It's all right, it's not an illness, and it's not even like a cut. It doesn't hurt. But you can have tummy-ache or backache. I myself have had headaches at the time."

I remembered now. M often had headaches, and was generally rather cross when she had them.

"Does Angela bleed?" I asked, still unbelieving.

"Yes, but I have told her never to talk to you about it, and you must promise me not to tell Jeanne."

Perhaps this was the reason Angela so often did not want to join in our games. She must have been bleeding at the time. Poor Angela . . .

"Now, run along, darling, and don't say anything about this to anyone. You will soon know when it happens to you."

I was dismissed. I left the morning room, closing the door behind me. Perhaps it would never happen. Perhaps I would yet turn into a boy. Lucky things, they only bled when they cut themselves or if they were like the Tsarevitch.

I soon forgot the whole business. In at one ear and out of the other, they used to say. And there was plenty to do, now that Miss Waddell, nicknamed Tod, came every day to give us lessons, and jolly interesting lessons too, history being the best, encouraging Angela and me to take sides. Angela was Lancastrian, I was Yorkist, Angela was a Cavalier, I was a Roundhead, and for prep after tea when Tod went back to her lodgings, which she called "digs," we would have to "Write an account of the Execution of Charles I," which, with his portrait in the hall, was fun to do. Even if my bad writing and spelling kept her awake at night, which she told me it did, this never seemed to matter, and she wasn't cross. And after prep, depending upon what I was reading at the time, whether *Nicholas Nickleby* or *Mr. Midshipman Easy*, the nursery—now called the schoolroom—could be turned into Dotheboys Hall or the deck of a ship, with Jeanne, now eight, a willing victim.

One morning, when I had raced round the garden after breakfast, before lessons, and was feeling rather tired, the maid who shared our bedroom with us, Alice, came to me with a solemn face and called me up to the night nursery.

"It's come," she said gloomily.

"What's come?" I asked.

"What your mother told you about, some weeks ago," she answered, and picking up my pyjamas from my bed, where I had thrown them, she showed me a curious stain. "Come with me," she said, in a voice of doom, "and I will fit you up with something to wear. Tell no one what has happened."

Yet everyone knew. Tod looked at me with sympathy when I walked stiffly into the schoolroom. Angela stared. M wore her *"pas devant les enfants"* expression at lunch. Only Jeanne, my constant companion and buddy, was her usual self. But deception, never practised before on her, must begin. Why, I asked myself, why? And must this continue, forever and ever? And M had been right. My back ached. I also felt sick. Nothing would ever be the same again. I no longer wanted to run around the garden, to kick a football, to play cricket. It was like having a temperature, it was like having "flu." So what was I to do? I felt the corners of my mouth turn down.

"I don't feel very well," I faltered.

"I think you had better go to bed," said M firmly, "with a nice hot-water bottle."

If this was what growing up meant, I wanted no part of it. Kindness and understanding from adults was no consolation. Jeanne's look of surprise round the bedroom door was a hit below the belt.

"Are you starting a cold?" she asked.

"Yes," I lied.

So it began. The deceit, the subterfuges, of the grown-up world, destroying forevermore the age of innocence.

Celebration

"Almost As If You Were Grown-up"

Paule Marshall
Brooklyn, 1930s

They lay in the ample silence of rock and trees, staring into the enormous blue expanse of sky and at the rock shutting out the sun. They heard a sharp crack and shouts from the baseball field and Beryl said, her eyes averted, "Remember what we were talking about in the zoo when you got so mad?"

"You got mad, not me."

"Okay. Well anyway what I was saying is true. I can prove it. I bleed sometimes," she said quietly.

"What?"

"I bleed sometimes."

"So what. Everybody does."

"Not from a cut or anything but from below. Where the baby pops out. Ina does too. That's why she gets pains every once in a while. I'll tell you, if you want to hear . . ."

"Tell me." And beneath her eagerness there was dread.

Beryl raised up, gathering her dress neatly under her. Her eyes flitted nervously across Selina's intense face. Then, with her head bowed and a squeamish look she explained it all. "That's why I'm getting these things," she concluded, jabbing her small breasts. "It happens to all girls."

Selina stared very quietly at her and, for that moment, she was quiet inside, her whole self suspended in disbelief. Then an inexplicable revulsion gripped her and her face screwed with disgust. "It's never gonna happen to me," she said proudly.

"If it doesn't happen by the time you're twenty you die."

"Well then I'll just die."

"It'll happen. It hurts sometimes and it makes you miserable in the summer and you can't jump rope when you have it but it gives you a nice figure after a time."

Her eyes searched Beryl's face. "How come?"

"I dunno. It just does. Look what's happening to Ina."

"Well if it ever happens to me nobody'll ever know. They'll see me change and think it's magic."

"Besides, it makes you feel important."

"How could anyone walking around dripping blood feel important?"

"It's funny but you do. Almost as if you were grown-up. It's like . . . oh, it's hard to explain to a kid . . ."

"Who's a kid?"

"You, because you haven't started yet."

"I'll never start!" And beneath her violent denial there was despair.

"Oh yes, you'll start." Beryl nodded wisely. "Wait, lemme try to explain how it makes you feel. The first time I was scared. Then I began to feel different. That's it. Even though nothing's changed and I still play kid games and go around with kids, even though my best friend's a kid"—she bowed to Selina—"I feel different. Like I'm carrying something secret and special inside . . . Oh, you can't really explain it to a kid . . ."

"Who's a kid? I was drinking rum today with Miss Suggie and I didn't bat an eye."

"Oh, Selina, nothing will help till you start."

Selina drew aside in a sullen despairing anger. A bit of the sun edged around the rock as though it had been hiding there listening and was coming now to upbraid

them. As she squinted through her tears at the sun's
bright fringe, the promise of the day was lost. The
mother had deceived her, saying that she was more of a
woman than Ina yet never telling her the one important
condition. She had deceived herself on the trolley and
on the rise in the park. She was not free but still trapped
within a hard flat body. She closed her eyes to hide the
tears and was safe momentarily from Beryl and Ina and
all the others joined against her in their cult of blood and
breasts.

After a time Beryl came and lay close to her. She
placed her arm comfortingly around her. "What was
that poem you wrote about the sky?" she asked. And always her voice calmed Selina. Her disappointment, her
anguish tapered slowly until finally her tears were gone
and she turned to Beryl and held her so that they were
like the lovers on the slope. "It wasn't about this kind of
sky," she said and began to recite, her thin voice striking
the rock and veering off into the sky, her eyes closed.
When she finished and opened her eyes Beryl's were
closed, her face serene in sleep. Whispering, Selina re-
cited then to the rock, to the dome of sky, to the light
wind, all the poems she had scribbled in class, that came
bright and vivid at night.

Beryl stirred in her sleep and pressed Selina closer.
Just then the sun rose above the rock. The strong light
seemed to smooth the grass, to set the earth steaming
richly. They were all joined it seemed: Beryl with the
blood bursting each month inside her, the sun, the
seared grass and earth—even she, though barren of
breasts, was part of the mosaic. With a cry she buried her
face between Beryl's small breasts, and suddenly her
happiness was like pain and a long leap into space.

Coming of Age the
Apache Way

Nita Quintero
Arizona, 1980

We call it Sunrise Dance. But it lasts through four days. It's the biggest ceremony of the White Mountain Apache —when a girl passes from childhood to womanhood. When my time came at fourteen, I didn't want to have one. I felt embarrassed. All my friends would be watching me. But my parents really wanted it. My mother— she never had one—explained it was important, "Then you will live strong to an old age." So I didn't say no.

My parents prepared for a year. They asked relatives, "Help us so our daughter's dance will be a good one." Older relatives—they know best—and a medicine man helped choose my sponsors, an older couple not related to us. I call them godparents. One morning my mother and father took an eagle feather to Godmother Gertrude Foster and placed it on her foot, saying, "Would you prepare a dance for my daughter?" Mrs. Foster picked up the feather. "Yes."

We held the dance at the fairgrounds at Whiteriver. There was room for everyone to camp. On Friday evening Godmother dressed me and pinned an eagle feather on my head. It will help me live until my hair turns gray. The abalone shell pendant on my forehead is the sign of Changing Woman, mother of all Apache people.

The most important thing Godmother does in the whole ceremony is to massage my body. She is giving me all her knowledge. That night for hours around the fire, I follow a crown dancer who impersonates a protective spirit.

Saturday is like an endurance test. Men begin the chants at dawn. They are really praying. Godmother tells me to dance while kneeling on a buckskin pad fac-

33

ing the sun—the creator. In that position, Apache
women grind corn. When the time comes for the running, I go fast around a sacred cane, so nobody evil will
ever catch up with me. My Aunt Dolly, in the pink dress,
runs behind me, followed by Godmother. Rain begins,
and my costume, which weighs ten pounds, gets heavier and heavier. But I don't fall. I don't even get
tired. . . .

On Sunday, Godfather paints me from the top of my
head to the bottom of my buckskin boots. I am blessed
and protected from all four sides. Four is the most important number to the Apache.

The paint is a mixture of pollen, cornmeal, and
ground-up stones of four colors. Later it brushes out of
my costume. I can wear the outfit again at any Apache
dance. I'm proud of it because a lot of people helped
make it. My Aunt Minda sewed the buckskin top; my
mother cut and rolled about 200 pieces of tin cans for the
jingles; they make me sound like wind in the trees when
I walk. Mom also beaded the necklace. Aunt Dolly made
my velvet camp dress. Godmother fixed a neck string
that holds a cloth to wipe my face and the traditional
reed drinking tube and the body scratcher. For the four
days I can't bathe, or touch my skin, or drink from a
glass.

Earlier the men raised a tepee frame. I dance through it
several times so I will always have a home. Here with my
mother behind me in the shadows, I go through for the
last time. The dancing is done.

On Monday morning there is more visiting and blessing. Aunt Dolly tells me I was really strong all the way; I
didn't cry like some girls do. Among the Apache, people
are most loyal to their mother's clan. So my mother's sister is a real important person in my life. Now Godmother is too. . . .

As for me, I'm finishing high school at Whiteriver.
Right now, I don't want to get married. I want to go
away to college and then come back home. I love sports,
especially basketball and volleyball. Just for fun I was
quarterback in a powder-puff football game during
homecoming.

I'm really glad I had a Sunrise Dance. It made me realize how much my parents care for me and want me to grow up right. They know my small age is past and treat me like a woman. If I have a daughter, I want her to have a Sunrise Dance too.

"On the Occasion of a Bat Mitzvah"

The Bat Mitzvah is an initiation rite for Jewish girls, usually occurring at age thirteen. This celebration in recent years has been created to offer girls the same communal affirmation that Jewish boys have traditionally enjoyed. Having prepared for many years, the girl is now ready to participate in this special ceremony in which she chants a section from the Bible in Hebrew, leads part of the service, and delivers a speech before family and friends. The ritual joyfully marks her entrance into a new phase of life as a Jewish woman. The following blessings are taken from an original Bat Mitzvah service.

Prayer of a Bat Mitzvah

O Lord!
Help me to understand that I am not alone
When I feel that I am so very small and the world
so very huge,
When I feel that the problems around me are very
great and I am very little,
When I hear of wars that I cannot stop, of
hungry people I cannot feed,
When I see people I cannot feed,
When I see people doing wrong and I cannot help
them;

When I hear of people hurting other people,
Help me to remember that you are with me—
Help me choose You, O Lord, again and again,
To choose the way of life You have taught people to
live,
That my world may be just a little better,
Just a little brighter,
Because I was in it.

Tamara Beth Jacobs

On the Occasion of a
Bat Mitzvah

Parents' Blessing

May you live to see your world fulfilled,
May your destiny be for worlds still to come,
And may you trust in generations past and yet to be.

May your heart be filled with intuition
and your words be filled with insight.
May songs of praise ever be upon your tongue
and your vision be on a straight path before you.
May your eyes shine with the light of holy words
and your face reflect the brightness of the heavens.
May your lips ever speak wisdom
and your fulfillment be in righteousness
even as you ever yearn to hear the words
of the Holy Ancient One of Old.

Berachot 17a, Talmud

O God, we have tendered
With hope this seed
of our youth.
We have watched
from springtime
the ripening and growth.
Now come the harvest days
And our child stands before You.
Bless this life with wisdom
To serve You with love.

A Jewish home opens its heart,
a child is born and its link
to the generations is proclaimed.

Today, that child, nearly grown,
is called to read from the Torah
and is welcomed into the congregation.

May this moment in time be blessed.

GINGER AND STEVEN:

We love you, Tammy, and we know that your existence is your possession, not ours.

With love and concern we come into your life for a little while to help you live and grow. It is our hope and our prayer that we will know when that time is done. For then, with grace and respect, we must return to you what has been ours only in trust—that which has always been rightfully yours: yourself.

Blessed are you, our child
in the joy of your existence.

Blessed are we
who have been enriched
by your life.

Rabbi Steven Jacobs
Ginger Jacobs
Los Angeles, December 27, 1980

When you phoned home from California to tell me it had started

A brilliant globule of blood
rolled out over the surface of the desert
up and down the Continental Divide
through the singing prairies
parting the Mississippi
leaping the Delaware Water Gap
until it spilled into this tall red kitchen
in Rocky Hill, New Jersey
where it skittered across the linoleum
and cracked into hundreds of little faceted jewels.

I will not diminish this day with labeling
I will not say foolishly
"now you are a woman"
I will never tell you
"don't talk to strangers"

because we are each of us strangers
one to another
mysterious in our bodies,
the connections between us
ascending like separate stone wells
from the same dark waters
under the earth

But tonight you delight me like a lover
so that my thigh muscles twitch
and the nipples of my breasts
rise and remember
your small mouth

until I am laughing to the marrow of my bones
and I want to shout
Bless you, my daughter, bless you, bless you;
I have created the world in thirteen years
and it is good.

Penelope Scambly Schott
New Jersey, 1979

CHAPTER TWO

The Spring of Pleasure: Sexuality

When maidens are young and in their spring,
    Of pleasure, of pleasure,
  Let 'em take their full swing,
    Full swing, full swing,
And love and dance, and play, and sing.

For Silvia, believe it, when youth is done,
There's naught but hum-drum, hum-drum,
    hum-drum,
There's naught but hum-drum, hum-drum,
    hum-drum.

Aphra Behn (1640–1689)
England

Young voices in this chapter speak to the discovery of heightened sexuality and the struggle to untangle the mysteries of love. In the first two sections, "First Stirrings" and "What Shall I Make Of This?," girls take pleasure in new sexual feelings and dream about being desirable. Brimming with curiosity, they seek information about their sensations by questioning their friends, by observing adults, and by making wild guesses about sex and the meaning of love.

In the third section, "I Will Lift My Gown," girls discover the power that comes with sexual attractiveness. Love poems from 15th-century B.C. Africa to 20th-century America show that young women learn the lessons of their culture at an early age—how to decorate their bodies, how to use coquetry and seduction, and how to initiate love relationships. At the same time, however, society places greater restrictions on girls than boys because of fear of pregnancy outside of marriage, and in the next section, "The Price of a Buffalo," we see the price paid by the girl who transgresses. The title comes from a Vietnamese folksong, the lament of a girl whose body is swelling up: "If I stay, the village will take away our buffalo as a fine." Writers represented in the final section, "I Shall Live All the Same!," show a desire for relationships that allow fulfillment in many areas. In 1918, Nelly Ptaschkina wrote in her diary, "If love comes I shall take it; and if not, I shall regret it, wildly regret it, but I shall live all the same." While dreaming about goals beyond love and marriage, young women like Nelly are confident of their abilities to make choices about their futures.

First Stirrings

"Sweet Secret"

Anne Frank
Amsterdam, 1944

During World War II, Anne's family and another family, the Van Daans, were forced into hiding in Amsterdam during the Nazi pogroms against the Jews. In their cramped living quarters Anne feels alienated from everyone, including seventeen-year-old Peter Van Daan, and confides only in her diary, which she calls "Kitty."

January 5, 1944

Dear Kitty,

Yesterday I read an article about blushing by Sis Heyster. This article might have been addressed to me personally. Although I don't blush very easily, the other things in it certainly all fit me. She writes roughly something like this—that a girl in the years of puberty becomes quiet within and begins to think about the wonders that are happening to her body.

I experience that, too, and that is why I get the feeling lately of being embarrassed about Margot, Mummy, and Daddy. Funnily enough, Margot, who is much more shy than I am, isn't at all embarrassed.

I think what is happening to me is so wonderful, and not only what can be seen on my body, but all that is taking place inside. I never discuss myself or any of these things with anybody; that is why I have to talk to myself about them.

Each time I have a period—and that has only been three times—I have the feeling that in spite of all the pain, unpleasantness, and nastiness, I have a sweet secret, and that is why, although it is nothing but a nuisance to me in a way, I always long for the time that I shall feel that secret within me again.

Sis Heyster also writes that girls of this age don't feel quite certain of themselves, and discover that they themselves are individuals with ideas, thoughts, and habits. After I came here, when I was just fourteen, I began to think about myself sooner than most girls, and to know that I am a "person." Sometimes, when I lie in bed at night, I have a terrible desire to feel my breasts and to listen to the quiet rhythmic beat of my heart.

I already had these kinds of feelings subconsciously before I came here, because I remember that once when I slept with a girl friend I had a strong desire to kiss her, and that I did do so. I could not help being terribly inquisitive over her body, for she had always kept it hidden from me. I asked her whether, as proof of our friendship, we could feel one another's breasts, but she refused. I go into ecstasies every time I see the naked figure of a woman, such as Venus, for example. It strikes me as so wonderful and exquisite that I have difficulty in stopping the tears rolling down my cheeks.

If only I had a girl friend!

Yours, Anne

January 6, 1944

Dear Kitty,

My longing to talk to someone became so intense that somehow or other I took it into my head to choose Peter.

Sometimes if I've been upstairs into Peter's room during the day, it always struck me as very snug, but because Peter is so retiring and would never turn anyone out who became a nuisance, I never dared stay long, because I was afraid he might think me a bore. I tried to think of an excuse to stay in his room and get him talking, without it being too noticeable, and my chance came yesterday. Peter has a mania for crossword puzzles at the moment and hardly does anything else. I helped him with them and we soon sat opposite each other at his little table, he on the chair and me on the divan.

It gave me a queer feeling each time I looked into his deep blue eyes, and he sat there with that mysterious laugh playing round his lips. I was able to read his inward thoughts. I could see on his face that look of helplessness and uncertainty as to how to behave, and, at the same time, a trace of his sense of manhood. I noticed his shy manner and it made me feel very gentle; I couldn't refrain from meeting those dark eyes again and again, and with my whole heart I almost beseeched him: oh, tell me, what is going on inside you, oh, can't you look beyond this ridiculous chatter?

But the evening passed and nothing happened, except that I told him about blushing—naturally not what I have written, but just so that he would become more sure of himself as he grew older.

When I lay in bed and thought over the whole situation, I found it far from encouraging, and the idea that I should beg for Peter's patronage was simply repellent. One can do a lot to satisfy one's longings, which certainly sticks out in my case, for I have made up my mind to go and sit with Peter more often and to get him talking somehow or other.

Whatever you do, don't think I'm in love with Peter—not a bit of it! If the Van Daans had had a daughter instead of a son, I should have tried to make friends with her too.

I woke at about five to seven this morning and knew at once, quite positively, what I had dreamed. I sat on a chair and opposite me sat Peter . . . Wessel. We were looking together at a book of drawings by Mary Bos. The dream was so vivid that I can still partly remember the drawings. But that was not all—the dream went on. Suddenly Peter's eyes met mine and I looked into those fine, velvet brown eyes for a long time. Then Peter said very softly, "If I had only known, I would have come to you long before!" I turned around brusquely because the emotion was too much for me. And after that I felt a soft, and oh, such a cool kind cheek against mine and it felt so good, so good. . . .

I awoke at this point, while I could still feel his cheek against mine and felt his brown eyes looking deep into my heart, so deep, that there he read how much I had loved him and how much I still love him. Tears sprang into my eyes once more, and I was very sad that I had lost him again, but at the same time glad because it made me feel quite certain that Peter was still the chosen one.

It is strange that I should often see such vivid images in my dreams here. First I saw Grandma[1] so clearly one night that I could even distinguish her thick, soft, wrinkled velvety skin. Then Granny appeared as a guardian angel; then followed Lies, who seems to be a symbol to me of the sufferings of all my girl friends and all Jews. When I pray for her, I pray for all Jews and all those in need. And now Peter, my darling Peter—never before have I had such a clear picture of him in my mind. I don't need a photo of him, I can see him before my eyes, and oh, so well!

Yours, Anne

January 24, 1944

Dear Kitty,

Something has happened to me; or rather, I can hardly describe it as an event, except that I think it is pretty crazy. Whenever anyone used to speak of sexual problems at home or at school, it was something either mysterious or revolting. Words which had any bearing on the subject were whispered, and often if someone didn't understand he was laughed at. It struck me as very odd and I thought, "Why are people so secretive and tiresome when they talk about these things?" But as I didn't think that I could change things, I kept my mouth shut as much as possible, or sometimes asked girl friends for information. When I had learned quite a lot and had also spoken about it with my parents, Mummy said one day, "Anne, let me give you some good advice; never speak about this subject to boys and don't reply if

[1] Grandma is grandmother on Father's side, Granny on Mother's side.

they begin about it.'' I remember exactly what my answer was: I said, ''No, of course not! The very idea!'' And there it remained.

When we first came here, Daddy often told me about things that I would really have preferred to hear from Mummy, and I found out the rest from books and things I picked up from conversations. Peter Van Daan was never as tiresome over this as the boys at school—once or twice at first perhaps—but he never tried to get me talking.

Mrs. Van Daan told us that she had never talked about these things to Peter, and for all she knew neither had her husband. Apparently she didn't know how much he knew.

Yesterday, when Margot, Peter, and I were peeling potatoes, somehow the conversation turned to Boche. ''We still don't know what sex Boche is, do we?'' I asked.

''Yes, certainly,'' Peter answered. ''He's a tom.''

I began to laugh. ''A tomcat that's expecting, that's marvelous!''

Peter and Margot laughed too over this silly mistake. You see, two months ago, Peter had stated that Boche would soon be having a family, her tummy was growing visibly. However, the fatness appeared to come from the many stolen bones, because the children didn't seem to grow fast, let alone make their appearance!

Peter just had to defend himself. ''No,'' he said, ''you can go with me yourself to look at him. Once when I was playing around with him, I noticed quite clearly that he's a tom.''

I couldn't control my curiosity, and went with him to the warehouse. Boche, however, was not receiving visitors, and was nowhere to be seen. We waited for a while, began to get cold, and went upstairs again. Later in the afternoon I heard Peter go downstairs for the second time. I mustered up all my courage to walk through the silent house alone, and reached the warehouse. Boche stood on the packing table playing with Peter, who had just put him on the scales to weigh him.

''Hello, do you want to see him?'' He didn't make any lengthy preparations, but picked up the animal, turned him over on to his back, deftly held his head and paws together, and the lesson began. "Those are the male organs, these are just a few stray hairs, and that is his bottom." The cat did another half turn and was standing on his white socks once more.

If any other boy had shown me "the male organs," I would never have looked at him again. But Peter went on talking quite normally on what is otherwise such a painful subject, without meaning anything unpleasant, and finally put me sufficiently at my ease for me to be normal too. We played with Boche, amused ourselves, chattered together, and then sauntered through the large warehouse towards the door.

"Usually, when I want to know something, I find it in some book or other, don't you?" I asked.

"Why on earth? I just ask upstairs. My father knows more than me and has had more experience in such things."

We were already on the stair, so I kept my mouth shut after that.

"Things may alter," as Brer Rabbit said. Yes. Really I shouldn't have discussed these things in such a normal way with a girl. I know too definitely that Mummy didn't mean it that way when she warned me not to discuss the subject with boys. I wasn't quite my usual self for the rest of the day though, in spite of everything. When I thought over our talk, it still seemed rather odd. But at least I'm wiser about one thing, that there really are young people—and of the opposite sex too—who can discuss these things naturally without making fun of them.

I wonder if Peter really does ask his parents much. Would he honestly behave with them as he did with me yesterday? Ah, what would I know about it!

Yours, Anne

April 16, 1944

Darlingest Kitty,

Remember yesterday's date, for it is a very important day in my life. Surely it is a great day for every girl when she receives her first kiss? Well, then, it is just as important for me too! Bram's kiss on my right cheek doesn't count any more, likewise the one from Mr. Walker on my right hand.

How did I suddenly come by this kiss? Well, I will tell you.

Yesterday evening at eight o'clock I was sitting with Peter on his divan, it wasn't long before his arm went round me. "Let's move up a bit," I said, "then I won't bump my head against the cupboard." He moved up, almost into the corner, I laid my arm under his and across his back, and he just about buried me, because his arm was hanging on my shoulder.

Now we've sat like this on other occasions, but never so close together as yesterday. He held me firmly against him, my left shoulder against his chest; already my heart began to beat faster, but we had not finished yet. He didn't rest until my head was on his shoulder and his against it. When I sat upright again after about five minutes, he soon took my head in his hands and laid it against him once more. Oh, it was so lovely, I couldn't talk much, the joy was too great. He stroked my cheek and arm a bit awkwardly, played with my curls and our heads lay touching most of the time. I can't tell you, Kitty, the feeling that ran through me all the while. I was too happy for words, and I believe he was as well.

We got up at half past eight. Peter put on his gym shoes, so that when he toured the house he wouldn't make a noise, and I stood beside him. How it came about so suddenly, I don't know, but before we went downstairs he kissed me, through my hair, half on my left cheek, half on my ear; I tore downstairs without looking round, and am simply longing for today!

Yours, Anne

April 17, 1944

Dear Kitty,

Do you think that Daddy and Mummy would approve of my sitting and kissing a boy on a divan—a boy of seventeen and a half and a girl of just under fifteen? I don't really think they would, but I must rely on myself over this. It is so quiet and peaceful to lie in his arms and to dream, it is so thrilling to feel his cheek against mine, it is so lovely to know that there is someone waiting for me. But there is indeed a big "but," because will Peter be content to leave it at this? I haven't forgotten his promise already, but . . . he *is* a boy!

I know myself that I'm starting very soon, not even fifteen, and so independent already! It's certainly hard for other people to understand, I know almost for certain that Margot would never kiss a boy unless there had been some talk of an engagement or marriage, but neither Peter nor I have anything like that in mind. I'm sure too that Mummy never touched a man before Daddy. What would my girl friends say about it if they knew that I lay in Peter's arms, my heart against his chest, my head on his shoulder and with his head against mine!

Oh, Anne, how scandalous! But honestly, I don't think it is; we are shut up here, shut away from the world, in fear and anxiety, especially just lately. Why, then, should we who love each other remain apart? Why should we wait until we've reached a suitable age? Why should we bother?

I have taken it upon myself to look after myself; he would never want to cause me sorrow or pain. Why shouldn't I follow the way my heart leads me, if it makes us both happy? All the same, Kitty, I believe you can sense that I'm in doubt, I think it must be my honesty which rebels against doing anything on the sly! Do you think it's my duty to tell Daddy what I'm doing? Do you think we should share our secret with a third person? A lot of the beauty would be lost, but would my conscience feel happier? I will discuss it with "him."

Oh, yes, there's still so much I want to talk to him about, for I don't see the use of only just cuddling each other. To exchange our thoughts, that shows confidence and faith in each other, we would both be sure to profit by it!

Yours, Anne

"The Secret Phrase"

Jessamyn West
California, 1940s

"I, Cress," said the girl, "in the October day, in the dying October day." She walked over to the fireplace and stood so that the slanting sunlight fell onto her bare shoulders with a red wine stain. The ashes smelled raw, rain wet. Or perhaps it's the water on the chrysanthemums, she thought, or the bitter, autumn-flavored chrysanthemums themselves.

She listened for her second heart-beat, the tap of the loosened shingle. But it was dead, it beat no more. For three days the Santa Ana had buffeted the house, but now at evening it had died down, had blown itself out. It was blown out, but it left its signs: the piled sand by the east doorsills; the tumbleweeds caught in the angle of the corral; the signboard by the electric tracks, face down; the eucalyptus with torn limb dangling.

"The Sabbath evening," said the girl, "the autumn Sabbath evening." And glowing and warm against the day's sober death, the year's sad end, burned her own bright living.

She walked to her own room, across her fallen nightgown, past her unmade bed, and opened the casement window and leaned out toward the west. There the sun was near to setting, red in the dust, and the lights in the distant well-riggings already blazed. She watched the sun drop until the black tracery of a derrick crossed its face.

"The day dies," murmured the girl, "its burnished wrack burns in yon western sky."

Then she was quiet so that no single word should fall to ripple the clear surface of her joy. The pepper tree rustled; there was a little stir in the leaves of the bougainvillaea. From the ocean, twenty miles away, the sea air was beginning to move back across the land. "It is as good against the dry face as water." She pushed her crackling hair away from her cheeks. "I won't have a windbreak as thin even as one hair against my face."

She arched her chest under the tightly wrapped lace scarf, so that she could project as much of herself as possible into the evening's beauty. "Now the sun is down and the day's long dream ended. Now I must make the air whistle about my ears."

She came out of the long black lace scarf like an ivory crucifix—with a body scarcely wider than her arms. Panties, slip, green rep dress on, and there she was—a girl of twelve again, and the supper to get, and the house to clean. She had the supper in her mind: a fitting meal for Sunday evening. Oyster soup. Oysters that actresses ate, floating in a golden sea of milk, and marble cupcakes veined like old temples for dessert.

She had supper ready when the car turned into the driveway bringing her family home from their drive— the cakes out of the oven, the milk just on for the soup.

"Well," said Mr. Delahanty when he entered the room, "this is pretty nice." He walked over and held his hand to the fire. "Woodbox full, too."

Her mother ran her finger over the top of the bookcase while she unwound her veil. "Cress, you'll burn us out dusting with kerosene."

Cress watched the scarlet accordion pleating in the opening of her mother's slit skirt fan out, as she held her foot toward the fire.

Father took Mother's coat. "You should have gone with us, Cress. The wind's done a lot of damage over in Riverside County. Lost count of the roofs off and trees down."

"Is supper ready?" Mother asked.

"Soon as the milk heats, and I put the oysters in."

"Oyster soup," exclaimed Father, "the perfect dish for a Sunday October evening. Did you get your studying done?" he asked curiously.

Cress nodded. Studying. Well, it was studying. There were her books and papers.

Father had said that morning before they left, "You're a bright girl, Cress. No need your spending a whole day studying. Do you more good to go for a ride with us."

"No, Father, I'm way behind." She could hardly wait until they left.

Finally at ten they got into the car, Mother on the front seat close to Father. Father backed out of the driveway and a dusty swirl of wind caught Mother's scarlet veil. They waved her a sad good-by.

She had watched the red car out of sight, then she turned and claimed the empty house for herself. . . .

She stood warming herself, happy and bemused, like a prisoner unexpectedly pardoned. Then she heard again the click, click she had not recognized. Brownie at the back door!

"Oh, poor Brownie, I forgot you. Poor kitty, are you hungry?" There was Brownie sitting on the back step, with fur blown and dusty, patiently waiting to be let in and fed. She was a young cat, who had never had a kit of her own, but she looked like a grandmother. She looked as if she should have a gingham apron tied around her waist, and spectacles on her nose, and now out of her grandmother's eyes she gave Cress a look of tolerance. Cress snatched the cat up and held her close to her face, and rubbed her nose in the soft, cool fur. When she got out the can of evaporated milk she sat Brownie by the fire and poured the milk into the bowl from which she had eaten her own lunch. Brownie lapped the yellow arc as it fell from can to bowl.

Cress crouched on the hearth with her eyes almost on a level with Brownie's. It was blissful, almost mesmeric to watch the quick, deft dart of the red tongue into the yellow milk. Her own body seemed to participate in that darting, rhythmic movement and was lulled and happy. "It is almost as if she rocked me, back and forth, back and forth, with her tongue," mused Cress.

When Brownie finished eating, Cress took her in her arms, felt the soft, little body beneath the shaggy envelope of cinnamon fur. She lay on the floor close to the fire and cradled Brownie drowsily. Suddenly she kissed her. "My darling, my darling," she said and caressed the cat the length of its long soft body. Her hand tingled a little as it passed over the little pin-point nipples.

Some day her mother would tell her the secret phrase,

the magic sentence—something the other girls already
knew. Then the boys would notice her. Then he would
come. Jo and Ina and Bernadine already had notes from
boys, and candy hearts on Valentine's day, and a piece
of mistletoe at Christmas time. The boys rode them on
their handlebars and showed them wrestling holds, and
treated them to sodas. "But no one," she mourned,
"ever looks at me." She pressed her apricot-colored hair
close to the cat's cinnamon fur. "It's because Mother
hasn't told me yet. Something the other girls know.
Sometime she'll tell me—some beautiful word I've been
waiting a long time to hear. Then I'll be like a lamp
lighted, a flower bloomed. Maybe she'll tell me tomorrow—and when I walk into school everyone will see the
change, know I know. How will they know? My lips, my
eyes, a walk, a gesture, the movement of my arms. But
there's not a boy here I'd have, but someone far away,
no boy. He will come and we will walk out along the
streets hand in hand and everyone will see us and say,
'They were made for each other.' His hair will be like
fur, soft and sooty black, and on his thin brown cheek
will be a long, cruel scar. He will say, 'Kiss it, Cress, and
I will bless the man who did it.' Ah, we shall walk together like sword and flower. All eyes will follow us and
the people will say, 'This is Cress. Why did we never see
her before.' "

Fire and wind were dying. Brownie slept on her arm.
"He will come, he will come." Cress lifted Brownie high
overhead, then brought her down sharply and closely to
her breast.

"He will come, he will come." She kissed Brownie
fiercely and put her on the floor, and ran to her mother's
room, undressing as she went. She stepped out of her
skirt and threw her jacket and sweater across the room
and sent her panties in a flying arc. She knew what she
wanted. She had used it before—Mother's long, black
lace shawl. She wound it tightly about herself from armpits to thighs. She unbraided her hair and let it hang
across her shoulders. Then she turned to the mirror. "I
have a beautiful body," she breathed, "a beautiful,
beautiful body."

And because she regarded herself, thinking of him, he

who was yet to come, it was as if he too, saw her. She loaned him her eyes so that he might see her, and to her flesh she gave this gift of his seeing. She raised her arms and slowly turned and her flesh was warm with his seeing. Somberly and quietly she turned and swayed and gravely touched now thigh, now breast, now cheek, and looked and looked with the eyes she had given him.

She moved through the gray dust-filled room weaving an ivory pattern. Not any of the dust or disorder of her mother's room fazed her, not its ugliness nor funny smell. Hair bubbled out of the hair receiver, the stopper was out of the cologne bottle, the mirror was spattered with liquid powder. She made, in her mind, a heap of all that was ugly and disordered. She made a dunghill of them and from its top she crowed.

"The curtains, green as vomit, and hanging crooked, the gray neckband on the white flannel nightgown, the dust on the patent leather shoes," she said, providing her imaginary stage with imaginary props, "I hate them and dance them down. Nothing can touch me. I am Cress. Or I can dance *with* them," she said and she clasped the nightgown to her and leaped and bent. "This is evil, to be naked, to like the feel of gritty dust under my feet, the bad smell, the dim light."

She regarded her face more closely in the spattered mirror. "There is something wanton and evil there," she thought, "something not good. Perhaps I shall be faithless," and she trembled with pity for that dark one who loved her so dearly. She shook back her hair and pressed her cool hands to her burning cheeks and danced so that the dust motes in the slanting shaft of light shot meteor-like, up and down.

"I can dance the word," she whispered, "but I cannot say it." So she danced it, wrapped in the black shawl, with the dust motes dancing about her. She danced it until she trembled and leaning on bent elbows looked deep into the mirror and said, "There is nothing I will not touch. I am Cress. I will know everything."

All at once she was tired. She turned and walked slowly to the living room. Brownie lay by the dead fire. "I, Cress," she had said, "in the October day, in the dying October day," and turned to do the evening work.

* * *

"If the milk boils, your soup will be spoiled," Mother said. "We've been here long enough for it to heat."

"Yes, sister, let's eat," said Father, "it's been a long day."

"Yes, let's eat," cried Cress. "It's been a long, beautiful day," and she ran to the kitchen to put the oysters in the milk.

Francina

Marta Brunet
Translated by Marilyn Bauman
Chile, 1920s

At the age of fourteen, uncoordinated due to normal child development, ugly, and unattractive, Francina had the soul of a child in the body of a woman. She remained an outcast from life, a dreamer clinging firmly to what was miraculous.

The great crisis of puberty passed without any anxiety; man existed for her only as a chimera. She did not bother about making herself pretty. She liked to wear a sack dress that gave her complete freedom, and in the evening, for the informal meals which were always the same—the mother was still sick and the father traveling —the only sign of coquetry shown was a ribbon tied around her neck, a ribbon that she thought might belong to a pet cat, perhaps that of Mucifuz, a pirate.

Accustomed to imaginary beings, flesh and blood people frightened her. No sooner had she spoken to them than she would hide. She only knew how to speak through the lips of her heroes. . . . The confusion of the streets terrified her. One time she was taken to the movies and they made such an impression that she came down with a nervous fever, and her mother, frightened, never allowed her to go to the theater again. Music was her delight, giving her trances which were almost ecstasy. But she continued to find her most complete happiness in books.

Then one day Francina met Marcial Luco and her life changed.

She was in the park, hurling stones at some imaginary monkeys which were bothering good old Robinson Crusoe on his island. She was Robinson. Suddenly, at her shoulder, a voice called, "Francina . . ."

She turned, startled.

Nearby, wearing a riding habit, a tall, dark-haired man with pearly teeth in a youthful mouth, and attentive, kindly eyes, was watching her. It was Prince Floridor . . . Of course! Prince Floridor! How exquisitely he walked! And he clapped his hands and smiled and gave a courtly salute, just like those that Princess Corysanda made.

"Sir," she said, "welcome to my island. You are speaking to Robinson."

Surprised, the youth looked at her.

"Child, don't you remember me? I am your Uncle Marcial, your father's cousin. Don't look at me with that frightened expression."

Francina began to remember . . . and terrified, she tried to flee, because she was so ashamed of having spoken as she did. But the young man anticipated her action and, resting a hand on her shoulder, stopped her.

"Were you playing?" he asked.

"Yes . . . No . . . The fact is—" and she could not say anything else, choked by fear and sorrow.

She wanted to hide, she wanted to flee, she wanted to kill herself rather than keep feeling the youth's hand still resting on her shoulder or seeing his eyes looking inquisitively at her.

And since she could not think of any way to avoid that examination, she covered her face with her hands and burst out crying inconsolably.

"Don't cry, little one . . . Have I frightened you?"

His serious voice made her nerves tingle. Was it true then that someone, anyone could possess such a voice —a voice she had thought the privilege of her legendary heroes? Could a man approach her and cause such a ripple of warmth that made her flush at an unknown pleasure?

"Have I frightened you?" insisted the youth.

"No . . . No. . ." She went on crying, in spite of the happiness that she felt, because it was another pleasure to see him through the tears, upset and trying to console her.

"What are you denying? Your fear? Or is it that you do not want me to see your tear-streaked face? Is that it?

Come! Run, wash your eyes and put on a little powder. I am eating lunch with you. While you are fixing yourself up, I'll stay here, smoking. Don't be long! I'll be waiting.''

He withdrew his hand from her shoulder, withdrew his hand which was petting her head. He moved farther into the park. The girl watched him go. He was not the hero Prince Floridor of her dreams: he was her flesh and blood uncle, Marcial. He was not a chimera: he was a reality.

What had he said? Fix herself up? Powder her nose? Waiting for her? Oh!

She examined her hands, covered with scratches. She examined her lanky legs and her feet, looking so enormous in tennis shoes. She looked at the unwashed, sailcloth sack dress. And she was ashamed of herself. An impulse made her run home, with her heart still bewildering her by its dull pounding, under its emotion. She reached her room gasping, her body trembling, her cheeks burning, her eyes shining.

She searched through her wardrobe, turned over everything in the bureau, opened drawers, upset boxes, rushed back and forth feverishly until she got together a dress, shoes, stockings, and a large ribbon to wear. Then with keen anxiety, she stared into the mirror to study herself.

Francina the child there met Francina the woman.

"The Kiss"

Nadine Gordimer
South Africa, 1940s

I did not know how long he was away. With nothing but
the waves' faint break in the darkness to measure the
passing of time, I could not tell if it was ten minutes or
half an hour, but suddenly he stepped into the enclosing
dark about me and he was there, toweling his hair. A
few drops of cold water shook from it onto my cheek. I
sat up, and a faint slither of sand ran like a breeze down
the back of my dress. I could hardly see him, yet he was
there vigorously, his sharp breathing, the smell of damp
towel, and as he bent, the fresh smell of khaki.

He said: "Where are you?"

"Here." —I put up my hand, but he could not see it.

"Was it cold?"

"No. There's a lot of seaweed about, tangling up your
legs. Come—" he said.

I got up obediently. We began to walk slowly along the
beach, quite far from the water, where the sand was dry
and coldly heavy to walk in. All my being was concen-
trated in my left hand, which hung beside him as we
walked. My whole body was poured into that hand as I
waited for him to take it. It seemed to me that he must
take it; I felt us walking up the beach together, with our
hands clasped. In my head I listened and heard again
him saying: "Come—"; so short, so intimate, and the
strange pleasure of my obedience, as if the word itself
drew me up out of the sand.

He began to talk, about the men with whom he lived
in camp. He talked on and on. I answered yes or no: I
was unable to listen, the way one cannot hear when one
is preoccupied by distress or anger. He did not seem to
notice. Now and then the uneven flow of the sand beneath our feet caused his shirt to brush my shoulder

with the faint scratch of material; my hand, numb with the laxity of waiting, felt as if it had been jammed.

We had reached the lagoon, pouring silently down the channel it had cut for itself into the sea. "Shall we get back now?" he said and, with a little groan, lowered himself down to the sand; he squatted with his arms folded on his knees. I stood awkwardly, with what must have been an almost pettish attitude of offense innocently expressed in my stiff body. But as he made no move to get up, I sat down too, facing past the hump of his knees.

"But you know," he said suddenly, as if it were the continuation of something we had discussed, "you're really only a little girl. I wonder. I wonder if you are." He took me by the elbows and drew me round, close against his knees and I saw his teeth, white for a moment, and knew that he had smiled. He enclosed my head and his knees in his arms and rocked them gently once or twice. The most suffocating joy took hold of me; I was terrified that he would stop, suddenly release me. So I kept as still as fear, my hands dangling against his shoes. He gave a curious sigh, as one who consents to something against his will. Then he bent to my face and lifted it with his own and kissed me, opening my tight pressing mouth, the child's hard kiss with which I tried to express my eagerness as a woman. The idea of the kiss completely blocked out for me the physical sensation; I was intoxicated with the idea of Ludi kissing me, so that afterward it was the idea that I remembered, and not the feel of his lips. I buried my face on his knees again and the smell of khaki, of the ironed khaki drill of his trousers, came to me as the smell of love. . . . I remembered the Cluff brothers at the dance . . . the smell of khaki . . . my heart beat up at the excitement of contrasting myself then with myself at this moment.

Ludi was feeling gently down my bare arm, as if to find out how some curious thing was made.

I do not know if I had ever been kissed before. Even if I had, it does not matter; it was as if it had never happened, the prim mouth of a frightened schoolboy dry on my lips, the social good-night kiss on the doorstep that would be smiled upon indulgently by Mine* parents, the contact that was an end in itself, like a handshake. Now I lay in my bed in the high little room in Mrs. Koch's house and kept my face away from the pillow because I wanted my lips free of any tactual distraction that might make it difficult for me to keep intact on my mouth the shape and sensation of Ludi's kiss. I thought about it as something precious that had been shown to me; vivid, but withdrawn too quickly for me to be able to re-create every detail as my anxious memory willed. That anxious memory trembling eagerly to forget nothing; perhaps that is the beginning of desire, the end of a childhood? Wanting to remember becomes wanting: the recurring question that has no answer but its own eventual fading out into age, as it faded in from childhood.

Suddenly sleep, arbitrary, uncaring, melted my body away from me. I had just time to recognize myself going; and with only my mind still left to me, the idea of the kiss became complete in itself: I held it warmed in my heart as a child holds the imaginative world in the clasped body of a Teddy bear.

* Refers to parents who work in the mine.

A Rush to Motherhood

Lucille Day
Oakland, California, 1962

The summer of 1962, there was nothing I liked better than to sit close to Frank on the back porch of his grandmother's cottage, sipping Olympia beer, making out, and listening to my transistor radio. I liked the way his arm felt, warm and heavy on my shoulder. When we kissed I felt we were partaking in a great romance—like Mitzi Gaynor and Rossano Brazzi in *South Pacific*, or Miko Taka and Marlon Brando in *Sayonara*.

The evening of June 6, we sat outside without sweaters, watching Frank's grandmother water the young bean and tomato plants in her garden. Occasionally, she bent to pull a weed, her housedress fluttering around her ankles. When she went inside, Frank picked me up and twirled me around, and when he stopped we kissed, standing and dizzy, before returning to the stoop.

From time to time I got up to dance, or just to step back and look at Frank. He wore Levi's, low on his hips, and a blue plaid Pendleton shirt. I admired his slouch and his thick brown hair, slicked back on the sides and falling in greasy waves across his forehead. A good catch. We'd been going steady since March.

We started talking about marriage, and I solemnly told him that I hoped someday to be a good wife and to mother four children. "There Goes My Baby," already an oldie but goodie, wailed on the radio.

"Well," he asked, "will you?"

"Will I what?"

"Marry me."

"Yes."

I was fourteen years old.

I'd been seriously looking for a husband since I was

twelve. I was tired of being a child, tired of being told what to do. I hated my classes at Piedmont Junior High School; I hated my school uniform; I hated my mother. I wanted to be free, and to be loved.

An only child and archetypal brat, I gave my parents a choice: I would run away (which I'd already done once), I would get pregnant, or they could let me get married. They opted for marriage. My mother had already had one nervous breakdown since my birth, when she was thirty-six. She thought my marriage would solve all her problems.

Frank and I first applied for a marriage license at the Oakland Courthouse. When I told the clerk my birth date, she thought I'd made a mistake. I told her there was no mistake, that I was fourteen. She looked at me as a mother would look at a naughty child, and said that California law requires an age of sixteen for both partners. I would have to see a judge to make a special request for the license.

I was escorted with my parents into the judge's wood-paneled chambers. I sat in a leather chair; the judge, stern and stocky, watched me from behind his desk.

"Why do you want to get married?" he asked.

"Because I'm in love."

"That's quite admirable, but at your age it's insufficient grounds. There have to be other circumstances. Are there any?"

I knew exactly what the other circumstances had to be, but I was honest. "No."

"I'm sorry, but I can't let you get married."

"Can't you make an exception? Isn't it better to get married because you're in love than because you're pregnant?"

"I agree with you entirely, but it's also best to wait until you're older. In California there's a law that says it's illegal to marry at your age. It's a good law; it was made to protect people.

"I wish you the best of luck, and I hope that someday you'll marry for love—when you're older."

Frank and I went to Nevada, where it was not only illegal to marry at my age, but also at his. In Nevada, the woman was supposed to be at least sixteen, and the man eighteen. Frank was seventeen.

We gave our real ages to the gray-haired justice of the peace in Minden, who both issued licenses and performed marriages. He advised us to come back when we were older.

By Reno we knew what we had to do. I said I was sixteen; Frank said he was eighteen. Both of our mothers were present to confirm this, and the license was issued as quickly as those of the other people waiting in line.

On September 8, 1962, three months before my fifteenth birthday, and the week before I should have started ninth grade, I was married at the First Methodist Church in Reno.

What Shall I Make
of This?

"Research"

Muriel Spark
Edinburgh, 1950s

"You know," Sandy said, "these are supposed to be the happiest days of our lives."

"Yes, they are always saying that," Jenny said. "They say, make the most of your schooldays because you never know what lies ahead of you."

"Miss Brodie says prime is best," Sandy said.

"Yes, but she never got married like our mothers and fathers."

"They don't have primes," said Sandy.

"They have sexual intercourse," Jenny said.

The little girls paused, because this was still a stupendous thought, and one which they had only lately lit upon; the very phrase and its meaning were new. It was quite unbelievable. Sandy said, then, "Mr. Lloyd had a baby last week. He must have committed sex with his wife." This idea was easier to cope with and they laughed screamingly into their pink paper napkins. Mr. Lloyd was the Art master to the senior girls.

"Can you *see* it happening?" Jenny whispered.

Sandy screwed her eyes even smaller in the effort of

seeing with her mind. "He would be wearing his pyjamas," she whispered back.

The girls rocked with mirth, thinking of one-armed Mr. Lloyd, in his solemnity, striding into school.

Then Jenny said, "You do it on the spur of the moment. That's how it happens."

Jenny was a reliable source of information, because a girl employed by her father in his grocer shop had recently been found to be pregnant, and Jenny had picked up some fragments of the ensuing fuss. Having confided her finds to Sandy, they had embarked on a course of research which they called "research," piecing together clues from remembered conversations illicitly overheard, and passages from the big dictionaries.

"It all happens in a flash," Jenny said. "It happened to Teenie when she was out walking at Puddocky with her boy friend. Then they had to get married."

"You would think the urge would have passed by the time she got her *clothes* off," Sandy said. By "clothes," she definitely meant to imply knickers, but "knickers" was rude in this scientific context.

"Yes, that's what I can't understand," said Jenny.

It had been raining and the ground was too wet for them to go and finish digging the hole to Australia, so the girls lifted the tea-table with all its festal relics over to the corner of the room. Sandy opened the lid of the piano stool and extracted a notebook from between two sheaves of music. On the first page of the notebook was written,

The Mountain Eyrie
by
Sandy Stranger and Jenny Gray

This was a story, still in the process of composition, about Miss Brodie's lover, Hugh Carruthers. He had not been killed in the war, that was a mistake in the telegram. He had come back from the war and called to enquire for Miss Brodie at school, where the first person whom he encountered was Miss Mackay, the headmistress. She had informed him that Miss Brodie did not desire to see him, she loved another. With a bitter, harsh laugh, Hugh went and made his abode in a mountain eyrie, where, wrapped in a leathern jacket, he had been discovered one day by Sandy and Jenny. At the present stage in the story Hugh was holding Sandy captive but Jenny had escaped by night and was attempting to find her way down the mountainside in the dark. Hugh was preparing to pursue her.

Sandy took a pencil from a drawer in the sideboard and continued:

"Hugh!" Sandy beseeched him, "I swear to you before all I hold sacred that Miss Brodie has never loved another, and she awaits you below, praying and hoping in her prime. If you will let Jenny go, she will bring back your lover Jean Brodie to you and you will see her with your own eyes and hold her in your arms after these twelve long years and a day."

His black eye flashed in the lamplight of the hut. "Back, girl!" he cried, "and do not bar my way. Well do I know that yon girl Jenny will report my whereabouts to my mocking erstwhile fiancée. Well do I know that you are both spies sent by her that she might mock. Stand back from the door, I say!"

"Never!" said Sandy, placing her young lithe body squarely in front of the latch and her arm through the bolt. Her large eyes flashed with an azure light of appeal.

Sandy handed the pencil to Jenny. "It's your turn," she said.

Jenny wrote: With one movement he flung her to the farthest end of the hut and strode out into the moonlight and his strides made light of the drifting snow.

"Put in about his boots," said Sandy.

Jenny wrote: His high boots flashed in the moonlight.

"There are too many moonlights," Sandy said, "but we can sort that later when it comes to publication."

"Oh, but it's a secret, Sandy!" said Jenny.

"I know that," Sandy said. "Don't worry, we won't publish it till our prime."

"Do you think Miss Brodie ever had sexual intercourse with Hugh?" said Jenny.

"She would have had a baby, wouldn't she?"

"I don't know."

"I don't think they did anything like that," said Sandy. "Their love was above all that."

"Miss Brodie said they clung to each other with passionate abandon on his last leave."

"I don't think they took their clothes off, though," Sandy said, "do you?"

"No. I can't see it," said Jenny.

"I wouldn't like to have sexual intercourse," Sandy said.

"Neither would I. I'm going to marry a pure person."

"Have a toffee."

They ate their sweets, sitting on the carpet. Sandy put some coal on the fire and the light spurted up, reflecting on Jenny's ringlets. "Let's be witches by the fire, like we were at Hallowe'en."

They sat in the twilight eating toffees and incanting witches' spells. Jenny said, "There's a Greek god at the museum standing up with nothing on. I saw it last Sunday afternoon but I was with Auntie Kate and I didn't have a chance to *look* properly."

"Let's go to the museum next Sunday," Sandy said. "It's research."

"Would you be allowed to go alone with me?"

Sandy, who was notorious for not being allowed to go out and about without a grown-up person, said, "I don't think so. Perhaps we could get someone to take us."

"We could ask Miss Brodie."

Miss Brodie frequently took the little girls to the art galleries and museums, so this seemed feasible.

"But suppose," said Sandy, "she won't let us look at the statue if it's naked."

"I don't think she would notice that it was naked," Jenny said. "She just wouldn't see its thingummyjig."

"I know," said Sandy. "Miss Brodie's above all that."

"How Beautiful!"

Raymonda Hawa Tawil
Israel, 1952

The girls at the convent school in Nazareth all came from Arab families, Moslem as well as Christian. But in 1952, when I moved to a convent school in Haifa, I suddenly found myself in a totally different milieu. I was the only Arab girl there; all the others were Jewish, most of them from Europe, where they had been baptized during the war so that they'd be saved from annihilation by the Nazis. After the physical danger passed, many of these families retained their Christian ties, giving their daughters a convent education. The Israeli authorities frowned on this tendency; they wanted Jewish children to go to Israeli government schools, where they would receive a "truly Jewish" education. In time, under constant pressure from the authorities, the number of Jewish girls in these establishments declined sharply. But during my schooldays, numerous Jewish girls attended convent schools. They brought with them much of the heritage of traditional European Jewish culture. They were highly gifted, with great talents in music and art and all forms of self-expression. At first, I felt a little overshadowed; I could not compete with their attainments. But the girls were very friendly toward me, never behaving in a superior manner or patronizing me. We soon developed feelings of deep sympathy, affection, and admiration for one another. At the same time, it was exciting for me to imbibe this creative, intellectual atmosphere. I tasted a new freedom, and I enjoyed myself thoroughly.

The attitude of the nuns was quite unlike what I was used to in the Nazareth convent. Here, in Haifa, they were also strict with us, but at the same time, there was a degree of open-mindedness and tolerance for more modern attitudes. I learned that once a week, a nun

would take us to the beach, where we were to put on
bathing costumes! I was astounded! The first time we
went, I felt terribly self-conscious. I could scarcely put on
my bathing suit; in Nazareth, we had been taught that it
is immoral to expose the body in any way—even short-
sleeved dresses were taboo. How could I wear a bathing
costume in public?

I was perplexed and confused: How could I reconcile
the teachings of the French nuns in Nazareth with the
teachings of the French nuns in Haifa?

My salvation came from the Jewish girls. In total contrast to my own angelic purity and innocence, they were
very free, open-minded, and, moreover, knowledgeable—and they were very patient and open in sharing
their knowledge with me. At first, I could scarcely understand their talk. What was the meaning of their
jokes? What were they laughing about? They were my
own age, but they seemed so much more sophisticated
and experienced. Most of them had boyfriends, whom
they went out with during their weekends at home. Returning to school, they always had mysterious and wonderful stories about these boys and what they did. I sat
in a corner, listening silently, shocked and fascinated,
nauseated and thrilled.

When I met Mother on weekends, I used to seek her
help, but I got little from her. For all her progressive out-
look, she gave evasive answers to my questions, contenting herself with some vague comment about the bad
housing conditions among the Jewish newcomers. Frequently, an entire immigrant family slept in a single
room, and my schoolmates often witnessed their parents' intimacies.

As for the nuns, their attitude toward sex was predict-
able. They tried to repress our desires, but they never
quite succeeded. We were healthy young girls, with a
healthy curiosity about life and above all about sex.
When the sisters went to the chapel for their daily prayers, we were left in the study room, free of their supervi-
sion. We were supposed to be doing our lessons, but on
occasion, while hymns and chants wafted in from the
chapel, one of the girls would walk up to the blackboard
and deliver an impromptu lecture about what our fa-

thers and mothers did in bed. The lecture was accompanied by crude but highly explicit sketches illustrating the various poses of lovemaking. At first, I scarcely understood what it was all about, nor why the other girls were laughing so much. When I began to catch on, I felt confused and embarrassed. Then a nun walked in, and we hurriedly thought up some explanation for all the giggling.

One day, a nun took us out for a walk along the seashore. By some ruse, we slipped away from her, and went off in search of adventure. One of the girls noticed a pair of lovers, and the others decided to climb a tree to get a better view. Once again, I felt confused and unsure; I didn't think it was right to spy, but I was afraid to say anything. We clambered up into the tree and held our breath. Down below us, we could see the couple, who did not know they were being watched. For what seemed like an eternity, we witnessed the elaborate ritual of lovemaking.

I gazed, fascinated. I felt a strange and overpowering mixture of curiosity and passion; I shall never forget that sensation. It was as though all my senses were being opened up, as though I had taken a single bound from childhood into adolescence.

When the couple finished, we gave way to a wave of gaiety. Triumphantly, we sang, *"Eize yoffi!"* (How beautiful!) Down below, the startled couple scrambled into their clothes. Suddenly, my mood changed again: I despised myself for helping to humiliate them. But I could not forget what I had seen.

"The Cushion"

Ella Leffland
Martinez, California, 1940s

Having nothing better to do one rainy noon in February, Eudene and I wandered into the auditorium where the orchestra was rehearsing. Jacket off and shirt sleeves rolled up, Mr. Kerr was working very hard conducting "Song of India." Hunched over, arms outspread, he waved his baton in one hand while with the other he made deep, scooping motions, as if to drag the musicians bodily from their chairs.

After a while Eudene yawned and scratched her sauerkraut hair. "Who wants to listen to that?"

"It's not bad," I objected, watching.

She smashed me with her elbow. "Let's go."

But my eyes were fastened, as if mesmerized, to Mr. Kerr's arms. They were hard-looking, hairy arms, and as they raised higher, the shirt stretched taut across a broad, muscular back.

"I'm going," said Eudene.

I beat her to it, getting up and walking hastily out the door.

"Have you got a cigarette?" I asked.

"Sure."

"Could we have a puff somewhere?"

"Sure."

I felt uneasy, not myself. In movies a smoke always helped.

The next day after my lesson, the sheet music happened to slip off my stand as Mr. Kerr departed. It fluttered down next to the chair he had used, and to reach it more easily, I slid over onto his cushion. As my thighs sank into the unexpected den of body heat, a keen sensation shot up my spine, an exciting, tingling rush of heat that seemed to envelop and melt my heart. I sat immo-

bile, staring straight ahead. It was an intensely pleasur-
able feeling, but its very intensity was alien, shocking.

It lasted only a moment. I scrambled back into my own
chair, feeling frightened and looking nervously around.
In the shadowy distance, Mr. Kerr was instructing the
boy with the French horn. I looked at him a long time, as
he stood there sallow-faced and irritable in the dim light.
Then my foot shot out, kicking his chair away from me.

All through the day I worried. It had happened. My
body had cried out to someone I didn't even like. Who
next? What next? What if I carried inside me a dark, secret weakness for any warm chair a man had sat in?

By the time the last class was dismissed I had decided
to try something. Setting my jaw, I slid into the still-
warm seat of the boy opposite me. Nothing. I tested the
next one. Nothing. I stood up, relieved.

But they were only schoolboys. Mr. Kerr was a grown
male, and that must be the difference. What if I was
powerless against the body heat of all grown males—half
the chairs of the world?

Throwing on my slicker, I hurried out into the rain and
walked directly to the Hatton house. I knew that Helen
Maria wasn't home today and that I had no excuse to go
inside, but I opened the door and stepped into the hall.
The hush of the rooms was so great that I went into the
Dungeon tiptoeing. There I took off my slicker and sat
down on the chesterfield, which still stood at its careless
angle from the wall. I gripped my hands in my lap. The
rain blew and spattered against the long dim windows.

After a while the front door opened. I stiffened at the
sound of Peggy's voice. Helen Maria said Peggy never
came home from school early anymore—why of all days
did she have to today? A sense of criminal guilt gripped
me, a housebreaker, and I fought down the urge to jump
up and hide behind the chesterfield.

She came through the archway with Bev and another
girl and stopped. I looked at the three faces, each with a
little bud of lipstick at its center.

"Hi," Peggy said, in a neutral tone, and I knew she
thought I had come to break into her charmed circle.

"I'm waiting for Helen Maria," I said stiffly.

"She won't be home till about nine tonight."

"I know. I'll wait."

She looked surprised. It was a ridiculous thing to say, but I couldn't think of anything else.

"Sure, if you want to," she said, and paused uncertainly, as if she felt she must ask me to come along with the others to her room.

"I'll wait here," I said more stiffly. "I want to read." I took a magazine from the side table.

"Okay," Peggy nodded, and they moved off. The two other girls smiled at me, nicely enough.

Watching them go out, I felt a sudden certainty that for all their grown-up ways they were more innocent than I, that they would be horrified to know the real purpose of my visit, that their lives were smooth, clear, and virtuous, deeply to be envied.

The magazine was a podiatrics journal. I put it back and resumed my wait, listening to Sinatra crooning through Peggy's closed door.

It was at least another hour and a half before the front door opened again. Mr. Hatton came into the Dungeon, the newspaper under his arm.

I cleared my throat. "Hello, Mr. Hatton."

He glanced over at me. "Hello, Suse," he murmured, opening the paper as he continued toward his room.

I watched him passing. One more step and it would be too late. I sat forward, squeezing my knees. "Could I talk with you?"

"Hm?" His eyes were on the paper.

I had planned what I would say. I spoke quickly. "I'd like to talk about your profession."

"Hm?"

"Would you—sit down for a minute?"

I could hardly get the words out; they seemed on top of everything else so rude and demanding. But with only a slight frown he came over, sitting down at my side. I had never seen him so close. He had many freckles. Even the bags under his eyes were freckled.

"I want to be a marine architect."

"Good. Fine. You'll like it."

He seemed already on the verge of rising.

"But I'm not strong in math."

"Got to be strong in math. Work on it."

"What about—what about English?"

"Got to know what you're reading, of course."

I ransacked my brain. "I like to read. I read a lot, because I like to read."

"Good. Always a good thing."

His eyes had strayed back to the newspaper in his hands.

"It sounds like a good profession," I said. "I know I'll like it."

"Got to like what you do."

"I think I'll be good at it."

But he was no longer responding. I feared an immediate departure. My eyes dropped to the headline. *Cassino Battle Rages!*

"They should have invaded in the north," I said.

"Too easy," he muttered, as if to himself. "This way they'll divert the whole German force for months." He slapped the headline. "Is it worth it, though? Look at the losses already. This monastery is something awful. A fortress."

"I know. It's held out for a month already."

"God-awful."

"I hope they shoot Mussolini."

He nodded, reading on. I hoped he would read for a long time. But after a few minutes he began rising.

"They should have gone in at Genoa. Don't you think so?"

He nodded again, but I could keep him no longer. Still reading, he shambled off. It had been long enough, though. I touched the cushion; it was sufficiently warmed. Holding my breath, I slid over and sank into its sultry depths. Nothing, nothing, and more nothing.

I sat quietly for a while, at peace. I didn't have to worry about every male in the world. Just Mr. Kerr, which narrowed it down to something manageable.

The Brassiere

Paul Fournel
France, 20th century

At Adeline's, they spoke freely of God, of Jesus Christ, of the Virgin Mary, they spoke also of flowers, of schoolwork and of whatever life chanced to put before them day by day. There was always, here or there, at the table or in the garden, an ear for listening and a tongue for chatting. The ear was better disposed than the one offered by the old parish priest behind the grate of the confessional and the tongue less solemn that that of the priest in the flesh. They got along well.

Nobody in the house, on the other hand, ever had anything to say about the way in which hairs and breasts grow and nobody explained to little girls that one day they would bleed without having hurt themselves.

Adeline knew all about Hell and the Devil: she had painted herself gripping pictures of the two of them that prompted her to be good and provoked astonishing shivers down her back. Sitting cross-legged in the middle of the enormous écru eiderdown of the bed in the upstairs bedroom she reckoned up her imaginings as seriously as she said her prayers; eyes closed and hands placed flat on her chest, she let her bust and her head nod gently and hummed a chant through her nose, beating time with her elbows, as if they were the wings of an angel who had dreamed of the Devil.

She was in that position when her grandmother brought in her first brassiere.

"There's your nothing bra," she said, throwing the little parcel onto the eiderdown.

"Help me."

Adeline pulled off her sweater and looked at her breasts. For some time the nipples had been red and swollen, they stuck out a good half-inch from her ribs.

78

She took the bra out of the paper bag. It bore as little resemblance as possible to the provocative strapless brassieres that she saw in the magazines, but it was a bra all right. For a moment she studied the catch and put her arms through the straps. Carefully, she placed the little cups over her breasts and her grandmother had to help her slip the hook into the elastic loop.

"You'll have to practice."

It made her smile and tilt her head. She also had a way of pursing her lips that said a lot about her opinion of the ideas held by the school doctor.

"Put your sweater back on, it's cold."

She took the paper bag, crumpled it in a ball, slipped it into the pocket of her apron and went back down to the kitchen.

Adeline stood up on the bed to see herself in the closet mirror. She stuck out her chest, wanted to turn around and tangled her feet in the eiderdown. She fell. Seated again, she looked at her breasts.

The brassiere made them look fatter. She slipped a finger under the straps, the way she had seen her mother do it, and ran her hands down her chest to set the cups well in place. She moved her arms and her shoulders, took in a deep breath to make sure that she wasn't too squeezed in, and put on her sweater again. Under the wool, the bra was even more noticeable: she really had breasts, this time. What were people going to call her from now on? Miss?

She went back to sitting cross-legged, closed her eyes again, but the pictures didn't come back, so she stayed still, her hands resting on her knees.

Pataud barked downstairs in the hall, the door creaked, the wooden heels of Swedish clogs clattered on the tiles then clumped heavily on the treads of the wooden staircase.

"Fat Josiane," thought Adeline immediately.

Fat Josiane always came by to say hello. She was too ample and too nice to be satisfied with her own existence alone, she always wanted to know how others were, overflowed with goodness, cried with the sad, laughed with the happy and ate snacks with everyone. She was the perfect chum, ready to organize picnics, ready to be number two anywhere at all, indefatigable.

She came into the room, out of breath and radiant. She brushed back the strand of hair stuck to her forehead.

Adeline immediately arched her back.

Josiane flopped onto the eiderdown, the box-spring creaked. Adeline started up.

"I'm done in," said Josiane. "Thérèse and Madeleine won't be able to come."

She noticed right away that Adeline was wearing a bra but for a moment she was trying to find what she could say to please her.

Adeline arched her back a bit more, already disappointed.

It was too late for an "oh" of surprise with a shake of the finger. She couldn't say "Aren't you the lucky one" to her, either, since she herself had been wearing a bra for almost a year. And she couldn't say flatly "You too"—that would have been drawing too much attention to herself.

Adeline was pretending to look at something out the window; leaning on one arm, she craned her neck and desperately thrust out her breasts.

If she simply said to her, "Well, so you have a bra," that would be too banal, out of proportion with the event; just as "Goon, enough of your act. I saw your bra!" would be vulgar and, after all, hardly friendly.

Adeline turned abruptly and looked Josiane straight in the eye. She had her nasty look.

The fat one opened her mouth to say anything at all right away but nothing came, a huge sob rose in her throat. Nothing else counted for her besides being nice and she couldn't bear the thought of not being always liked. She stretched out a hand looking for help, something to go on, a bit of warmth, and her fat fingers like so many little sausages touched Adeline's right breast accidentally. Her face lit up right away and Josiane got the impression that the breast was offering itself slightly for a caress. She caressed it. The brassiere was hard under the wool sweater.

"Let me see it?"

Adeline pulled up the bottom of her sweater and

showed the bra. Josiane helped her and in her eagerness
made her take the pullover off all the way.

"It's very nice."

"I hardly feel it."

Josiane passed her hand back and forth over the cups.
Adeline was happy, there was not a shadow left in her
expression and she accepted Josiane's inspection grate-
fully. Josiane was knowledgeable, she appreciated the
quality of the straps, she even slipped a finger under the
elastic to try the tension. Adeline had risen to her knees
and pivoted her bust according to the whim of her fat
chum who was pink with pleasure and was breathing
harder and harder.

"Turn around. . . . Mine doesn't fasten like that, it's
a simple hook."

"Do you like it?"

"This one must hold better. . . . Wait."

To see, Josiane unfastened the hook, and the new elastic releasing with a snap slipped away from her. She
laughed and Adeline turned back to face her laughing
too.

"It would make a good slingshot!"

"Look, you have a red mark."

Adeline sat back on her heels and looked. Josiane's index finger ran over the line left by the elastic right below
her bust.

"I don't feel anything."

The finger rose to the nipple of the left breast, light,
gentle, then circled slowly around the pink tip. The first
finger of her left hand met the right breast and gave it a
parallel caress.

Adeline felt as if her breasts were getting hard. A
shiver ran from her stomach up to her chin. She
breathed in through the nose and her lips closed in a
smile of well-being.

Josiane placed her palms frankly on the breasts, the
tips of her fingers lightly brushing the skin almost up to
the armpits. Adeline heard her friend's forced breathing
and saw nothing but the top of her skull; the brassiere
was hanging in the air, like a curtain in front of her
hands; she closed her eyes.

What she saw then upset her so much that she froze,

abandoning her bust to Josiane. She saw the usual cave,
she made out in the background the tall red flames risen
from the bowels of the earth, she saw the gnomes, the
elves, the soot-colored squirrels, she saw the swords,
the pitchforks, the tridents, the flashes of lightning. She
heard bursts of voices. The earth in front of the cave
scorched. Animals fled, sick with terror. The Devil,
dressed like Batman with horns and a tail, came out of
the cave, his long red cape flecked with sparks. He came
up to her and took her in his arms. Head hanging and
her hair brushing the ground, she read upside down the
sign "Hell" over the entrance to the cave. Inside she
saw, still upside down, the old parish priest who was
laughing as he bounced her livid mother on his knees, as
in the photograph, and her grandmother, who was
holding out her arms and whose tears, hardly out of her
gray eyes, evaporated in the heat of the flames. She began the incredible descent of the tortuous staircase that
would never end. The pointed nails of the Devil were
digging in below her breast. She was lost and was beginning nothing less than the infernal rosary of a hundred
million sorrows.

Josiane, undone by so much immobility, wasn't quite
so sure anymore what to do with her caresses. She took
back her hands, rubbed them on her skirt, and since
Adeline still wasn't moving, got up, said, "Well, I've got
to go," and left.

The steps creaked, the clogs clumped, Pataud yapped,
the door slammed. Adeline put her bra back in place
convulsively, pulled on her sweater, crossed her arms
over it and remained prostrate until her grandmother returned.

For twenty days and twenty nights, she held out and
never took off her brassiere. She washed through the
gaps. It grew dull, it became dirty.

The twenty-first morning her grandmother became
aware of it, got angry and scolded her. Adeline's head
fell.

She was severely punished and immediately felt
better.

"That Invisible 'They'"

Deborah Hautzig
New York, 1970s

In the novel, Hey, Dollface, Val tries to understand the sexual current between herself and her best friend, Chloe, a feeling "that was unlike anything I'd ever experienced before." One night the two are discovered by Chloe's mother in an embrace. Distraught, Val runs home, but later musters enough courage to talk about the incident with Chloe.

"Chloe, remember what we—what we were doing—"

She gave a harsh little laugh. "As if I could forget!"

I attempted a smile and failed. "Well, Chloe, I—" I knew I was going to cry. She got down on the floor with me and poked my nose gently.

"Whatsa matter, dollface?"

I hid my face in my hands. "Get away! I'm not a doll, I'm me and I'm awful and I'm sorry!" Two tears squeezed out, and I wiped them away and looked at her. "Chloe, your mother saw us."

"I know."

My head began to spin. How could she know?

"I was awake too. I didn't want you to know. I was—scared. That's why I didn't call."

"You were scared of me," I said, more to myself than to her. So I was right; I had scared her.

"No."

"Of your mother?"

"No, Val—of myself, I guess."

I began fiddling with the fringe on my bedspread. "Did your mother say anything?"

Chloe got up and sat back down on the radiator. "No. Not a word. That's what was so creepy." All this time I'd been worried Mrs. Fox had forbidden her to see me again, and she hadn't even mentioned it! "But you know what she did do?'' I raised my eyebrows questioningly. ''She found that box with my beautiful-lady collection under my bed and she threw it out.''

''She—what? What did she do that for?''

''She said, 'What kind of girl are you?' She made me feel like some sort of pervert for collecting them. She doesn't understand. But she wouldn't have done it if she hadn't seen us. She thinks we—you know,'' she said haltingly.

''She thinks we made love, doesn't she?'' I said acidly. ''She must love me now. Christ, she'll never want me over again. Oh, Chloe, can't you tell her it isn't true?'' I said, feeling like a hypocrite and hating myself for it the instant I said it.

''And—and what if it were true?'' Chloe said defiantly.

I could see her lip tremble slightly. ''What do you mean?''

''Well—look at all the men and women having sex who don't even like each other, let alone love each other. Isn't that the real sin?''

''Yes,'' I whispered, holding my chin up. ''Yes, that's the sin. And how would your moral mother feel about that?''

''I bet my mother thinks sex is sinful in any case,'' she said dryly. Then she leaned toward me. ''Val, don't you understand? It doesn't matter what she thinks. You're my best friend. When I decide to go to bed with a man I'll be lucky if I'm half as crazy about him as I am about you. I don't have to defend anything! Nothing can change how I feel about you!''

''No?'' I said, nastily, wanting to cry.

''No. Because I love you.''

''I love you too,'' I said, wondering why it had never occurred to me.

''You know, sometimes they all make me sick!'' Chloe yelled.

Who's ''they''? I thought.

''We do something like—what we did once,'' she faltered. ''And then there's a choice; either I'm a lesbian forever or I stop being myself with you. When I don't want either one.'' I watched her carefully, not saying anything. ''I mean—gosh, other people must think about stuff like this.''

''Really? Do you really think they do?'' I said hopefully.

''Sure they do. They must. But just because you think about something doesn't mean you're guilty of it.''

''Guilty!'' I pounced. ''See? You said 'guilty.' But, Chloe, we didn't just think.''

''But we didn't do what my mother thought either. Maybe—maybe I've thought about it,'' she said, blushing.

''Well—maybe I have too.''

''Maybe I've even wished it. Maybe I'll wish it again. But I'll bet if you gave everyone what they wished for, it would turn out it wasn't what they really wanted after all. I just want us to be the way we always were.'' My ivy plant was making shadows on her face, and I watched her cautiously.

''I know,'' I said finally. ''Chloe? I'm not a—a lesbian,'' I said. ''I'm not anything at all. Some guys turn me on a lot, but I'm not ready to have sex yet. What we did—I mean—I did what I wanted to do. I didn't even think about it first. It just came naturally, because I—'' What am I trying to say? I thought helplessly. Why is it coming out so mixed up? ''You're my best friend,'' I said. ''And now—you won't be—''

''I will be. I'll always be your friend.''

You know what it is? I thought. We're scared of each other. I'm scared that she'll be afraid of me and she's probably thinking the same thing. I wonder if we'd have been scared if her mother never saw. Maybe we'd never have had to admit to each other that any of this had crossed our minds. We could have just gone on being best friends and maybe fantasizing once in a while or being affectionate and pretending that sexual attraction never occurred to us. But Mrs. Fox *had* seen; Chloe had admitted what she felt, and so had I. There was no turning back. How do you separate loving as a friend and sexual love—or do they cross over sometimes?

''It isn't fair,'' Chloe burst out angrily. ''God, I can't believe how hung up we've gotten, just because of my mother!''

"But Chloe, it isn't just because of your mother," I said gently. She jerked her head round to face me, her eyes filled with tears.

"What do we do?" she said.

Chloe—is that you? I thought. Always rebelling and always so certain of what you think—what's happened to you?

"What do we do?" I echoed. "I'll tell you what we do. Do you want to be my friend?"

"Of course, I—"

"Are you sure? You're not afraid, or turned off?"

"Yes, I'm sure."

"O.K. Do you want to be my—my lover?" Am I *saying* this? I thought incredulously. Am I admitting that it's a possibility?

"No," she mouthed inaudibly. "Sometimes I thought I did. I just want us to be friends like we always were, and to think what I want. Like everybody else."

"But," I said, less sure of myself, "I can still kiss you good-bye and stuff—like we always do—" I paused and looked at her bleakly. Is it the world out there making us feel guilty? I thought. Is it the world saying, either you're a lesbian or you're not, with no room for Chloe and me? "I mean, I feel like we don't fit into any slots at all, and they want us to, but we can't," I said. There was that invisible "they" again. Who are "they"? Nobody knows about the feelings we have for each other; nobody is literally trying to force us to choose anything. And then gradually it came to me; "they" must just be us. *We're* trying to put *ourselves* into slots, and condemning ourselves for not being able to.

"We don't have to fit into any slots," Chloe said. "So let's stop trying."

I moved closer to her and looked up at her face. Suddenly it didn't matter to me anymore whether things were "right" or whether they were "wrong," whether the attraction we felt for each other was "good" or "bad." I'd been looking for some kind of judgment or approval, but when I asked adults like Miss Udry or Mom they didn't know any more than I did. But *I* can decide! I thought. I've been so worried about what other people would think I never asked myself what *I* thought.

It isn't wrong, I thought; it isn't bad. Maybe for someone else it would be, but it isn't for me.

"Chloe, that guy you played tennis with—that's just the beginning. Pretty soon you'll forget all about me," I said flatly.

"Are you nuts?"

"No, it's true. Once my cousin Shirley was supposed to have me sleep over at her apartment, and then at the last minute she told me I'd have to come some other time 'cause she had a date. She said that's the way it is when you get older."

Chloe looked ready to scream. "Well, your cousin is full of shit! I'm *never* going to be like that. Never!"

"Really, Chloe? You mean it?"

"Damn right I mean it. Ooooh, I can't stand people like that. Don't you ever get like that," she said, pointing a finger at me.

"Honey, the day I have that choice I might lose my head," I said jokingly, but she jumped down and took my chin firmly in her hand.

"That's exactly it. People like your stupid cousin think if you say no to someone they won't come back. Well, maybe they *wouldn't*, for *her*. But any guy worth anything will come back for you. You hear me?"

I smiled. "Chloe, I love you."

"You have to promise me you won't turn out that way. Do you swear it?"

"I take a sacred vow. I, Valerie Hoffman, shall never dump my friends on account of some guy. And since you're my only friend," I added, "I swear I shall never dump *you* on account of some guy. Do you swear it too?"

"I swear it."

"O.K., that's settled then."

I'm in Love with the
Son of Sidi Daud

I'm in love with the son of Sidi Daud.

Why won't he look at me?

She's in love with the son of Sidi Daud.

Who wants to guess why he won't look at her?
——Because his father was with him!
——Because your breast popped out of your blouse!
——Because he's worried about money!
——Because a wasp stung his nose!
——Because the shaykh signed him up for forced
labor!
——Because the tea gave him a stomach ache!
——Because you're so beautiful. He's afraid to look
at you!
——Because he loves you, and your look burns him
to the heart!
Tell him you'll meet him tonight in the village square
And tomorrow it's you who won't dare look at him!

Improvised song
Translated by Elizabeth Warnock Fernea
Berber tribe, Morocco

What She Said to Her Girl-Friend

On beaches washed by seas
older than the earth,
in the groves filled with bird-cries,
on the banks shaded by a punnai
clustered with flowers,
        when we made love
my eyes saw him
and my ears heard him;
my arms grow beautiful
in the coupling
and grow lean as they come away.
        What shall I make of this?

Venmanippūti from the Kuruntokai
Translated by A.K. Ramanūjan
India, 1st–3rd centuries

"How Will I Know?"

Sheila Schwartz
New York, 1970s

Neither Henrik nor my mother had any money, so they never went anywhere. They just kind of sat around being peaceful together. I think his friendship was good for my mother; it calmed her and made her more secure. Henrik told her about court cases, crimes, his own research; and he showed her a side of campus life that she had previously never even thought about.

"Mom," I asked her one day, "are you in love with Henrik?"

"I'm very fond of him," she said. "If you mean do we have a romantic attachment, the answer is no."

"Why not?"

"Just not."

"Were you in love with Percy?"

"I think so."

"How could you be in love with Percy and not with Henrik?"

"Honey, please drop the subject," she said. Then, turning away, she added, "Henrik didn't even finish college."

"So what? I think he's a great human being. He's a lot better than some of those phony English professors you know."

She was getting mad. "Look, let's drop Henrik and Percy. Let's talk about *your* boy friends."

"Ha, ha, very funny. You know I don't have any."

"Well, when you do you'll find that you don't like my interference."

"I probably won't have any until I'm too old to do anything with them."

"Darling, be patient. You'll find love soon enough."

"How will I know when I'm in love?" I asked.

"You just will. It's something that happens without volition."

"And you can't make yourself love Henrik?"

"No."

"Or not love Percy?"

Her eyes looked watery. "No."

"Are you telling me that a person has absolutely no control over love?" I looked at her with wonder.

"None at all."

"How awful," I gasped. "It sounds kind of like a disease or a plague from heaven."

"Or a gift from heaven," my mother said.

"Let me get this clear." I thought for a minute. "You kind of wait around for love to strike, like in *Romeo and Juliet?*"

"Exactly."

"But suppose love never strikes? Then what can people do?"

"They do without, they settle, they lie to themselves, they pretend, they think that by adopting love's postures they will actually find themselves in love."

"Does that happen to many people?"

"I'm afraid so."

"Well, if they don't *know* they aren't in love, maybe it doesn't seem so bad."

"Maybe."

"Still," I mused, "it doesn't seem fair. Some people just live and other people love them, and some people never get loved. It's kind of like some people are born with musical talent, or sports talent. And some people are born with love talent."

"Right."

"Can even rich and beautiful people not have love?"

"Yes."

"And an ugly, unimportant person can?"

"Sure."

It seemed pretty scary and chancy to me. Sort of like playing Bingo. I thought for a moment, then asked, "Isn't it possible that someone might find love in one place and not in another? I mean, you might not find love here, but you might find it in New York City?"

"That's right." She laughed. "That's why people travel. It's the basis of the tourist business."

I giggled. "You mean people don't really go to see famous churches?"

"Only secondarily."

She seemed so positive. Of course, she hadn't done much traveling, so maybe she didn't know. But it was true that my father had gone off to Denmark with his student. Why Denmark? Why couldn't he have stayed here, near me?

"Let me get this straight," I said. "Love just hits you, like in *Romeo and Juliet*, and there's nothing you can do to get it."

"Yes, that's my opinion. But I'm not exactly the world's greatest authority on love. In fact, you might well describe it as one of my failure areas."

Her mood was changing. I didn't mean to make her feel depressed.

"Why are you asking me all these questions?" she asked.

"I don't want to upset you," I said cautiously. "I'm just trying to find out. I mean, kids in school talk a lot about getting laid, but nobody seems to understand anything about being in love."

She reached out and hugged me, cheerful again. "All right, what else do you want to know?"

"I want you to describe to me how you feel when you're in love, so I'll recognize it when it hits me."

She thought for a moment, then said, "You like the way a person smells and tastes—and you feel lonely and unsettled unless you're with that person. You feel that you're more *with* that person than without him." . . .

"Oh, Mom," I said.

"It's all so sad. You don't know when love will strike you, and you don't know when you will lose it, and you can't do anything about it either way. It's not fair."

She wiped her eyes. "So who says anything is fair?"

"Don't tell me that. It's got to be fair. Otherwise, nothing has any meaning. It's all so passive. According to your theory, you could even be an amoeba, a blob doing nothing, and somebody might love you. And you

could be a beautiful movie actress, and nobody might.
Then, even if you get love, you have no certainty of
keeping it. Honestly, it's all so terrible, it's enough to
make me give up."

"Look at it another way, Jen. It's so wonderful that
you can always keep hoping."

"It's a terrible mystery."

"No," she laughed gently, "it's a wonderful mystery.
Don't ever give up. I'm still hoping, even at my age, and
you have a long life of loving ahead. You're just at the
beginning of your life."

Well, I can't say I felt better after our talk, but I certainly didn't feel worse about love. As a matter of fact, it
kind of did leave me hoping. *Serendipity*, my mother
called it. That means something good waiting for you
just around the bend, just when you least expect to find
it.

I Will Lift
My Gown

Love Song

I painted my eyes with black antimony
I girded myself with amulets.

I will satisfy my desire,
you my slender boy.
I walk behind the wall.
I have covered my bosom
I shall knead coloured clay
I shall paint the house of my friend,
O my slender boy.
I shall take my piece of silver
I will buy silk.
I will gird myself with amulets
I will satisfy my desire
the horn of antimony in my hand,
Oh my slender boy!

Traditional song
Translated by H. Gaden
Bagirmi kingdom, Africa

I Will Lift My Gown

If you think much of me
you may look when I lift my gown
in fording the Tsin; but
should you not like me
surely others will,
stupid lad!

   Yes, if you love me
   I will lift my gown
   when I cross the Wei;
   but if you have no thoughts for me
   you will leave me to others,
   silly boy!

Book of Odes
China, 500 B.C.

Love Charm

All during the night I dream of him.
And as soon as it is daylight
I get up and dress
And slip out and wait for him
To see if perhaps he will come by.

And when at last I see him coming toward me
My heart pounds
And I am afraid to look at him.
I do not raise my eyes.

He passes close by me
And sometimes he gives me a flower
He has picked
Or a sweet grass he has twisted
Into a bracelet.
And I wear the flower
Even when it is wilted.
And I wear the bracelet
Until it falls to pieces.

But when he is gone again
I raise my eyes
And look at him.
And I say this charm while I look at him
So that he must come back to me.

I say:

Suwa!
May you turn back
And look at me!

May you see only me
Wherever you look!

May you think about me
All through the day and the night!

May you come here to me every day!
May you love me as I love you!

I say this and I cry to myself. I cry and cry.

Traditional chant
Translated by Theodora Kroeber
Yana tribe, California

Love Song

I passed by the house of the young man who loves me;
I found the door was open.
He sat at his mother's side,
In the midst of his brothers and sisters.
Everyone who passes in the roadway loves him.
He is a fine young man, a man with no equal,
A love of rare character.
And how he stared out at me as I passed by the house!
(I was walking abroad on my own, for my own enjoy-
    ment.)
And how my heart leaped up with love,
My dearest lover, when I set eyes on you!
Ah! If only my mother knew what was in my heart
She would go and visit him in a flash!
O golden goddess, inspire in her this thought!
Oh, how I wish to go to my love,
To embrace him openly in front of his family,
And weep no longer because of people's attitude,
To be happy because everyone knows at last
That he and I are in love with each other.
I would hold a little festival in honour of my goddess!

My heart is on fire with the idea of venturing abroad
    again tonight

In order to catch another glimpse of my lover . . .

Translated by J.E. Manchip White
North Africa, 1400 B.C.

I Dial . . . I Dial

The old clock chimed eight, it's Saturday night.
I slink out of the house and walk in a coolish gait.
I enter O'Flanagan's Drugstore, and into a phone booth.
A dime sings down the phone—
      I dial,
      I dial,
I dial a little more.
"Doing somethin' ta nite?
Great, pick ya up soon,
We'll eat at the cafe.
Cafe Blue Moon."
I run out of the booth;
I dance like a whirl.

That was done pretty good,
    for a first time,
        by a girl!

Debbie Hoeltzell
Greenvale, New York, 1973

"The World Her Oyster"

Ella Leffland
California, 1940s

One afternoon, sitting under the walnut tree with my book, I saw the back porch door open, and Peggy came out.

"Want to take a walk?" she asked, crossing the glare of the yard.

I dropped the book and scrambled to my feet. "Maybe. I don't care."

"How do you think I look? Your mother said I looked terrific."

"My mother doesn't say terrific."

"Well, she said *nice*."

She did look nice. She must have lost another five or six pounds by now, and though she wasn't slim, she wasn't a big fat girl anymore. She wore a crisp chalky blue full skirt and a crisp white peasant blouse and spotless white Wedgies matched by a dainty white purse. The most outstanding thing was her hair, which hung to her shoulders all of a piece like a big catcher's mitt, a dense complex of fiery glints and gleams.

She touched it. "Rosemary oil, I just discovered it. It works wonders."

"Where do you want to go?"

"Oh, just around." She started down the driveway with small, new, dainty steps. "I really like your mother, I always have. She's so nice. And she's so attractive. And she has such a cute accent."

"She doesn't have an accent."

"Of course she does. They both do. It's so cute."

"Cute? They're not cute."

"I didn't say *they* were cute, their *accent's* cute."

"But they don't have one."

"You just don't notice it, you're always around them. When's Karla coming home?"

"I don't know." How could they have an accent? I would have heard it. You couldn't live with somebody for twelve years and not notice something like that. What was all this small talk about family anyway, as if she had suddenly become one of the iced-tea ladies? That tiny purse. That mincing walk.

Except that she was going faster now, and from the tiny purse she grabbed a stick of gum, unwrapped it, and slapped it into her mouth. All at once she was her old corky self, chewing openmouthed as we hastened along, scratching an itch on her behind, even banging out a belch from times gone by.

But it was all nerves, I realized later, for on Main Street the gum flew to the pavement and she pushed open the door to Buster Brown's, saying over her shoulder, "Don't you want to say hello to Peter?"

He was trying shoes on a customer. We waited at the counter. I saw that Peggy's face had become a mask of apprehension, as if earwigs were crawling up her leg. When Peter came behind the counter to make out the sales slip, she kept shifting from foot to foot and staring over his head at different places on the wall. The cash register rang. The shoes were wrapped. She began clearing her throat in a low, testing way; beads of sweat stood out on her upper lip. The customer departed. Peter stuck his pencil behind his ear.

"Say, who's this? Don't tell me it's Peggy?"

"Hello, Peter," she said in soft, sliding tones, breathlessly, and took hold of my hand. "We were just going by and we thought, why not drop in for a minute? So here we are . . . it's certainly a hot day, isn't it? And how's the shoe business these days?"

She was twisting my hand painfully as she got through all this, but above the tortured activity her face wore the calm, round-eyed expression she used on parents and teachers, only the smallest blush hinting at her inner turmoil. Finally I yanked my fingers free and held them up, blowing on them, but this had no effect on Peggy. Her eyes were filled with Peter.

He was saying business wasn't bad, and it was hot all

right, 104 degrees, and as he spoke, I saw with horror that she was very slowly sucking in her cheeks and that the left eyebrow was rising high, high, in Dietrich's sultry arch.

Coupled with the still-round eyes, this expression gave her an effect of weird astonishment. Peter glanced away, rearranging some pads and pencils, and I saw a hint of a smile on his lowered face. But when he looked up, he was serious.

"Well, I'm glad you dropped by. You look very nice today, Peggy. Nice hairdo."

She had to release her cheeks to reply. "Thank you, Peter," she drawled in a low, husky voice, "I'm so glad you think so." Then, as the eyebrow came slowly down, she turned gracefully away, saying that we had to be going, and gave him a last look over her shoulder, drawling once more in the low, husky voice, " 'Bye, Peter . . . see you later."

Outside, she walked to the next building and leaned against it, heaving a deep sigh.

"You acted like a nut. Peter thought you were a nut."

"He did not."

"You were making insane faces."

"I was not."

Just then our ears were assailed by a piercing whistle as a soldier passed by. Looking back over his shoulder, he winked hard at Peggy, screwing up his face in a virile knot.

"He winked!" she whispered, clutching my arm.

"So what, they'll wink at anything."

But she was already walking on, her eyes bright and darting, the world her oyster.

The Price of
a Buffalo

Folksong

The middle part of my body is swelling up:
Mother, I can no longer stay at home.
If I stay, the village will take away our buffalo
as a fine,
Therefore, I have to go away in a hurry.

Traditional song
Vietnam

Ballad

I loved
secretly,
but now
the pain!
My belly
is huge,
and birth
is near.

Mother yelled,
Father slapped
me. Both
fumed. I'm
alone in
this room,
and can't
play outside.

Neighbors
look at me
as at a
monster. They
stare, poke each
other, and
clam up till
I walk by.

They always
point at me
with fingers.
I'm a wonder.
They wink
obscenely.
They damn me
for one sin.

Why am I
talking?
I'm gossip
in every mouth.
Pain grows
and now
my friend
is gone.

He ran off
for good,
back to France.
Without him
I hurt,
almost die.
I cry
for myself.

Translated by Willis Barnstone
Medieval Europe, ca. 1200

Sister

Sister, don't scold me.
I know I shouldn't have slept in the *azib*.
You know, sister, what can happen there
On a warm night, close to a young man . . .
Am I the only girl to give in
To the wishes of a young man?
How could I know that this night
Would bring a heavy stomach?
Sister, keep my secret!
Old Tamoucha knows the virtues of plants,
Of plants that will quickly deliver me.
Sister, you know well that afterwards
There won't be a trace.
Tamoucha has the alum and resin ready
To restore my virginity.
She has even promised to mention marriage
(Is it possible?) to our dear cousin . . .
Tell me, sister, will he make a good husband?

Mririda n'Ait Attik
Translated by Daniel Halpern and Paula Paley
Morocco, 20th century

"The Lesson"

Betty Smith
Brooklyn, New York, 1930s

"Today, I am a woman," wrote Francie in her diary in the summer when she was thirteen. She looked at the sentence and absently scratched a mosquito bite on her bare leg. She looked down on her long thin and as yet formless legs. She crossed out the sentence and started over. "Soon, I shall become a woman." She looked down on her chest which was as flat as a washboard and ripped the page out of the book. She started fresh on a new page.

"Intolerance," she wrote, pressing down hard on the pencil, "is a thing that causes war, pogroms, crucifixions, lynchings, and makes people cruel to little children and to each other. It is responsible for most of the viciousness, violence, terror and heart and soul breaking of the world."

She read the words over aloud. They sounded like words that came in a can; the freshness was cooked out of them. She closed the book and put it away.

That summer Saturday was a day that should have gone down in her diary as one of the happiest days of her life. She saw her name in print for the first time. The school got out a magazine at the end of the year in which the best story written in composition class from each grade was published. Francie's composition called "Winter Time" had been chosen as the best of the seventh grade work. The magazine cost a dime and Francie had had to wait until Saturday to get it. School closed for the summer the day before and Francie worried that she wouldn't get the magazine. But Mr. Jenson said he'd be working around on Saturday and if she brought the dime over, he'd give her a copy.

Now in the early afternoon, she stood in front of her door with the magazine opened to the page of her story. She hoped someone would come along to whom she could show it.

She had shown it to mama at lunch time but mama had to get back to work and didn't have time to read it. At least five times during lunch, Francie mentioned that she had a story published. At last mama said,

"Yes, yes. I know. I saw it all coming. There'll be more stories printed and you'll get used to it. Now don't let it go to your head. There are dishes to be washed."

Papa was at Union Headquarters. He wouldn't see the story till Sunday but Francie knew he'd be pleased. So she stood on the street with her glory tucked under her arm. She couldn't let the magazine out of her hands even for a moment. From time to time she'd glance at her name in print and the excitement about it never grew less.

She saw a girl named Joanna come out of her house a few doors away. Joanna was taking her baby out for an airing in its carriage. A gasp came up from some housewives who had stopped to gossip on the sidewalk while going to and fro about their shopping. You see, Joanna was not married. She was a girl who had gotten into trouble. Her baby was illegitimate—bastard was the word they used in the neighborhood—and these good women felt that Joanna had no right to act like a proud mother and bring her baby out into the light of day. They felt that she should have kept it hidden in some dark place.

Francie was curious about Joanna and the baby. She had heard mama and papa talking about them. She stared at the baby when the carriage came by. It was a beautiful little thing sitting up happily in its carriage. Maybe Joanna *was* a bad girl but certainly she kept her baby sweeter and daintier than these good women kept theirs. The baby wore a pretty frilled bonnet and a clean white dress and bib. The carriage cover was spotless and showed much loving handiwork in its embroidery.

Joanna worked in a factory while her mother took care of the baby. The mother was too ashamed to take it out so the baby got an airing only on week-ends when Joanna wasn't working.

Yes, Francie decided, it was a beautiful baby. It looked just like Joanna. Francie remembered how papa had described her that day he and mama were talking about her.

"She has skin like a magnolia petal." (Johnny had never seen a magnolia.) "Her hair is as black as a raven's wing." (He had never seen such a bird.) "And her eyes are deep and dark like forest pools." (He had never been in a forest and the only pool he knew was where each man put in a dime and guessed what the Dodgers' score would be and whoever guessed right got all the dimes.) But he had described Joanna accurately. She was a beautiful girl.

"That may be," answered Katie. "But what good is her looks? They're a curse to the girl. I heard that her mother was never married but had two children just the same. And now the mother's son is in Sing Sing and her daughter has this baby. There must be bad blood all along the line and no use getting sentimental about it. Of course," she added with a detachment of which she was astonishingly capable at times, "it's none of my business. I don't need to do anything about it one way or the other. I don't need to go out and spit on the girl because she did wrong. Neither do I have to take her in my house and adopt her because she did wrong. She suffered as much pain bringing that child into the world as though she *was* married. If she's a good girl at heart, she'll learn from the pain and the shame and she won't do it again. If she's naturally bad, it won't bother her the way people treat her. So, if I was you, Johnny, I wouldn't feel too sorry for her." Suddenly she turned to Francie and said, "Let Joanna be a lesson to *you*."

On this Saturday afternoon, Francie watched Joanna walk up and down and wondered in what way she was a lesson. Joanna acted proud about her baby. Was the lesson there? Joanna was only seventeen and friendly and she wanted everybody to be friendly with her. She smiled at the grim good women but the smile went away when she saw that they answered her with frowns. She smiled at the little children playing on the street. Some smiled back. She smiled at Francie. Francie wanted to smile back but didn't. Was the lesson that she mustn't be friendly with girls like Joanna?

The good housewives, their arms filled with bags of vegetables and brown paper parcels of meat, seemed to have little to do that afternoon. They kept gathering into little knots and whispered to each other. The whispering stopped when Joanna came by and started up when she had passed.

Each time Joanna passed, her cheeks got pinker, her head went higher and her skirt flipped behind her more defiantly. She seemed to grow prettier and prouder as she walked. She stopped oftener than needed to adjust the baby's coverlet. She maddened the women by touching the baby's cheek and smiling tenderly at it. How dare she! How dare she, they thought, act as though she had a right to all that?

Many of these good women had children which they brought up by scream and cuff. Many of them hated the husbands who lay by their sides at night. There was no longer high joy for them in the act of love. They endured the love-making rigidly praying all the while that another child would not result. This bitter submissiveness made the man ugly and brutal. To most of them the love act had become a brutality on both sides; the sooner over with, the better. They resented this girl because they felt this had not been so with her and the father of her child.

Joanna recognized their hate but wouldn't cringe before it. She would not give in and take the baby indoors. Something *had* to give. The women broke first. They couldn't endure it any longer. They had to do something about it. The next time Joanna passed, a stringy woman called out:

"Ain't you ashamed of yourself?"

"What for?" Joanna wanted to know.

This infuriated the woman. "What for, she asks," she reported to the other women. "I'll tell you what for. Because you're a disgrace and a bum. You got no right to parade the streets with your bastard where innocent children can see you."

"I guess this is a free country," said Joanna.

"Not free for the likes of you. Get off the street, get off the street."

"Try and make me!"

"Get off the street, you whore," ordered the stringy woman.

The girl's voice trembled when she answered. "Be careful what you're saying."

"We don't have to be careful what we say to no street walker," chipped in another woman.

A man passing by stopped a moment to take it in. He touched Joanna's arm. "Look, Sister, why don't you go home till these battle-axes cool off? You can't win with them."

Joanna jerked her arm away. "You mind your own business!"

"I meant it in the right way, Sister. Sorry." He walked on.

"Why don't you go with him," taunted the stringy woman. "He might be good for a quarter." The others laughed.

"You're all jealous," said Joanna evenly.

"She says we're jealous," reported the interlocutor. "Jealous of what, You?" (She said "you" as though it were the girl's name.)

"Jealous that men like me. That's what. Lucky you're married already," she told the stringy one. "You'd never get a man otherwise. I bet your husband spits on you—afterwards. I bet that's just what he does."

"Bitch! You bitch!" screamed the stringy one hysterically. Then, acting on an instinct which was strong even in Christ's day, she picked a stone out of the gutter and threw it at Joanna.

It was the signal for the other women to start throwing stones. One, droller than the rest, threw a ball of horse manure. Some of the stones hit Joanna but a sharp pointed one missed and struck the baby's forehead. Immediately, a thin clear trickle of blood ran down the baby's face and spotted its clean bib. The baby whimpered and held out its arms for its mother to pick it up.

A few women, poised to throw the next stones, dropped them quietly back into the gutter. The baiting was all over. Suddenly the women were ashamed. They had not wanted to hurt the baby. They only wanted to drive Joanna off the street. They dispersed and went home quietly. Some children who had been standing around listening, resumed their play.

Joanna, crying now, lifted the baby from the carriage. The baby continued to whimper quietly as though it had no right to cry out loud. Joanna pressed her cheek to her baby's face and her tears mixed with its blood. The women won. Joanna carried her baby into the house not caring that the carriage stood in the middle of the side-walk.

And Francie had seen it all; had seen it all. She had heard every word. She remembered how Joanna had smiled at her and how she had turned her head away without smiling back. Why hadn't she smiled back? Why hadn't she smiled back? Now she would suffer—she would suffer all the rest of her life every time that she remembered that she had not smiled back.

Some small boys started to play tag around the empty carriage, holding on to its sides and pulling it way over while being chased. Francie scattered them and wheeled the carriage over to Joanna's door and put the brake on. There was an unwritten law that nothing was to be molested that stood outside the door where it belonged.

She was still holding the magazine with her story in it. She stood next to the braked carriage and looked at her name once more. "Winter Time, by Frances Nolan." She wanted to do something, sacrifice something to pay for not having smiled at Joanna. She thought of her story, she was so proud of it; so eager to show papa and Aunt Evy and Sissy. She wanted to keep it always to look at and to get that nice warm feeling when she looked at it. If she gave it away, there was no means by which she could get another copy. She slipped the magazine under the baby's pillow. She left it open at the page of her story.

She saw some tiny drops of blood on the baby's snowy pillow. Again she saw the baby; the thin trickle of blood on its face; the way it held out its arms to be taken up. A wave of hurt broke over Francie and left her weak when it passed. Another wave came, broke and receded. She found her way down to the cellar of her house and sat in the darkest corner on a heap of burlap sacks and waited while the hurt waves swept over her. As each wave spent itself and a new one gathered, she trembled. Tensely she sat there waiting for them to stop. If they didn't stop, she'd have to die—she'd have to die.

After a while they came fainter and there was a longer time between each one. She began to think. She was now getting her lesson from Joanna but it was not the kind of lesson her mother meant.

She remembered Joanna. Often at night, on her way home from the library, she had passed Joanna's house and seen her and the boy standing close together in the narrow vestibule. She had seen the boy stroke Joanna's pretty hair tenderly; had seen how Joanna put up her hand to touch his cheek. And Joanna's face looked peaceful and dreamy in the light from the street lamp. Out of that beginning, then, had come the shame and the baby. Why? Why? The beginning had seemed so tender and so right. Why?

She knew that one of the women stone-throwers had had a baby only three months after her marriage. Francie had been one of the children standing at the curb watching the party leave for the church. She saw the bulge of pregnancy under the virginal veil of the bride as she stepped into the hired carriage. She saw the hand of the father closed tight on the bridegroom's arm. The groom had black shadows under his eyes and looked very sad.

Joanna had no father, no men kin. There was no one to hold her boy's arm tight on the way to the altar. That was Joanna's crime, decided Francie—not that she had been bad, but that she had not been smart enough to get the boy to the church.

Francie had no way of knowing the whole story. As a matter of fact, the boy loved Joanna and was willing to marry her after—as the saying goes—he had gotten her into trouble. The boy had a family—a mother and three sisters. He told them he wanted to marry Joanna and they talked him out of it.

Don't be a fool, they told him. She's no good. Her whole family's no good. Besides, how do you know you're the one? If she had you she had others. Oh, women are tricky. We know. We are women. You are good and tender-hearted. You take her word for it that you are the man. She lies. Don't be tricked, my son, don't be tricked, our brother. If you must marry, marry a good girl, one who won't sleep with you without the priest saying the words that make it right. If you marry this girl, you are no longer my son; you are no longer our brother. You'll never be sure whether the child is yours. You will worry while you are at your work. You'll wonder who slips into your bed beside her after you have left in the morning. Oh, yes, my son, our brother, that is how women do. *We* know. *We* are women. *We* know how they do.

The boy had let himself be persuaded. His women folk gave him money and he got a room and a new job over in Jersey. They wouldn't tell Joanna where he was. He never saw her again. Joanna wasn't married. Joanna had the baby.

The waves had almost stopped passing over Francie when she discovered to her fright that something was wrong with her. She pressed her hand over her heart trying to feel a jagged edge under the flesh. She had heard papa sing so many songs about the heart; the heart that was breaking—was aching—was dancing— was heavy laden—that leaped for joy—that was heavy in sorrow—that turned over—that stood still. She really believed that the heart actually did those things. She was terrified thinking her heart had broken inside her over Joanna's baby and that the blood was now leaving her heart and flowing from her body.

She went upstairs to the flat and looked into the mirror. Her eyes had dark shadows beneath them and her head was aching. She lay on the old leather couch in the kitchen and waited for mama to come home.

She told mama what had happened to her in the cellar. She said nothing about Joanna. Katie sighed and said, "So soon? You're just thirteen. I didn't think it would come for another year yet. I was fifteen."

"Then . . . then . . . this is all right what's happening?"

"It's a natural thing that comes to all women."

"I'm not a woman."

"It means you're changing from a girl into a woman."

"Do you think it will go away?"

"In a few days. But it will come back again in a month."

"For how long?"

"For a long time. Until you are forty or even fifty." She mused awhile. "My mother was fifty when I was born."

"Oh, it has something to do with having babies."

"Yes. Remember always to be a good girl because you can have a baby now." Joanna and her baby flashed through Francie's mind. "You mustn't let the boys kiss you," said mama.

"Is that how you get a baby?"

"No. But what makes you get a baby often starts with a kiss." She added, "Remember Joanna."

Now Katie didn't know about the street scene. Joanna happened to pop into her mind. But Francie thought she had wonderful powers of insight. She looked at mama with new respect.

Remember Joanna. Remember Joanna. Francie could never forget her. From that time on, remembering the stoning women, she hated women. She feared them for their devious ways, she mistrusted their instincts. She began to hate them for this disloyalty and their cruelty to each other. Of all the stone-throwers, not one had dared to speak a word for the girl for fear that she would be tarred with Joanna's brush. The passing man had been the only one who spoke with kindness in his voice.

Most women had the one thing in common: they had great pain when they gave birth to their children. This should make a bond that held them all together; it should make them love and protect each other against the man-world. But it was not so. It seemed like their great birth pains shrank their hearts and their souls. They stuck together for only one thing: to trample on some other woman . . . whether it was by throwing stones or by mean gossip. It was the only kind of loyalty they seemed to have.

Men were different. They might hate each other but they stuck together against the world and against any woman who would ensnare one of them.

* * *

Francie opened the copybook which she used for a diary. She skipped a line under the paragraph that she had written about intolerance and wrote:

"As long as I live, I will never have a woman for a friend. I will never trust any woman again, except maybe mama and sometimes Aunt Evy and Aunt Sissy."

I Shall Live
All the Same

Rejection of a Lover

My younger brother is yellow like the evening star.
My elder brother is beautiful like the morning star.
If the two of them were a coloured cloth
I would not bother to pick it up.

The tree is large and good to lean against it,
its leaves are broad, and its sun roof
offers the coolest shade.

But I prefer to stay in the sun.

Traditional poem
Translated by Ulli Beier
Sumbawa, Indonesia

"My Golden Horizon"

Nelly Ptaschkina
Translated by Pauline D. Chary
Soviet Union, 1918

During the cataclysmic years of the Russian Revolution, Nelly Ptaschkina fled with her family from Moscow to Paris. At age fourteen, she recorded in her diary her dream of rising above what she perceived as the drab fate of ordinary women.

January 26, 1918

. . . Whatever turns events may take, whatever may happen in Russia, nothing can stop the march of time. The years will pass, I shall grow up and enter life. What do I need then? Education and knowledge.

Whatever I neglect now I shall have to pay for later. What I mean by this is that my studies represent to me my very life, the greatest part of my interests, and that is why I am so anxious about their fate.

And after all my ego stands in the first place: events and all the rest only occupy the background. My own life obscures them. . . .

February 18, 1918

. . . A passionate joy comes over me when I look into the distance; there, beyond the houses, the towns, the people, all is radiant, all is full of sunshine. . . . Then it dawns upon me that my life will be different from that of theirs . . . bright, interesting. . . .

Then I see young girls, such as I shall become in three or four years' time. They live, like everyone else, from day to day, waiting for something. They live drab, dull lives. . . . Probably they too had visions of a bright, happy future, and gazed into the golden distance. . . . But now . . . where is that golden distance? Did they not

117

reach it? *Can* one never reach it? Does it exist really, or only in our dreams?

For, surely, I am not the only dreamer. Are they not dreamers too? Shall I live on as they do, following the pattern woven by routine on the canvas of life? Waiting for someone?

There will be nothing. . . . No, no, not that! I am frightened. Give me my golden horizon. Let me live a full life, with all the strength of my soul.

October 14, 1918

And, even if I should fall in love and meet with no response, my life will not suffer from this; I shall arrange it, so as not to depend on love, let alone wait for it as so many girls do. I shall live. If love comes I shall take it; and if not, I shall regret it, wildly regret it, but I shall live all the same.

I see in my imagination a small flat furnished with exquisite comfort. Beauty everywhere, softness, coziness. And I am the mistress of it—a woman and a personality at the same time. I live an interesting life: writers, artists, painters foregather at my house, a really interesting circle, a close, friendly community. I know no picture more attractive than this. I am free, independent. In these surroundings, in which there is even no place for it, I shall not regret love. Life is full without it. It is only the dawn of love which I should miss . . . those moments, the memory of which beautifies all the life of man.

I see children in my imagination and think with joy about them. The husband is a figure that has never appeared in my fancies, quite a stranger in fact; I have never once thought about him.

On one side I see my little home—on the other I think with delight of my children.

"When I Grow Up,
I Won't Marry"

Nisa, as told to Marjorie Shostak
!Kung tribe, Kalahari Desert
Africa, 1930s

In this excerpt from her oral history, Nisa recalls her coming-of-age years in a remote corner of Botswana. In the hunter-gatherer !Kung tribe, girls are expected to marry during early puberty, often to men ten years older than themselves. More than once Nisa's parents made special efforts to arrange a marriage with the kind of man who would give her time to mature. Yet, contented with the life she had, Nisa did everything in her power to remain at home with her parents.

When adults talked to me, I listened. When I was still a young girl with no breasts, they told me that when a young woman grows up, her parents give her a husband and she continues to grow up next to him.

When they first talked to me about it, I said, "What kind of thing am I that I should take a husband? When I grow up, I won't marry. I'll just lie by myself. If I married, what would I be doing it for?"

My father said, "You don't know what you're saying. I, I am your father and am old; your mother is old, too. When you marry, you will gather food and give it to your husband to eat. He also will do things for you. If you refuse, who will give you food? Who will give you things to wear?"

I said, "There's no question about it, I won't take a husband. Why should I? As I am now, I'm still a child and won't marry." I said to my mother, "You say you have a man for me to marry? Why don't you take him and set him beside Daddy? You marry him and let them be co-husbands. What have I done that you're telling me I should marry?"

My mother said, "Nonsense. When I tell you I'm
going to give you a husband, why do you say you want
me to marry him? Why are you talking to me like this?"

I said, "Because I'm only a child. When I grow up and
you tell me to take a husband, I'll agree. But I haven't
passed through my childhood yet and I won't marry!"

A long time passed before my mother talked about it
again. "Nisa, I want to give you a husband. Who shall it
be?" I knew there was another man she wanted me to
marry. I said, "I won't marry him." I almost added,
"You marry him and set him beside Daddy," but I
stopped. This time I was ashamed of myself and didn't
say anything more. . . .

One day . . . I went with my friend Nukha to get
water at the well. That's when Tashay saw me. He
thought, "That woman . . . that's the young woman
I'm going to marry." He called Nukha over to him
and asked, "Nukha, that young woman, that beautiful
young woman . . . what is her name?" Nukha told him,
"Her name is Nisa." He said, "Mmm . . . that young
woman . . . I'm going to tell my mother and father
about her. I'm going to ask them if I can marry her."

Nukha came back and we finished filling the water
containers. We left and walked the long way back to our
village. When Nukha saw my mother, she said, "Nisa
and I were getting water and while we were there, some
other people came to the well and began filling their
water containers. That's when a young man saw Nisa
and said he would ask his parents to ask for her in marriage."

I didn't say anything. Because when you are a child
and someone wants to marry you, you don't talk. But
when they first talked about it, my heart didn't agree.
Later, I did agree, just a little; he was, after all, very
handsome.

The next night there was a dance at our village. We
were already singing and dancing when Tashay and his
family came. They joined us and we danced and sang
into the night. I was sitting with Nukha when Tashay
came over to me. He touched my hand. I said, "What?
What is the matter with this person? What is he doing?
This person . . . how come I was just sitting here and he

came and took hold of me?'' Nukha said, ''That's your husband . . . your husband has taken hold of you. Is that not so?'' I said, ''Won't he take you? You're older. Let him marry you.'' But she said, ''He's my uncle. I won't marry my uncle. Anyway, he, himself, wants to marry you.''

Later his mother and father went to my mother and father. His father said, ''We came here and joined the dance, but now that the dancing is finished, I've come to speak to you, to Gau and Chuko. Give me your child, the one you both gave birth to. Give her to me and I will give her to my son. Yesterday, while he was at the well, he saw your child. When he returned, he told me that in the name of what he felt, I should today ask for her. Then I can give her to him. He said he wants to marry her.''

My mother said, ''Eh, but I didn't give birth to a woman, I gave birth to a child. She doesn't think about marriage, she just doesn't think about the inside of a marriage hut.'' Then my father said, ''Eh, it's true. The child I gave birth to is still a child. She doesn't think about her marriage hut. When she marries a man, she just drops him. Then she gets up, marries another, and drops him, too. She's already refused two men.''

My father continued, ''There is even another man, Dem, his hut stands over there. He is also asking to marry her. Dem's first wife wants Nisa to sit beside her as a co-wife. She goes out and collects food for Nisa. When she comes back, she gives Nisa food to cook so Nisa can give it to her husband. But when the woman unties the ends of her kaross and leaves it full of food beside Nisa, Nisa throws the food down, ruins it in the sand and kicks the kaross away. When I see that, I say that perhaps Nisa is not yet a woman.''

Tashay's father answered, ''I have listened to what you have said. That, of course, is the way of a child; it is a child's custom to do that. When she first marries, she stays with her husband for a while, then she refuses him. Then she goes to another. But one day, she stays with one man. That is also a child's way.''

They talked about the marriage and agreed to it. I was in my aunt's hut and couldn't see them, but I could hear their voices. Later, I went and joined them in my father's hut. When I got there, Tashay was looking at me. I sat down and he just kept looking at me.

When Tashay's mother saw me, she said, "Ohhh! How beautiful this person is! You are certainly a young woman already. Why do they say that you don't want to get married?" Tashay said, "Yes, there she is. I want you to give me the one who just arrived." . . .

We began to live together, but I ran away, again and again. A part of my heart kept thinking, "How come I'm a child and have taken another husband?"

One night, I ran away and slept in the bush, the far away bush. We had been lying together inside the hut, sleeping. But I woke up and quietly tiptoed around his feet and then, very quickly, ran off. I went far, very far, past the mongongo groves near where we were living. It was very dark and I had no fire. I lay down beside the base of a tree and slept.

Dawn broke. People started to look for me and then saw my tracks. They followed them past the mongongo groves and came to where I had slept that night. But I had already left and was digging sha roots in the shade of some trees far away. They came closer. Nukha rushed ahead and, following my tracks, found me. She said that she had come alone looking for me and that the others were elsewhere. She said that we should stay together and dig roots together. I thanked her and told her she was a good friend.

We dug sha roots, and after a while she said, "Let's sit in the shade of that tree. After we rest awhile, we'll dig more roots. I'll stay with you the rest of the day, but when the sun is late in the sky, I'll leave you and return to the village. You can stay alone in the bush again. Tomorrow, I'll roast some of the roots and come back and give them to you to eat." I praised her, "My friend! You are very kind. But when you return to the village, don't tell them you saw me."

We sat in the shade together, resting. Then I looked around and saw the others approaching. I said, "Nukha, people are coming! You lied to me. You said they were in the village, but they're already here. I can't leave now. I'll just have to sit here with you."

The others found us sitting in the shade, full with the sha roots we had dug. They sat down with us. They were many—my older brother, my father, and Tashay. My father said, "What's the matter with you, leaving in the middle of the night like that, running away and sleeping among things of the night? If a lion had seen you, it would have killed you. Or a hyena. Or wild dogs. Any one of them would have killed you. What's the matter with you? Who is responsible for this? You are. You're the one trying to kill yourself."

I said, "Yes, if I want to sleep among the things of the night, what am I taking with me that belongs to any of you? I didn't take anything. I just left and slept by myself. Even if my heart desired it right now, I'd go as far as I wanted. Because that *is* what I want to do, to go far away. If I go back and stay with you, you'll just find me another husband. But everything that I am at this moment refuses one."

My older brother said, "Why should a husband be refused? Isn't a husband like a father? He helps you live and he gives you food. If you refuse to marry, where do you think you'll find food to eat?" I cried, "As I am now, if you take me and bring me back to the village, I will take a poison arrow and kill myself. I don't want to be married!"

My older brother answered, "If you say you are going to stick yourself with a poison arrow, then I'll beat you until you understand what a poison arrow is and what you think you are going to do with it. You're insulting your very self. You are a person, a woman, and you aren't alive to talk like that; you are alive to play and to be happy."

He continued, "Look at your friends, all of them are married. Even Nukha, who is sitting with you, has taken herself in marriage. Why don't you think about how you and Nukha will be married and have homes? Why should your friend have a home and not you?"

I said, "This friend of mine may have taken a husband, but she is certainly older than I am. She is already a grown woman. But me, I'm a child and don't know what I would do with a husband."

He said, "Mm . . . put the roots in your kaross and

let's go, because the person who sits here *is* your husband and he isn't anyone else's. He is the man we gave you. You will grow up with him, lie down with him, and give birth to children with him.''

We all got up and returned to the village. I didn't go to my hut but went to my mother's hut, put down the sha roots, and stayed there. Tashay went and sat by our hut. After a while he called to me, ''Nisa . . . Nisa . . .'' I thought, ''What does he want?'' and went over to him. He gave me some roots he had dug. I took a few and gave them to my mother; I took the others and went back to our hut and stayed there. In the late afternoon, when dusk was falling and the red sky began to stand, I started roasting food by the fire outside our hut. I took the food out of the coals and set it aside. Then I took some and gave it to Tashay. When they had cooled, we ate them—together.

"Can We Be Friends?"

Ursula LeGuin
West Coast, 1976

In the novel Very Far Away from Anywhere Else, *Owen and Natalie at seventeen are nonconformists who have found solace in sharing their interests with each other. Owen, who narrates the story, values Natalie's friendship and encourages her in her dream to become a composer. Then Owen "falls in love" with his best friend.*

I kept wondering things like whether she had ever had another man friend, and what she planned to do about men in amongst her other plans, and what she thought about me in that particular way, and not daring to ask her any of it. The closest I got was once when we were walking the fat off Orville again in the park. I said, "Do you think people can combine love with a career?" It came out and sort of hung there like a corpse. It sounded exactly like a question out of some magazine for Homemakers. Natalie said, "Well of *course* they can," and gave me an extremely peculiar look. Then Orville met a Great Dane on the path and tried to kill and eat it. When that was over, we had gotten past the stupid question. But I kept on being sort of solemn and moody. As we were coming home, Natalie said in a sort of wistful voice, "How come you never do the ape act any more?"

That burned me. That really burned me. When I got home, I was in a foul mood. What I want to do is take this girl suddenly in my arms and kiss her and say "I love you!" and what she wants is for me to jump around with a banana peel looking for fleas in it.

I worked myself up good and proper. I resented her for being so friendly and matter of fact, and I deliberately thought about the way her hair looked when she'd just washed it and it was all sleek and soft, and the texture of her skin, which was white and very fine. And pretty soon I had managed to develop her into the real thing, the mysterious female, the cruel beauty, the untouchable desirable goddess, you name it. So that instead of being my first and best and only real friend, she was something that I wanted and hated. Hated because I wanted it, wanted because I hated it.

In February we drove over to the coast again.

There's always a week around Washington's Birthday that is fantastic. It stops raining. The sun gets warm. The leaf buds start showing on the trees, and some first flowers come out. It's the first week of spring, and in some ways the best, because it's the first, and because it's so short.

You can count on that week, and I'd planned ahead. I got her to get a substitute at the music school and postpone her lessons, so that we could drive over to Jade Beach on Saturday. If her father made any static about it, I didn't care. She had to handle him. We were adults, and she had to learn to do without his approval for everything. I was all ready to tell her exactly that, if she mentioned her father; but she didn't. She didn't seem very enthusiastic about this trip, but I guess she knew I wanted it, so she did what I wanted, like a friend.

When we got to the beach about eleven in the morning, it was low tide, and there were some people clamming. We'd worn shorts under our jeans this time, and we played in the surf again, but it was different. There was a low fog over the sand, not thick and cold, just a kind of dimming as if the air was made of mother-of-pearl, and the waves were quiet and broke slowly, curving over themselves in long blue-green lines, dreamy and regular and hypnotic. We didn't stay together, but drifted apart, wading in the breakers. When I looked, Natalie was way up the beach, walking slowly in the foam, kicking up spray. She walked a little hunched with her hands in her pockets and looked very small and frail there between the misty beach and the misty sea.

The clammers left when the tide began to come back in. After about an hour Natalie came wandering back. Her hair was all tangled in strings and she kept sniffing. The sea air made her nose run, and we hadn't brought any tissues. She looked serene and distant, the way her mother always looked. She'd picked up some rocks, but most of them were the kind that are beautiful when wet, but nothing much when they dry. "Let's eat," she said. "I'm starving."

I'd built a fire with driftwood in the same place as last time, in the hollow sheltered by the big log. She sat down right by the fire. I sat down next to her. I put my arm on her shoulders. Then my heart started hammering in this terrifying way, and I felt really crazy and dizzy, and I took hold of her really hard and kissed her. We kissed, and I couldn't get my breath. I hadn't meant to grab her like that; I meant to kiss her and tell her, "I love you" and talk about it, about love, and that was all. I hadn't thought any farther. I didn't know what would happen to me, that it would be like when you're in deep and a big breaker hits you and pulls you over and down and you can't swim and you can't breathe, and there is nothing you can do, nothing.

She knew when the breaker hit me. And I guess it scared her too, but she wasn't caught in it. Because she pulled free after a bit and drew back, away from me. But she kept hold of my hand, because she saw that I was drowning.

"Owen," she said, "hey, Owen sweetheart, Owen, don't."

Because I was sobbing. I don't know whether it was crying, or because I couldn't breathe.

I came out of it gradually. I was still too shaken up to be embarrassed or ashamed yet, and I reached for her other hand, so we were kneeling in the sand face-to-face, and I said, "Natalie, why can't—we're not kids—don't you—"

She said, "No, I don't. I don't, Owen. I love you. It isn't right."

She didn't mean morally right. She meant right the way the music or the thought comes right, comes clear, is true. Maybe that's the same thing as moral rightness. I don't know.

It was she who said, "I love you." Not me. I never did say it to her.

I said what I'd said before, stammering—I couldn't

stop—and pulling her towards me. All of a sudden her
eyes got very bright, and she scowled and pulled away
and stood right up. "No!" she said. "I *won't* get into this
bind with you! I thought we could manage it, but if we
can't, we can't, and that's it. That's all. If what we have
isn't enough, then forget it. Because it's all we do have.
And you know it! And it's a lot! But if it's not enough,
then let it be. Forget it!" And she turned and walked off,
down the beach to the sea, in tears.

I sat there for a long time. The fire went out. I went
and walked up the beach by the foam line, till I saw her
sitting on a rock over the tide pools at the foot of the
northern cliffs.

Her nose was all red, and her legs were covered with
goose pimples and looked very white and thin against
the barnacle-rough rock.

"There's a crab," she said, "under the big anemone."

We looked into the tide pool a while. I said, "You
must be starving, I am." And we walked back along the
foam line and built up the fire, and pulled on our jeans,
and ate some lunch. Not very much, this time. We didn't
talk. Neither of us knew what to say any more. There
were ten thousand things going on in my head, but I
couldn't say any of them.

We started home right after lunch.

About at the summit of the Coast Range, I found the
one thing I thought needed saying, and said it. I said,
"You know, it's different for a man."

"Is it?" she said. "Maybe. I don't know. You have to
decide."

Then my anger came out and I said, "Decide what?
You've already decided."

She glanced at me. She had that remote look. She
didn't say anything.

The anger took over entirely, and I said, "I guess
that's always the woman's privilege, isn't it?" in this
sneering, bitter voice.

"People make the real choices together," she said.
Her voice was much lower and smaller than usual. She
started blinking and looked away, as if she was watching
the scenery.

I went on driving, watching the road. We drove seventy miles without saying anything. At her house she said, "Good-bye, Owen," in the same small voice, and got out, and went into the house. . . .

Later, after a long absence from each other, they discuss the incident which has divided them.

"About Jade Beach and all that."

"Oh, yeah. Well, that's all right."

I didn't want to talk about it. It loomed up out of the fog much too big and solid and hard. I wanted to turn away and not look at it.

"I've been thinking about it a lot," she said. "See, I thought I had all that figured out. At least for a while. For the next couple of years anyhow. The way I figured, I didn't want to get really involved with anybody. Falling in love or love affairs or marrying or anything like that. I'm pretty young, and there's all these things I have to do. That sounds stupid, but it's the truth. If I could take sex lightly the way a lot of people do, that would be fine, but I don't think I can. I can't take anything lightly. Well, see, what was so beautiful was that we got to be friends. There's the kind of love that's lovers, and the kind of love that's friends. And I really thought it was that way. I thought we'd really made it, and everybody's wrong when they say men and women can't be friends. But I guess they're right. I was . . . too theoretical. . . ."

"I don't know," I said. I didn't want to say anything more, but it got dragged up out of me. "I think you were right, actually. I was pushing the sex stuff in where it didn't belong."

"Yeah, but it does belong," she said in this defeated, morose voice. And then in the fierce voice, "You can't just tell sex to go away and come back in two years because I'm busy just now!"

We went on another block. The rain was fine and misty so that you hardly felt it on your face, but it was beginning to drip down the back of my neck.

"The first fellow I went out with," she said, "I was sixteen and he was eighteen; he was an oboeist, oboeists are all crazy. He had a car and he kept parking it in places with a nice view and then, you know, sort of launching himself onto me. And he started saying, 'This is bigger than either of us, Natalie!' And it made me mad, and I finally said, 'Well it may be bigger than you, but it isn't bigger than me!' That sort of finished that. He was a jerk anyhow. So was I. But anyhow. Now I know what he meant."

After a while she went on, "But all the same . . ."

"What?"

"It doesn't belong. Does it?"

"What?"

"With you and me. It just doesn't work. Does it?"

"No," I said.

She got mad then. She stopped walking and looked at me with that scowl. "You say yes, you say no, you say there isn't anything to decide—Well, there is! And did I decide right or didn't I? *I* don't know! Why do I have to make the decision? If we're friends—and that's the whole point of it, can we be friends?—then we make the decisions together—don't we?"

"OK. We did."

"Then why are you mad at me?"

We were standing there under a big horse chestnut tree in a parking lot. It was dark under the branches, and they kept most of the rain off. Some of the flowers shone like candles in the streetlight, above us. Natalie's coat and hair were all like shadows, all I could see of her was her face and eyes.

"I'm not," I said. It was like the ground was shifting under me, the world reorganizing itself, an earthquake, nothing to hold onto. "I'm really mixed-up. It's just that I can't make sense out of anything. I can't handle it."

"Why not, Owen? What's wrong?"

"I don't know," I said, and I put my hands on her shoulders, and she came up close and held me around the ribs.

"I get scared," I said.

She said, "What of?" into my coat.

"Being alive."

She held onto me, and I held onto her.

"I don't know what to do," I said. "See, I'm supposed to go on living all these years and I don't know how."

"You mean you don't know why?"

"I guess so."

"But, for this," she said, holding on. "For this. For you, for the stuff you have to do, for time to think; for time to hear the music. You know how, Owen. Only you listen to the people who don't!"

"Yeah, I guess so," I said. I was shaking. She said, "It's cold. Let's go home and make some weird tea. I've got some Chinese tea that's supposed to be very calming and aids longevity."

"Longevity is just what I need right now."

We started back. I don't think we said anything much going back or while we were standing around in the kitchen waiting for the water to boil. We took the teapot and cups up to the practice room and sat on the Oriental rug. The Chinese herb tea tasted really vile. It left your mouth feeling scoured out, but then it was kind of pleasant once you got used to it. I was still feeling shaken-up, but I was getting used to that, too.

"Did you ever finish the Thorn Quintet?" I said.

Actually it had only been eight weeks since I had seen her, but it seemed like eight years, and we were in a whole new place.

"Not yet. The slow movement's done, and I have the idea for the last movement."

"Listen, Nat. Your stuff last night, the songs, you know. It made me cry. The second one."

"I know. That's why I had to talk to you again. I mean, because I knew we could. I mean, because . . ."

"Because that's the way you really talk. The rest is just words."

She looked at me straight on and she said, "Owen, you are the neatest person I ever knew. Nobody else understands that. I don't even know any other musicians who understand that. I can't really say anything. I can't even really be anything. Except in music. Maybe later. Maybe when I get good at music, maybe when I learn how to do that, then I'll be able to do some of the rest, too. Maybe I'll even become a human being. But you *are* one."

"I'm an ape," I said. "Trying to do the human act."

"You're good at it," she said, "the best I ever knew."

I lay down on the rug on my stomach and looked down into my cup of tea. It was a sort of murky yellow brown, with bits of Chinese sediment floating around in it.

"If this stuff is really calming," I said, "I wonder if it works on the central nervous system, or the cerebrum, or the cerebellum, or where."

"It tastes like steel wool pads; I wonder if they're calming."

"I don't know, I never ate one."

"For breakfast, with milk and sugar."

"Five thousand percent of the minimum daily adult iron requirement."

She laughed and wiped her eyes. "I wish I could talk," she said. "I wish I was like you."

"What did I ever say?"

"I can't tell you, because I can't talk. I can play it, though."

"I want to hear it.". . .

She looked at me and I looked at her, and we kissed each other on the mouth. But modestly: six seconds at the maximum. . . .

Natalie and I saw each other several times a week in May and June. It was difficult sometimes, because we did not always manage to stick to the six-second maximum. As she said, neither of us are good at taking things lightly. We had several sort of quarrels, because we would both be somewhat frustrated and take it out on the other. But they lasted only about five minutes, because we both were basically certain that we couldn't make any commitment yet, and that sex was no good to us without a commitment, but that we were no good without love. So the best we could do was just go on as we were, together. It was a very good best.

CHAPTER THREE

The Wish: Appearance

My God, grant that I may never have the small pox; that I may grow up pretty; that I may have a beautiful voice; that I may be happily married.

> Marie Bashkirtseff, *Diary*,
> Translated by Mary J. Serrano
> Russia, 1884

"She spends her life in the bathroom" is the perennial complaint of many mothers speaking of their teen-age daughters. Dramatic physical changes take place early in puberty, and a narcissistic pleasure and concern with one's appearance is universal. "Lia, do you think I'm pretty? There was a silence. It seemed as if the light shifted a little around them, as if time slid out of focus and stood still for a moment, as if they were set apart in something old, a ritual, a first knowing" ("Am I Pretty?" by Gunilla Norris).

From the time she is young, a girl learns that it is the beautiful woman who gains power by attracting men and wealth. Until puberty even the ugly duckling has been reassured that beauty will accompany the other changes in her body. Now the transformation into "the swan" must occur, and the adolescent girl often becomes obsessed with the question "Am I pretty?" The opening sections, "Prayer for Beauty" and "The Price," show the intensity of this preoccupation as girls pray for, pursue, and sometimes pay a price to attain an ideal of beauty. Girls are especially vulnerable in these years of transition when conformity rather than uniqueness is valued. For the girl who does not conform to the dominant standard, the question "Am I pretty?" becomes particularly painful. In the section "Not Born to the Clan," we see the anguish of the girl who is born into a minority racial or ethnic group. She can never become the Ideal, as Nellie Wong recalls in her poem, "I read magazines and saw movies, blond movie stars, white skin . . . I began to wear imaginary white skin." Finally, in the concluding section, "Mine and Beautiful," girls triumph over the pressures to conform to a single standard. They are willing to be unique, they accept themselves as they are, and they take pride in their natural beauty.

Prayer for Beauty

Prayer

The light of four suns
and the light of five moons
shall reflect in my eyes.
Let my chin glimmer like a dying star.
Let my eyebrows be moons
my lips a column of ants
and my teeth a herd of elephants.

Traditional
Translated by Ulli Beier
Indonesia

The Crisis

Paul Fournel
France, 1960s

The door of the bathroom swings full tilt and slams. The tooth glass on the shelf under the mirror trembles, wavers and topples. The toothbrush bounces on the basin and the glass shatters on the tile floor.

Clementine puts her finger in her mouth, makes a face, shuffles on the debris. She takes the finger out, looks. A drop of blood appears under the nail bent back by the door. She turns on a thin stream of cold water. The blood drips into the basin and dilutes.

Without turning around, Clementine hooks with the tip of her right foot the stool on which she perches to raise her face to the level of the mirror. She gets up on it. The splinters of glass grate under the wooden legs. She leans her thighs against the rim of the basin and brings her nose to within an inch or less of the mirror.

This morning's socks were too much, and that's all there is to it, and the nice round white collar under the blue sweater too, and the braids, and the pleats in the skirt, and the flat moccasins and the book bag. You are patient for one year, two years, seven years, eight years, and you explode; even when you're nice without trying and sweet without doing it on purpose.

Between her thumb and second finger (the first will stick out straight until the bleeding stops) she picks up the tiny little brush. She spits, the way she has seen her mother do it, on the little strip of mascara set in the plastic box, scrubs the brush to coat it well and darkens her eyelashes. Her hand trembles, the brush touches the cornea, the eye begins to weep. She keeps on.

Being old is to say in the morning with a yawn
"What a filthy mug I've got," and to emerge from
the bathroom painted, radiant and courageous as
an Indian brave.

Time for the grease pencil, black, its tip squashes.
With a single stroke it covers the eyelid. A broad stroke
to the right, a broad stroke to the left, a bit shaky, catch
the balance by backing up, to see. The sockets are black
as coal, deep, lugubrious, with the whites of the eyes
tiny, far in the background. Very good. Adds five years.

Being old is not wearing a hood when it's raining.

Rouge on the cheeks. Two thick patches. Back up. Too
much. It looks healthy and whoever says healthy thinks
little girl and implies country. Blend it with a plastering
of white that reaches to the nostrils. Adds ten years.

Being old is strapping your papers and your
books with a belt.

The lipstick. She chooses the brightest, between an
orangish and a blood. And lays it on. Her lips swell,
spread, run over onto the chin, underline the nose.
Adds fifteen years and that's it.

Being old is having boots and being able to hide
your socks inside them.

Her hair falls to her shoulders in soft ringlets. She
grasps them and crimps them severely until they
wreathe her daubed face. Back up. She looks like a sor-
ceress.
She gets down off the stool.

No longer will she allow them to place a hand tenderly on her head, like a measuring stick.

The splinters of glass grate between the tile floor and
her sneakers.
She goes to the closet where her mother hangs her

clothes. Over her sweater she hooks a brassiere. Over that, she puts on a slip, then a dress. She swims in it. She puts on another, then still another and on top of everything, the muslin dress that her mother wears to go out in the evening.

The teacher: "My little Clementine."
Her father: "My little apple."
Bite them.

She looks for the high heels, the blue ones, the patent leathers. By staying in her sneakers, she just manages to keep them on. A white scarf from her father's drawer. A glance in the mirror. Off we go.

She'll be a singer, it's a life that ages one quickly.

The bathroom door slams again, the heels clop on the stone floor of the entry, the front door slams. It is raining.

She takes the road that goes by the sea. She walks. She twists her ankles, she staggers. She accelerates. She walks.

The rain plasters her hair to her cheeks. She looks straight ahead. The water traces furrows through her make-up, drops of red, white and black stain the front of the dress.

The soaked material sticks to her skin. She brushes strands of hair out of the way. She is so hot that on contact with the summer rain her clothes steam.

"I'll keep walking," she says between clenched teeth, "until I've grown breasts."

"The Question"

Anaïs Nin, *Diary*
New York, 1918

There is another mirror framed in brown wood. The girl is looking at the new dress which transfigures her. What an extraordinary change. She leans over very close to look at the humid eyes, the humid mouth, the moisture and luminousness brought about by the change of dress. She walks up very slowly to the mirror, very slowly, as if she did not want to frighten reflections away. Several times, at fifteen, she walks very slowly towards the mirror. Every girl of fifteen has put the same question to a mirror: "Am I beautiful?" The face is masklike. It does not smile. It does not want to charm the mirror, or deceive the mirror, or flirt with it and gain a false answer. The girl is in a trance. She does not want to frighten the reflection away herself. Someone has said she is very pale. She approaches the mirror and stands very still like a statue. Immobile. Waxy. She never makes a gesture. Surprised. Somnambulistic? She only moves to become someone else, impersonating Sarah Bernhardt, Mélisande, *La Dame aux Camélias*, Madame Bovary, Thaïs. She is never Anaïs Nin who goes to school, and grows vegetables and flowers in her backyard. She is immobile, haunting, like a figure moving in a dream. She is decomposed before the mirror into a hundred personages, recomposed into paleness and immobility. Silence. She is watching for an expression which will betray the spirit. You can never catch the face alive, laughing, or loving. At sixteen she is looking at the mirror with her hair up for the first time. There is always the question. The mirror is not going to answer it. She will have to look for the answer in the eyes and faces of the boys who dance with her, men later, and above all the painters.

"Just You Wait"

Alix Kates Shulman
Baybury Heights, Ohio, 1940s

Until I donned my dental armor it had always been my mother's comforting word against everyone else's that I was pretty. Though I sat before my three-way mirror by the hour studying myself, I couldn't figure out whether to believe my doting mother or the others. I would scrutinize my features, one at a time, then all together, filling in the answers at the end of our common bible, *The Questions Girls Ask*, but I always wound up more confused than when I started.

Does your hair swing loose? Do you tell your date what time you must be home when he picks you up? Do you brush the food particles out of your teeth after every meal? Do you avoid heavy make-up? Do you stand up straight? Do you see to it that your knees are covered when you sit down? Are your cheeks naturally pink? Do you consume enough roughage? Are your ears clean? Do you wear only simple jewelry? Do you protect against body odor? Do you powder your feet? Do you trim your cuticle? Are you a good listener?

It seemed as impossible for me to know how I looked as it was important. Some people said I looked exactly like my mother, the most beautiful woman in the world; others said I resembled my father who, though very wise, was not particularly comely.

But once the grotesque braces were on, all my doubts disappeared. It became obvious that my mother's word, which she didn't alter to accommodate my new appearance, was pure prejudice. While to her, busily imagining the future, the advent of my braces only made the eventual triumph of my beauty more certain—indeed, it was for the sake of my looks that they had been mounted at all—to me they discredited my mother's optimism.

Sometimes at night, after a particularly harrowing day

at school, after receiving some cutting insult or subtle slight, I would cry into my pillow over my plainness. My mother took my insults personally when I told her about them. "What do they know?" she would say, comforting me. "Why, you're the prettiest girl in your class." And when I protested between sobs that no, I was awkward, skinny, and unloved, she would take me in her arms and *promise* me that someday when my braces were removed they would all envy me and be sorry. "You'll see," she would say, stroking my lusterless hair, her eye on some future image of me or some past one of herself. "Just you wait."

I longed to believe her but didn't dare. Before bed each night I would walk to the gable window in my room that seemed to form a perfect shrine and on the first star I saw wish with a passion that lifted me onto my tiptoes to be made beautiful. I performed the rite just so, as though I were being watched. I thought if I wished earnestly enough my life would change and everything I wanted would come true. My grandmothers, teachers, uncles and aunts, and especially my father, were always encouraging me with their constant homilies: if at first you don't succeed try try again; hard work moves mountains; God helps those who help themselves. Nor was there any lack of precedent: from the seminal Ugly Duckling, a tale which never failed to move me to tears, to Cinderella and Snow White and Pinocchio, there were deep lessons to learn. All those step-daughters and miller's daughters and orphan girls who wound up where I wanted to go likely started out having it even worse than I. I wallowed in fable, searching for guidance. White-bearded Aesop stretched his long bony finger across the centuries to instruct me in prudence, while from Walt Disney's Hollywood studio I learned how to hope. "Someday my prince will come" echoed in my ears even as it stuck in my throat. From my first glimpse of the evening star until the ritual wish was over I would not utter a syllable; but pressing my hands tightly together like a Catholic at prayer to dramatize my earnestness, I would summon a certain Blue Fairy, blond-haired and blue-eyed and dressed in a slinky blue satin gown, to materialize. "Star bright, star light, first star I see to-

night, I wish I may I wish I might, have the wish I wish
tonight." I believed she would one day grow before my
eyes from the dot size of the star to life size, and landing
on my window sill reach out with her sparkling wand,
which would glint off my braces and illuminate my darkened room, and touch me lightly, granting my wish. I
had actually seen her only once, in Walt Disney's *Pinocchio*, but I believed in my power to summon her. If it
wasn't ludicrous for my simpering brother Ben to see
himself a general, it couldn't be ludicrous for me to wish
for a minor miracle of my own. When I had finished
wishing, I would stand in my gable until I could spot five
other stars (on a clear night ten), then climb solemnly
into bed.

If during those years I wore braces there was ever any
sign that I might turn out lovely, no one except my
mother noticed it. Certainly not I. Each morning I examined myself anew in the mirror for the fruits of my
wishes; each morning I saw only the glum reality of my
flaws. Faced with my reflection, I shuddered and looked
inward. Those steel bands that encircled my teeth like
fetters and spanned my mouth like the Cuyahoga Bridge
were far more remarkable, more dazzling, than any
other aspect of my countenance; exhibiting obscenely
the decaying remains of the previous day's meal, no
matter how thoroughly I had brushed my teeth the night
before, they completely monopolized my reflection. The
pain they produced in my mouth was nothing to the
pain they caused in my heart. . . .

I placed all my faith in the miracle. I wished nightly on
my star and daily on dandelion puffs to be beautiful. I
wished on fallen eyelashes, on milkweed, on meteors,
on birthday candles, on pediddles, on wishbones, on
air. Seeking some sign of the coming miracle I told my
fortune with cards and drew prophecies from tea leaves.
"Rich man, poor man, beggarman, thief, doctor, law-
yer, merchant, chief": only a beauty could land one of
the desirables. I examined my palm, my horoscope.
I avoided stepping on cracks. I depetaled daisies. I
knocked on wood, set the knives and forks on the table
exactly so, whispered magical syllables and incanta-
tions. I ate gelatin to make my nails hard and munched

carrots to make my hair curl. I crossed my fingers, bit my tongue, held my breath, and wished steadfastly for the single thing in the world that mattered.

Then suddenly, in August 1945, as the boys of Baybury Heights reeled in ecstasy over the impact of the A-bomb and the girls of my class assembled their wardrobes for the coming encounter with junior high—on the very eve of my entering a new world—the Blue Fairy, that lovely lady, came through. My braces came off, and the world was mine.

The Price

"How Small Are Her Feet?"

Ning Lao T'ai-t'ai, as told to Ida Pruitt
China, 1876

They did not begin to bind my feet until I was seven because I loved so much to run and play. Then I became very ill and they had to take the bindings off my feet again. I had the "heavenly blossoms" and was ill for two years and my face is very pockmarked. In my childhood everyone had the illness and few escaped some marking.

When I was nine they started to bind my feet again and they had to draw the bindings tighter than usual. My feet hurt so much that for two years I had to crawl on my hands and knees. Sometimes at night they hurt so much I could not sleep. I stuck my feet under my mother and she lay on them so they hurt less and I could sleep. But by the time I was eleven my feet did not hurt and by the time I was thirteen they were finished. The toes were turned under so that I could see them on the inner and under side of the foot. They had come up around. Two fingers could be inserted in the cleft between the front of the foot and the heel. My feet were very small indeed.

A girl's beauty and desirability were counted more by the size of her feet than by the beauty of her face. Matchmakers were not asked "Is she beautiful?" but "How small are her feet?'' A plain face is given by heaven but poorly bound feet are a sign of laziness.

My feet were very small indeed. Not like they are now. When I worked so hard and was on my feet all day I slept with the bandages off because my feet ached, and so they spread.

"I Pumiced and I Brushed and I Sprayed"

Caryl Rivers
Massachusetts, 1960s

Do you have gritty elbows? *Glamour* asked. (I looked. Oh God, yes, I had gritty elbows. They looked like cobblestone streets that hadn't been washed in years.) Use a pumice stone each night to keep them smooth.

Do you have ugly feet? (I looked at them. Blaugh. Ugly feet. Not even a mother could love such feet.) Use skin oil daily and keep your toes well groomed and polished.

Do you want shining hair? (YES YES YES.) Brush at least one hundred strokes a night.

Are your eyes small and beady? Beauty advisor asked. (I peered in the mirror. Definitely small and beady. Like a myopic snake.) Apply three shades of eye shadow. Blue Coral, Misty Ash and Tahiti Green, white near the corner of the eye, liner three quarters of the way under the eye and use waterproof Roman Brown mascara.

Is your skin caressable? (I slid an index finger down my arm. It felt more like burlap than velvet. Uncaressable.) Bathe in Sardo oil.

Does your hair need sheen? Are your knees bumpy? Teeth stained? Hips big? Calves skinny? Do you have dandruff? Bad breath? Body odor? Psoriasis? Split ends?

I read, sitting there on the glider, and I believed. I was perfectible. After all, had I not seen perfection emerge like a statue by Praxiteles out of human clay in *Glamour* Makeovers and *Ladies Home Journal* Beauty Biographies? It could be done.

So I pumiced and I brushed and I sprayed and I bleached and I trimmed and I squirted and I slathered and I rubbed. I did all the things the magazines told me to do. And I discovered a terrifying fact. If I did all the things the magazines told me to do I would spend my entire life in the bathroom. I would be a shining, perfect creature, but the only people who would ever see me—briefly—were members of my own family and the occasional guest who wandered into the john.

"The Elite European Hairdressing and Beauty Salon"

Han Suyin
China, 1932

My appointment at the hairdresser's was at five thirty.

"I have a ticket for you, for the musical evening at the German Club," Mrs. Bürger had said to me a few days previously. The proceeds were to go to relief for the flood victims, and there were five million of them in that February of 1932. "It will be a nice party; decent people you will meet."

This was my first grown-up party. What would I wear? Mother advised pale-blue wool with collar and sash of white silk; the little tailor in Eight-side Tumble Street made the dress with a swinging skirt, a big hem, in case I grew taller. I bought a pair of silk stockings; on Hilda's advice, a long pair, American, but as I did not know about girdles they were held up with elastic garters. Underwear was a complication. Shoes were a difficulty. They must be high-heeled for such a grown-up party. The problem was solved by purchasing second-hand high-heeled shoes from Annabelle Lee, an American-Chinese secretary who was to marry a doctor and generously parted with a pair for six dollars. A Tangee lipstick, some Pan-stik make-up, recommended by Hilda. Mrs. Bürger had her hair set and curled for parties and I must do the same; at the Beauty Salon on Hatamen Street, where a Max Factor beauty counsellor, newly arrived that winter, gave lessons in make-up. "Try it, it's plush," said Hilda, who now arrived in the morning with a faint tinge of powder, lipstick, eye shadow; and with her expensive suede-brimmed felt hat achieved a haunting look. But it cost something like ten dollars to have a complete lesson in make-up; and I could not afford it. "You should have a manicure," Olga advised,

149

but this also was beyond my means. I would have my hair done, and dispense with manicure.

The dress cost me twelve dollars; the shoes six dollars; a slip four, panties one dollar sixty cents, altogether twenty-nine dollars and sixty cents, or three-fifths of my month's salary, for one grown-up party. The hairdresser would be an adventure: first step into womanhood. I recapture its swivel chairs, the tang of hot irons, the smell of burnt hair, the permanent clips hanging from corkscrewing wires overhead, the sneezy soap-water smell, the reek of ammonia. And clinking around the past image, seven silver dollars, bright and round, to put some curls into straight straight hair, for a grown-up party in aid of five million peasants famished in China's plains. . . .

"Ja," said Mrs. Bürger, "you will look nice with curls."

Wind-ragged snowmounds piled unmelted on the sidewalk; the stones were slippery with ice. The hairdresser's window had a haughty wax face with a pompadour, a corkscrew curl loping down the neck, staring at the Chinese street below gold lettering proclaiming it the Elite European Hairdressing and Beauty Salon. Some beggars shivering with cold were picking a garbage bin. I pushed the outside door with its mattressed inner protection, and then the inside door, for in Peking's winter two doors kept the bitter cold out. The White Russian assistant looked like the wax head, even her hair the same gold. Her beauty completed my overthrow.

"Yes?" The glance went from my flat boots, warm stockings, up my coat to my unmaxfactored face with chapped lips. I stammered that I had an appointment.

She flicked the pages of a book, "Miss Suzy, shampoo and curl for this lady." Then to me: "Take a seat. We aren't ready for you yet."

Around me, beautiful European women sat under the driers or under clips firmly gripping their heads, or stretched on chairs, wrapped in white protectors, a hand out to the manicurist, or chatted to the Russian assistants while their hair was being brushed with those new brushes just come on the market, made with rubber bristles widely spaced.

"I said to him: Hey what do you take me for? I'm not going out at *this* time of the night."

"And what do you think? The damn Chink over-charged me ten dollars so I had him take it all back and give me back the money."

"And I said to the doctor: Now you just wait. I'll start pushing, get ready to catch. And sure enough out it popped."

I pored over a magazine. Page after page of delectable cakes, bigger and more luscious than anything in the Greek Bakery of my friend Vera Thassounis, glamorous women with beautiful legs and hips, handsome smiling young men bent over them showing all their teeth . . . Mum, Odorono, Kotex, Camel, the so-important doctor, white-gowned, holding up the Listerine bottle: "Statistics prove . . ." Dread of halitosis, b.o., sweat, unpopularity, assailed me. Should I get Listerine for tonight? What if I had halitosis and offended? I stared at that wonderful world, the rich, the smooth, the happy, where wind did not blow sand into one's eyes, where beggars did not root into garbage, rot and die on the streets, where no corpses floated on rivers, where no one was shot or beheaded on calm Saturday afternoons for being a Communist, and where there were not five million people dying of hunger, to be rescued by musical evenings and theatricals. And here, glamorously curled, Cleopatra using Mum and Kotex, and some film star darting from a sofa with her hip out, and someone else getting divorced and remarried . . . It was feared that there would be typhus, in Manchuria there was bubonic plague, and in Shanghai the Japanese were bombing refugees . . . and in America, too, there were marchers, and hunger, and soup kitchens, and in England much talk of socialism and strikes . . .

"Your turn, Miss." A swivel chair, crescent-shaped leather-padded neck-rest. "Lean back and let your hair loose" into an enamel basin behind it. The first glamour is gone, everything reeks of ammonia and of woman. Woman, soap, disinfectant, ammonia, singed hair, woman. Miss Suzy pulls a comb through my hair, then rubs some jellied stuff into it, then her red nails dig in, kneading. "My you got lots of hair"—as if it was wrong to have so much hair. The red nails draw out grey frothy blobs. "My it's dirty." Tepid water pours down. "Put your head well back." Splash splash. Towels. Then under the drier which is too hot. In the mirror, a sallow face. "You should use our Cold Cream, our complexion softener." I am ugly, I am ugly, I shall never be beautiful. Mouth too large, eyes too small. "Side parting, Miss?" Affably Miss Suzy holds up the curling-irons. A work of art. Woof woof. Brilliantine spray. Does one tip? How can one tip such an incredibly superior Miss Suzy? Do I have enough money to tip?

Mr. Vogel wants thirty-six dollars a month for his physics teaching. Henri Vetch of the French bookstore wants seven dollars for the last book bought yesterday. Tonight I must be attractive, almost pretty. Glacé kid high-heeled shoes at six dollars a little too big, silk stockings a little too pink against the new blue dress, but the curls will save the day. People will pause. Is this indeed Rosalie Chou, who types in the Comptroller's office at the Peking Union Medical College, this poised and beautiful person with Max Factor Pan-stik make-up and Tangee lipstick, gliding effortlessly about under all those lovely curls? They make my face twice as broad as usual, but perhaps that is as it ought to be, perhaps I shall be beautiful tonight; a big wave on the forehead wavering almost between my eyes; the nape of the neck with little curls, a miracle of art. "That's very nice thank you very much." "Six dollars." Six dollars and one for the tip, already the feeling that I am different, almost like the wax face in the window. Some of the curls are stiff to touch, and now in the clear cold there is a light aroma of burning coming to me from my own head. But Mama approves; Tiza pins two curls already uncurling themselves; when the dress is on, and the shoes and the stockings, Mother's face is smiling; "Don't come back too late," she says.

A rickshaw has been called, it is impossible to bicycle there, all dressed up. In the cold the rickshaw shambles on, coughing, panting, and the lamps are just coming out, along the Eastern Main Street, and already outside the German Club are some cars, and also some private rickshaws, with their fur blankets for the passengers and their gleaming lanterns. The German Club has a fair-sized hall with ferns, aspidistra, winter cherry. There is a black piano in one corner, at which a man in a black suit with a black tie and a stiff collar sits and plays, singing to himself, one of his feet goes on the pedals, the soft, the loud, to and fro. He is playing a march; two women walk about in long satin dresses with fur jackets on their shoulders, ordering the servants to put chairs here and there. In comes Mrs. Bürger in scarlet silk with fur stole, her hair is so short, it looks as if half of it were missing, she has rouge upon her cheeks and it makes her face longer, older. The ladies' room gossip is that she is two years older than her husband and two years seems an enormous long time, to me. Recently an American missionary lady has married a Chinese convert, her own student, who is now going to study in the U.S.A. on a missionary scholarship; she is twelve years older than he is and the secretaries pretend to be horrified. With Mrs. Bürger is her husband and Eugen, the brother of Fredi, and a tall corpulent man with a monocle and suit with tails who says: "Ja, ah ahhahahah ja" with great gusts of laughter in between his ahs. It is the German doctor in charge at the hospital who, Hilda has told me, offers to fit young girls who need it with contraceptive caps. "He is very modern-minded." Another couple, the man astonishingly bald, overwhelming pink baldness, a frieze of hair round the polished smooth glistening round cranium. I find my lower jaw hanging loose and snap my mouth shut; so absorbed looking at all those people coming in, short or tall, thin or fat, like a procession; I feel myself blush and turn and meet the blue eyes of the man at the piano; he has stopped the march and is drumming with one hand and smiles. His teeth are rather long and his face not unpleasant, his hair soft, hanging over his forehead, like pale yellow silk.

Mrs. Bürger comes up with a careful smile as if smiling too much might shatter something in her face.

"You are early, that is good, you did not wish to miss any fun. I think it is going to be a nice evening. Come and I will introduce . . . Herr Will, Herr Fruber, Miss Chou. Otto, good evening . . ." She waves to the man at the piano. "Come and talk. This is Otto Kurtens."

Some click heels, others shake hands, the man called Otto gets up and winks at me. I blush again.

Emilie Bürger moves on to the platform, I feel unwanted and return to my chair and find the piano-playing man sitting on the next chair. "Let us talk. How old are you?" "Sixteen." He eyes me. His eyes are a little bloodshot. "You are only a little girl." That hurts. I pat my curls, "I earn my own living." "What do you do?" "I'm a secretary." "Oh," he bows with mock respect. "A secre-t-a-ary. My, my, how important." "And what do *you* do, if I may ask?" "I am . . . a flyer." He makes a gesture of wings. "You know . . . aeroplanes." I bend forward, inquisitive: "Do you know about the man who was shot down somewhere in Mongolia and put in jail and had to have his leg cut off?"

"Yes, I am that man."

I can't say anything, only look at him and feel the hot red flow mounting and spreading. He bows mockingly, then stands and goes back to the piano, and again begins to play.

The curtains loop, the costumed singers begin singing and thumping their feet. The man at the piano plays on and on. I am still thinking of the terrible thing I have done. Because I read in the papers about this German pilot of the Eurasia airline, which is actually a German company, being shot down by Mongolian marauders, a few months ago. At the interval Emilie comes: "Have you enjoyed it?" I nod. Some people circulate with cakes, and sandwiches, and there is coffee to drink. Otto Kurtens is again there, a big cream cake on a plate, he hands it to me. "But I am already eating one." "Have two, all children like cakes." Then we sit and I tell him I have just finished reading Ibsen at the P.U.M.C. library, and he says: "You should read Goethe," and then teaches me a few words of German: "Auf Wiedersehen, guten Morgen." When the last act is over everyone claps, Emilie says: "I am asking Otto to take you home." "I have a car, may I have the pleasure?" says Otto. He drives me back through the quiet night. From time to time, a rickshaw comes out of the darkness, the man's legs flash in the car lights, his body hurling forwards, then becomes a dark shadow behind us. We arrive home and Otto gets out of the car, stiffly, one leg does not bend. "Well, good night, sweet dreams, little girl." He kisses me lightly on the cheek. "Thus we do in Germany." He pronounces it Chermany. I stand looking at him. He says: "What is it?" I do not answer but shut the door on him, and now I go to bed, feeling grown up. I have been to a party, met a man who has lost his leg, who has taken me home in his car, and who has actually kissed me! Immense the great space traversed in one evening. He said "Little girl," but it is not true. I am growing up. And now all this world I covet, world where everything is knowledge and happiness and there is no torment, no worrying, will be mine—all that, and becoming a doctor, and doing something about the beggars.

"Thin Fever"

Aimee Liu
Glenridge, Connecticut, 1960s

In her autobiography, Solitaire, *Aimee Liu recalls her desperate struggle at sixteen to be thin, an obsession which ultimately resulted in* anorexia nervosa.

The mannequins behind my reflection wore skimpy knit blouses and long, flared skirts cinched at the waist. They were flat, thin, and tall. I compared myself with them and felt round, heavy, and short. The scale at home told me I weighed ninety-seven; I obviously needed to lose at least another seven pounds. There was little I could do to augment my height, but if I were skinnier I might appear taller. Is illusion the key to life?

It was funny. Sometimes I felt so solid and slender, all muscle and bone. But then I would see another model, or look in a magazine or store window, and all of a sudden I felt like a tub of lard. Walking, I could feel my thighs shake and my breasts jiggle. I would clench my arms to tighten the muscles across my chest, harder and harder, until it hurt. I would suck in my cheeks, like a high fashion model's, and tighten my stomach muscles into knots. But when I relaxed my body fell apart again, and I hated myself as much as ever.

Love, hate, love, hate. Which would it be? Did I consider myself lovely or loathsome? I could never decide. In some pictures there was no doubt—I was very pretty, if not ravishing. And sometimes when I studied myself in the mirror I was truly pleased. But the rest of the time I seemed as gruesome as the witch who once chased me around a childhood nightmare. I could stand to improve myself, that much was evident. I must work harder, lose more weight, and perhaps one day I'd fit the bill.

* * *

*A much-admired friend, Kimmy, later confesses to Aimee
her desire to lose weight too, and asks advice from the expert.
Concerned about her own looks, Aimee wants to find out how
Kimmy sees herself.*

"Do you think of yourself as beautiful?" I asked her.

She tugged at a stray wisp of hair. It reminded me of
white gold. The girl looked like a goddess. "I suppose
it's inevitable, since everybody keeps telling me I am.
And sometimes, like when I go shopping and stare at
myself in a dressing room mirror or something, I really
impress myself. But other times, early in the morning, or
after I've been studying for a midterm, I feel like a total
turn-off." Kim wished she were a better student. She
was bright, not brilliant. "With me, that's something
that changes constantly. If my self-esteem is up, chances
are I think I'm gorgeous. I've been awfully dissatisfied
with myself lately, though, and consequently I've been
hating the way I look. Why, don't you consider yourself
pretty?"

"Funny that it's such a sticky issue, isn't it?" I hedged
the question, just as she had. "Modeling has sort of
warped my perspective, I think. To be honest, I guess I
went into the business to prove to myself that I was
worth looking at. Not to seem like a crybaby, but I was
always such a loser socially at school, I never could quite
understand compliments when they came, you know,
from adults or my brother and his friends. If I'd been
popular like you, I doubt I would have even thought of
modeling."

"Oh, you'd be surprised," Kimmy retaliated, "how
little confidence that kind of attention gives you. Everybody stares at you all the time, but no one ever *talks* to
you. They talk *at* you. They all think you've got life made
—the old bowl-of-cherries story, you know? I mean, I
feel guilty if it seems like there's a problem, or if I feel
down. You can't complain, ever, because you have no
right to. You have to uphold this image of innocence and
perfection, or they'll treat you like a traitor. Honestly,
half the time I feel like a prisoner. . . . The neat thing
about you is that you cut out and created a life beyond all
this petty bullshit."

The vehemence of her protest startled me. I glanced into her eyes, to make sure she wasn't playacting. They were like cats' eyes, flaming and icy at the same time, glowing green.

"Believe me, my situation is no better than yours," I said softly. I had at least to try to set her straight, but I wasn't at all sure I was up to the task. "All I've managed to do is to find new and different ways to disappoint myself. I don't feel that I belong in New York any more than I do here, so I dabble on the edges of both scenes, and constantly feel like a freak—only not a rebel, not a strong, beautiful eccentric. Just a misfit. In the city I'm too young, too naive to feel comfortable with the other models and photographers. I'm too stupid to handle the men on the streets, and the come-ons of the business. And worst of all, I can't even make enough money to make it worthwhile. There are all sorts of excuses—I'm not blond, tall, or American, or on the other hand, I'm not Oriental enough either. The few jobs I do get are a kick, admittedly, but it's a real schizophrenic kind of existence. You walk out of one studio feeling like garbage, and walk into another to hear them praising you like some sort of rare doll. I keep telling myself that there's more to me than my looks, but sometimes it's almost impossible to believe it."

"How does your weight fit into the picture?" Kimmy asked. "I mean, does it make you feel better about yourself if you don't eat? Or do you eat to reward yourself?" It wasn't a serious question. She knew perfectly well how I'd respond, but I told her anyway.

"I loathe myself when I eat. The only time I ever feel proud of myself is when my stomach is totally empty, when I climb on the scale and see that I've lost a pound—or two, or three, or four. When I eat I become an automaton. It's as though my subconscious takes over to punish me. I know. It's very weird." I felt as though I'd exposed an open wound, self-inflicted. It embarrassed me, and I hurriedly changed the subject.

"What I said about fasting, though . . . it's wrong. Just because I'm too weak-willed to do it any other way, you really should diet sensibly. Cut down, not out, as the experts say. You have to eat to stay healthy. Even as much fasting as I've done, I've really screwed up my body." Kimmy looked at me curiously. "I haven't had a period in three years."

"What does your doctor say?" she asked. "Has he told you it's because of your weight?"

"No. He says he has no idea what's wrong with me. Last year he ran me through a whole battery of tests and X-rays. They took pints of blood. Ugh! That was especially bad because the veins in my arms are so tiny that they kept missing, shoving the needle in over and over. And after it was all over they said they couldn't find a thing wrong. It's fine with me, actually. My mother keeps wailing and worrying, but as long as the doctor tells her I'm okay, what can she do!"

"I wouldn't mind having that problem. I can't stand periods. It seems so unfair that girls have to go through all that nuisance, when boys get away scot-free, doesn't it? I mean, if I wanted to have kids, I could justify it, but I have the maternal instinct of a rock."

"Funny. I don't ever want to have kids, either."

"But you've found a way out," she said pointedly. I supposed I had, in a way.

We reached the end of Brookfield Lane. Kimmy turned here. I went straight. It was still difficult for me to believe that she had approached me for advice, or that what I had said would have any effect on her. Despite everything she had told me, I found it inconceivable that she should want out of her spotlight position. She was the queen bee, the jewel of the community. To think that she even remotely identified with me! I would be interested to see whether she changed or remained the same.

We saw little of each other during the remainder of that spring. In the summer I devoted myself exclusively to modeling and solitary walks. True to my vow, I began again to lose weight and, as a consequence, most of my bookings. I was actually too small to fit the clothes my clients wanted photographed. But our conversation haunted me, kept reminding me of the spiritual significance of losing weight, of discipline, of sacrifice. Even at the expense of my modeling career, I was determined to keep reducing. It strengthened the soul, so to speak. In a way it made me a little smug to think that I was actually thinner than the average model. I had always considered myself much fatter than the norm, and still, inside, felt that I was. It was an odd kind of tug-of-war now. I wrote in my diary:

I weighed under ninety-five again this morning. It really feels strange at times. I'm skinny one minute, fat the next. I should know better than to weigh myself every five minutes! I wonder if I'm not quite right, staring into mirrors and seriously thinking, "You are actually very beautiful." What's strange is that I feel almost sure of my near perfection, but that makes me feel so guilty. I must restrain myself, not eat, not eat, not *eat!* It's so hard, when you look at yourself and argue that you're thin enough, to keep down to five hundred calories.

But at the end of the summer and the beginning of school I realized that I had a long way to go before I reached "thin enough." Kimmy this time, not I, was the guide.

The Complaint of a
Beautiful Girl

I was a beautiful talented girl.
I furtively think of the early days of my life:
Full-grown, I was like a rose in the daylight.
The rose hadn't opened its corolla to smile,
Other flowers soon faded and became vile.

Things have changed.
Now, things have changed: He has abandoned me;
Once a wise lady, I now become a little silly.
Oh my august friend, you have so flighty a heart,
Now, I regret my spring and endure this ill luck.

I think of the moment when, in the Tan palace,
You picked a willow branch, in its early freshness.
The vernal gown I wore when I was close to you
Is still here, to testify to our tender love.

Now, my lord, you have resolutely disdained me,
So, unexpectedly, friendless I've turned out to be.
Oh Heaven, why do you challenge me by confining
Me in this hell, with a lamp growing dim?

I care about my growing age, like a faint moon,
Or a fallen flower, which can attract no one.
How sad my love is and how charmless the world.

My pretty face worried the hearts of other belles,
My lovely glance could even collapse a citadel.
When my graceful shadow loomed up through a blind,
Plants and weeds would have their sexual instincts
   aroused.

Seduced, a fish would dive deep into the waters,
A high-flying swallow would feel dizzy and falter.
By my heavenly charms, a flower would be enticed,

Miss Tay-Thi would be dazed, Miss Moon would be surprised.

I was famous, in wait for an idyll.
My gifts and beauty were famous in the kingdom,
The suitors increasingly loitered near my home.
They had only heard of my charms and not seen me,
Yet, their passion had risen fiercely.

*I was passionately loved, but my happiness was
ephemeral.*
Frequently, in moonlight, he gently embraced me,
And often, in the palace, we laughed together lovingly.
He was very pleased with my natural grace,
I was equally pretty without rouging my face.

The monarch cherished me like a precious sapphire,
He coddled me and yielded to all my desires.
Indeed, a woman's beauty, having no venom,
Can poison everyone and overthrow a kingdom!

Nguyen Gia Thieu
Vietnam, 18th century

The Little Bouilloux Girl

Colette
Translated by Una Vicenzo Trowbridge
and Enid McLeod
France, 20th century

The little Bouilloux girl was so lovely that even we children noticed it. It is unusual for small girls to recognize beauty in one of themselves and pay homage to it. But there could be no disputing such undeniable loveliness as hers. Whenever my mother met the little Bouilloux girl in the street, she would stop her and bend over her as she was wont to bend over her yellow tea-rose, her red flowering cactus or her Azure Blue butterfly trustfully asleep on the scaly bark of the pine tree. She would stroke her curly hair, golden as a half-ripe chestnut, and her delicately tinted cheeks, and watch the incredible lashes flutter over her great dark eyes. She would observe the glimmer of the perfect teeth in her peerless mouth, and when, at last, she let the child go on her way, she would look after her, murmuring, "It's prodigious!"

Several years passed, bringing yet further graces to the little Bouilloux girl. There were certain occasions recorded by our admiration: a prize-giving at which, shyly murmuring an unintelligible recitation, she glowed through her tears like a peach under a summer shower. The little Bouilloux girl's first communion caused a scandal: the same evening, after vespers, she was seen drinking a half pint at the *Café du Commerce*, with her father, the sawyer, and that night she danced, already feminine and flirtatious, a little unsteady in her white slippers, at the public ball.

With an arrogance to which she had accustomed us, she informed us later, at school, that she was to be apprenticed.

163

"Oh! Who to?"

"To Madame Adolphe."

"Oh! And are you to get wages at once?"

"No. I'm only thirteen, I shall start earning next year."

She left us without emotion, and coldly we let her go. Already her beauty isolated her and she had no friends at school, where she learned very little. Her Sundays and her Thursdays brought no intimacy with us; they were spent with a family that was considered "unsuitable," with girl cousins of eighteen well known for their brazen behavior, and with brothers, cartwright apprentices, who sported ties at fourteen and smoked when they escorted their sister to the Parisian shooting-gallery at the fair or to the cheerful bar that the widow Pimelle had made so popular.

The very next morning on my way to school I met the little Bouilloux girl setting out for the dressmaker's workrooms, and I remained motionless, thunderstruck with jealous admiration, at the corner of the Rue des Soeurs, watching Nana Bouilloux's retreating form. She had exchanged her black pinafore and short childish frock for a long skirt and a pleated blouse of pink sateen. She wore a black alpaca apron and her exuberant locks, disciplined and twisted into a "figure of eight," lay close as a helmet about the charming new shape of a round imperious head that retained nothing childish except its freshness and the not yet calculated impudence of a little village adventuress.

That morning the upper forms hummed like a hive.

"I've seen Nana Bouilloux! In a long dress, my dear, would you believe it? And her hair in a chignon! She had a pair of scissors hanging from her belt too!"

At noon I flew home to announce breathlessly:

"Mother! I met Nana Bouilloux in the street! She was passing our door. And she had on a long dress! Mother, just imagine, a long dress! And her hair in a chignon! And she had high heels and a pair of . . ."

"Eat, Minet-Chéri, eat, your cutlet will be cold."

"And an apron, mother, such a lovely alpaca apron that looked like silk! Couldn't I possibly . . ."

"No, Minet-Chéri, you certainly couldn't."

"But if Nana Bouilloux can . . ."

"Yes, Nana Bouilloux, at thirteen, can, in fact she should, wear a chignon, a short apron and a long skirt—it's the uniform of all little Bouilloux girls throughout the world, at thirteen—more's the pity."

"But . . ."

"Yes, I know you would like to wear the complete uniform of a little Bouilloux girl. It includes all that you've seen, and a bit more besides: a letter safely hidden in the apron pocket, an admirer who smells of wine and of cheap cigars; two admirers, three admirers and a little later on plenty of tears . . . and a sickly child hidden away, a child that has lain for months crushed by constricting stays. There it is, Minet-Chéri, the entire uniform of the little Bouilloux girls. Do you still want it?"

"Of course not, mother. I only wanted to see if a chignon . . ."

But my mother shook her head, mocking but serious.

"No, no! You can't have the chignon without the apron, the apron without the letter, the letter without the high-heeled slippers, or the slippers without . . . all the rest of it! It's just a matter of choice!"

My envy was soon exhausted. The resplendent little Bouilloux girl became no more than a daily passer-by whom I scarcely noticed. Bareheaded in winter and summer, her gaily colored blouses varied from week to week, and in very cold weather she swathed her elegant shoulders in a useless little scarf. Erect, radiant as a thorny rose, her eyelashes sweeping her cheeks or half revealing her dark and dewy eyes, she grew daily more worthy of queening it over crowds, of being gazed at, adorned and bedecked with jewels. The severely smoothed crinkliness of her chestnut hair could still be discerned in little waves that caught the light in the golden mist at the nape of her neck and round her ears. She always looked vaguely offended with her small, velvety nostrils reminding one of a doe.

She was fifteen or sixteen now—and so was I. Except that she laughed too freely on Sundays, in order to show her white teeth, as she hung on the arms of her brothers or her girl cousins, Nana Bouilloux was behaving fairly well.

"For a little Bouilloux girl, very well indeed!" was the public verdict.

She was seventeen, then eighteen; her complexion was like a peach on a south wall, no eyes could meet the challenge of hers and she had the bearing of a goddess. She began to take the floor at fetes and fairs, to dance with abandon, to stay out very late at night, wandering in the lanes with a man's arm round her waist. Always unkind, but full of laughter, provoking boldness in those who would have been content merely to love her.

Then came a St. John's Eve when she appeared on the dance floor that was laid down on the *Place du Grand-Jeu* under the melancholy light of malodorous oil lamps. Hobnailed boots kicked up the dust between the planks of the "floor." All the young men, as was customary, kept their hats on while dancing. Blonde girls became claret-colored in their tight bodices, while the dark ones, sunburned from their work in the fields, looked black. But there, among a band of haughty workgirls, Nana Bouilloux, in a summer dress sprigged with little flowers, was drinking lemonade laced with red wine when the Parisians arrived on the scene.

They were two Parisians such as one sees in the country in summer, friends of a neighboring landowner, and supremely bored; Parisians in tussore and white serge, come for a moment to mock at a village midsummer fete. They stopped laughing when they saw Nana Bouilloux and sat down near the bar in order to see her better. In low voices they exchanged comments which she pretended not to hear, since her pride as a beautiful creature would not let her turn her eyes in their direction and giggle like her companions. She heard the words: "A swan among geese! A Greuze! A crime to let such a wonder bury herself here. . . ." When the young man in the white suit asked the little Bouilloux girl for a waltz she got up without surprise and danced with him gravely, in silence. From time to time her eyelashes, more beautiful than a glance, brushed against her partner's fair mustache.

After the waltz the two Parisians went away, and Nana Bouilloux sat down by the bar, fanning herself. There she was soon approached by young Leriche, by

Houette, even by Honce the chemist, and even by Possy the cabinetmaker, who was ageing, but none the less a good dancer. To all of them she replied, "Thank you, but I'm tired," and she left the ball at half-past ten o'clock.

And after that, nothing more ever happened to the little Bouilloux girl. The Parisians did not return, neither they, nor others like them. Houette, Honce, young Leriche, the commercial travelers with their gold watch-chains, soldiers on leave and sheriff's clerks vainly climbed our steep street at the hours when the beautifully coiffed sempstress, on her way down it, passed them by stiffly with a distant nod. They looked out for her at dances, where she sat drinking lemonade with an air of distinction and answered their importunities with "Thank you very much, but I'm not dancing, I'm tired." Taking offense, they soon began to snigger: "Tired! Her kind of tiredness lasts for thirty-six weeks!" and they kept a sharp watch on her figure. But nothing happened to the little Bouilloux girl, neither that nor anything else. She was simply waiting, possessed by an arrogant faith, conscious of the debt owed by the hazard that had armed her too well. She was awaiting . . . not the return of the Parisian in white serge, but a stranger, a ravisher. Her proud anticipation kept her silent and pure; with a little smile of surprise, she rejected Honce, who would have raised her to the rank of chemist's lawful wife, and she would have nothing to say to the sheriff's chief clerk. With never another lapse, taking back, once and for all, the smiles, the glances, the glowing bloom of her cheeks, the red young lips, the shadowy blue cleft of her breasts which she had so prodigally lavished on mere rustics, she awaited her kingdom and the prince without a name.

Years later, when I passed through my native village, I could not find the shade of her who had so lovingly refused me what she called "The uniform of little Bouilloux girls." But as the car bore me slowly, though not slowly enough—never slowly enough—up a street where I have now no reason to stop, a woman drew back to avoid the wheel. A slender woman, her hair well dressed in a bygone fashion, dressmaker's scissors

hanging from a steel "châtelaine" on her black apron.
Large, vindictive eyes, a tight mouth sealed by long silence, the sallow cheeks and temples of those who work
by lamplight; a woman of forty-five or . . . Not at all; a
woman of thirty-eight, a woman of my own age, of exactly my age, there was no room for doubt. As soon as
the car allowed her room to pass, "the little Bouilloux
girl" went on her way down the street, erect and indifferent, after one anxious, bitter glance had told her that
the car did not contain the long-awaited ravisher.

Not Born to
the Clan

"Why Am I So Ugly?"

Jean Auel
Europe, Late Pleistocene Epoch

In Jean Auel's novel The Clan of the Cave Bear, *the Others
(Cro-Magnon people) are living in the same ice-age world as
the Cave Bear Clan (Neanderthal people). The two groups
rarely meet but one day Ayla, an Other baby, is discovered by
the Clan's medicine woman, Iza. The group considers the child
deformed, but Iza convinces them to adopt Ayla, whom she
raises as heir to her healing power. At puberty Ayla learns
about her responsibilities as a woman and begins to think about
a mate.*

On a sunny spring morning not long after she returned,
Ayla went to fill a waterbag at the spring-fed pool near
the cave. No one else was out yet. She knelt down and
bent over, ready to dip the bag in, then suddenly
stopped. The morning sun slanting across the still water
gave it a mirror-like surface. Ayla stared at the strange
face looking her out of the pool; she had not seen a reflection of herself before. Most water near the cave was
in the form of running streams or creeks, and she didn't
usually look in the pool until after she had dipped in the
container she wanted to fill, disturbing the tranquil surface.

The young woman studied her own face. It was somewhat square with a well-defined jaw, modified by cheeks still rounded with youth, high cheekbones and a long, smooth neck. Her chin had the hint of a cleft, her lips were full, and her nose straight and finely chiseled. Clear, blue-gray eyes were outlined with heavy lashes a shade or two darker than the golden hair that fell in thick soft waves to well below her shoulders, glimmering with highlights in the sun. Eyebrows, the same shade as her lashes, arched above her eyes on a smooth, straight, high forehead without the slightest hint of protruding brow ridges. Ayla backed stiffly away from the pool and ran into the cave.

"Ayla, what's wrong?" Iza motioned. It was obvious something was troubling her daughter.

"Mother! I just looked in the pool. I'm so ugly! Oh, mother, why am I so ugly?" was her impassioned response. She burst into tears in the woman's arms. For as long as she could remember, Ayla had never seen anyone except people of the clan. She had no other standard of measure. They had grown accustomed to her, but to herself, she looked different from everyone around her, abnormally different.

"Ayla, Ayla," Iza soothed, holding the sobbing young woman in her arms.

"I didn't know I was so ugly, mother. I didn't know. What men will ever want me? I'll never have a mate. And I'll never have a baby. I'll never have anyone. Why do I have to be so ugly?"

"I don't know if you're really so ugly, Ayla. You're different."

"I'm ugly! I'm ugly!" Ayla shook her head, refusing to be comforted. "Look at me! I'm too big, I'm taller than Broud and Goov. I'm almost as tall as Brun! And I'm ugly. I'm big and ugly and I'll never have a mate," she gestured with fresh sobs.

"Ayla! Stop it!" Iza commanded, shaking her shoulders. "You can't help the way you look. You were not born to the Clan, Ayla, you were born to the Others, you look the way they look. You can't change that, you must accept it. It's true you may never have a mate. That can't be helped; you must accept that, too."

When I Was Growing Up

I know now that once I longed to be white.
How? you ask.
Let me tell you the ways.

   when I was growing up, people told me
   I was dark and I believed my own darkness
   in the mirror, in my soul, in my own narrow vision

      when I was growing up, my sisters
      with fair skin got praised
      for their beauty, and in the dark
      I fell further, crushed between high walls

   when I was growing up, I read magazines
   and saw movies, blonde movie stars, white skin,
   sensuous lips and to be elevated, to become
   a woman, a desirable woman, I began to wear
   imaginary pale skin

      when I was growing up, I was proud
      of my English, my grammar, my spelling
      fitting into the group of smart children
      smart Chinese children, fitting in,
      belonging, getting in line

   when I was growing up and went to high school,
   I discovered the rich white girls, a few yellow girls,
   their imported cotton dresses, their cashmere sweaters,
   their curly hair and I thought that I too should have
   what these lucky girls had

      when I was growing up, I hungered
      for American food, American styles,
      coded: white and even to me, a child
      born of Chinese parents, being Chinese
      was feeling foreign, was limiting,
      was unAmerican

   when I was growing up and a white man wanted
   to take me out, I thought I was special,

an exotic gardenia, anxious to fit
the stereotype of an oriental chick

> when I was growing up, I felt ashamed
> of some yellow men, their small bones,
> their frail bodies, their spitting
> on the streets, their coughing,
> their lying in sunless rooms,
> shooting themselves in the arms

when I was growing up, people would ask
if I were Filipino, Polynesian, Portuguese.
They named all colors except white, the shell
of my soul, but not my dark, rough skin

> when I was growing up, I felt
> dirty. I thought that god
> made white people clean
> and no matter how much I bathed,
> I could not change, I could not shed
> my skin in the gray water

when I was growing up, I swore
I would run away to purple mountains,
houses by the sea with nothing over
my head, with space to breathe,
uncongested with yellow people in an area
called Chinatown, in an area I later learned
was a ghetto, one of many hearts
of Asian America

I know now that once I longed to be white.
How many more ways? you ask.
Haven't I told you enough?

> Nellie Wong
> California, 1960s

"The Disrupter of Seasons"

Toni Morrison
Ohio, 1940s

My daddy's face is a study. Winter moves into it and presides there. His eyes become a cliff of snow threatening to avalanche; his eyebrows bend like black limbs of leafless trees. His skin takes on the pale, cheerless yellow of winter sun; for a jaw he has the edges of a snowbound field dotted with stubble; his high forehead is the frozen sweep of the Erie, hiding currents of gelid thoughts that eddy in darkness. Wolf killer turned hawk fighter, he worked night and day to keep one from the door and the other from under the windowsills. A Vulcan guarding the flames, he gives us instructions about which doors to keep closed or opened for proper distribution of heat, lays kindling by, discusses qualities of coal, and teaches us how to rake, feed, and bank the fire. And he will not unrazor his lips until spring.

Winter tightened our heads with a band of cold and melted our eyes. We put pepper in the feet of our stockings, Vaseline on our faces, and stared through dark icebox mornings at four stewed prunes, slippery lumps of oatmeal, and cocoa with a roof of skin.

But mostly we waited for spring, when there could be gardens.

By the time this winter had stiffened itself into a hateful knot that nothing could loosen, something did loosen it, or rather someone. A someone who splintered the knot into silver threads that tangled us, netted us, made us long for the dull chafe of the previous boredom.

This disrupter of seasons was a new girl in school named Maureen Peal. A high-yellow dream child with long brown hair braided into two lynch ropes that hung down her back. She was rich, at least by our standards, as rich as the richest of the white girls, swaddled in com-

fort and care. The quality of her clothes threatened to de-
range Frieda and me. Patent-leather shoes with buckles,
a cheaper version of which we got only at Easter and
which had disintegrated by the end of May. Fluffy
sweaters the color of lemon drops tucked into skirts with
pleats so orderly they astounded us. Brightly colored
knee socks with white borders, a brown velvet coat
trimmed in white rabbit fur, and a matching muff. There
was a hint of spring in her sloe green eyes, something
summery in her complexion, and a rich autumn ripeness
in her walk.

She enchanted the entire school. When teachers called
on her, they smiled encouragingly. Black boys didn't
trip her in the halls; white boys didn't stone her, white
girls didn't suck their teeth when she was assigned to be
their work partners; black girls stepped aside when she
wanted to use the sink in the girls' toilet, and their eyes
genuflected under sliding lids. She never had to search
for anybody to eat with in the cafeteria—they flocked to
the table of her choice, where she opened fastidious
lunches, shaming our jelly-stained bread with egg-salad
sandwiches cut into four dainty squares, pink-frosted
cupcakes, stocks of celery and carrots, proud, dark apples. She even bought and liked white milk.

Frieda and I were bemused, irritated, and fascinated
by her. We looked hard for flaws to restore our equilib-
rium, but had to be content at first with uglying up her
name, changing Maureen Peal to Meringue Pie. Later a
minor epiphany was ours when we discovered that she
had a dog tooth—a charming one to be sure—but a dog
tooth nonetheless. And when we found out that she had
been born with six fingers on each hand and that there
was a little bump where each extra one had been removed, we smiled. They were small triumphs, but we
took what we could get—snickering behind her back and
calling her Six-finger-dog-tooth-meringue-pie. But we
had to do it alone, for none of the other girls would coop-
erate with our hostility. They adored her.

When she was assigned a locker next to mine, I could
indulge my jealousy four times a day. My sister and I
both suspected that we were secretly prepared to be her
friend, if she would let us, but I knew it would be a dan-

gerous friendship, for when my eye traced the white border patterns of those Kelly-green knee socks, and felt the pull and slack of my brown stockings, I wanted to kick her. And when I thought of the unearned haughtiness in her eyes, I plotted accidental slammings of locker doors on her hand.

As locker friends, however, we got to know each other a little, and I was even able to hold a sensible conversation with her without visualizing her fall off a cliff, or giggling my way into what I thought was a clever insult.

One day, while I waited at the locker for Frieda, she joined me.

"Hi."

"Hi."

"Waiting for your sister?"

"Uh-huh."

"Which way do you go home?"

"Down Twenty-first Street to Broadway."

"Why don't you go down Twenty-second Street?"

" 'Cause I live on Twenty-first Street."

"Oh. I can walk that way, I guess. Partly, anyway."

"Free country."

Frieda came toward us, her brown stockings straining at the knees because she had tucked the toe under to hide a hole in the foot.

"Maureen's gonna walk part way with us."

Frieda and I exchanged glances, her eyes begging my restraint, mine promising nothing.

It was a false spring day, which, like Maureen, had pierced the shell of a deadening winter. There were puddles, mud, and an inviting warmth that deluded us. The kind of day on which we draped our coats over our heads, left our galoshes in school, and came down with croup the following day. We always responded to the slightest change in weather, the most minute shifts in time of day. Long before seeds were stirring, Frieda and I were scruffing and poking at the earth, swallowing air, drinking rain. . . .

As we emerged from the school with Maureen, we began to moult immediately. We put our head scarves in our coat pockets, and our coats on our heads. I was wondering how to maneuver Maureen's fur muff into a gutter when a commotion in the playground distracted us. A group of boys was circling and holding at bay a victim, Pecola Breedlove.

Bay Boy, Woodrow Cain, Buddy Wilson, Junie Bug— like a necklace of semiprecious stones they surrounded her. Heady with the smell of their own musk, thrilled by the easy power of a majority, they gaily harassed her.

"Black e mo. Black e mo. Yadaddsleepsnekked. Black e mo black e mo ya dadd sleeps nekked. Black e mo . . ."

They had extemporized a verse made up of two insults about matters over which the victim had no control: the color of her skin and speculations on the sleeping habits of an adult, wildly fitting in its incoherence. That they themselves were black, or that their own father had similarly relaxed habits was irrelevant. It was their contempt for their own blackness that gave the first insult its teeth. They seemed to have taken all of their smoothly cultivated ignorance, their exquisitely learned self-hatred, their elaborately designed hopelessness and sucked it all up into a fiery cone of scorn that had burned for ages in the hollows of their minds—cooled—and spilled over lips of outrage, consuming whatever was in its path. They danced a macabre ballet around the victim, whom, for their own sake, they were prepared to sacrifice to the flaming pit.

> Black e mo Black e mo Ya daddy sleeps nekked.
> Stch ta ta stch ta ta
> stach ta ta ta ta ta

Pecola edged around the circle crying. She had dropped her notebook, and covered her eyes with her hands.

We watched, afraid they might notice us and turn their energies our way. Then Frieda, with set lips and Mama's eyes, snatched her coat from her head and threw it on the ground. She ran toward them and brought her books down on Woodrow Cain's head. The circle broke. Woodrow Cain grabbed his head.

"Hey, girl!"

"You cut that out, you hear?" I had never heard Frieda's voice so loud and clear.

Maybe because Frieda was taller than he was, maybe because he saw her eyes, maybe because he had lost interest in the game, or maybe because he had a crush on Frieda, in any case Woodrow looked frightened just long enough to give her more courage.

"Leave her 'lone, or I'm gone tell everybody what you did!"

Woodrow did not answer; he just walled his eyes.

Bay Boy piped up, "Go on, gal! Ain't nobody bothering you."

"You shut up, Bullet Head." I had found my tongue. "Who you calling Bullet Head?"

"I'm calling you Bullet Head, Bullet Head."

Frieda took Pecola's hand. "Come on."

"You want a fat lip?" Bay Boy drew back his fist at me.

"Yeah. Gimme one of yours."

"You gone get one."

Maureen appeared at my elbow, and the boys seemed reluctant to continue under her springtime eyes so wide with interest. They buckled in confusion, not willing to beat up three girls under her watchful gaze. So they listened to a budding male instinct that told them to pretend we were unworthy of their attention.

"Come on, man."

"Yeah. Come on. We ain't got time to fool with them."

Grumbling a few disinterested epithets, they moved away.

I picked up Pecola's notebook and Frieda's coat, and the four of us left the playground.

"Old Bullet Head, he's always picking on girls."

Frieda agreed with me. "Miss Forrester said he was incorrigival."

"Really?" I didn't know what that meant, but it had enough of a doom sound in it to be true of Bay Boy.

While Frieda and I clucked on about the near fight, Maureen, suddenly animated, put her velvet-sleeved arm through Pecola's and began to behave as though they were the closest of friends.

"I just moved here. My name is Maureen Peal. What's yours?"

"Pecola."

"Pecola? Wasn't that the name of the girl in *Imitation of Life?*"

"I don't know. What is that?"

"The picture show, you know. Where this mulatto girl hates her mother 'cause she is black and ugly but then cries at the funeral. It was real sad. Everybody cries in it. Claudette Colbert too."

"Oh." Pecola's voice was no more than a sigh.

"Anyway, her name was Pecola too. She was so pretty. When it comes back, I'm going to see it again. My mother has seen it four times."

Frieda and I walked behind them, surprised at Maureen's friendliness to Pecola, but pleased. Maybe she wasn't so bad, after all. Frieda had put her coat back on her head, and the two of us, so draped, trotted along enjoying the warm breeze and Frieda's heroics.

"You're in my gym class, aren't you?" Maureen asked Pecola.

"Yes."

"Miss Erkmeister's legs sure are bow. I bet she thinks they're cute. How come she gets to wear real shorts, and we have to wear those old bloomers? I want to die every time I put them on."

Pecola smiled but did not look at Maureen.

"Hey." Maureen stopped short. "There's an Isaley's. Want some ice cream? I have money."

She unzipped a hidden pocket in her muff and pulled out a multifolded dollar bill. I forgave her those knee socks.

"My uncle sued Isaley's," Maureen said to the three of us. "He sued the Isaley's in Akron. They said he was disorderly and that that was why they wouldn't serve him, but a friend of his, a policeman, came in and beared the witness, so the suit went through."

"What's a suit?"

"It's when you can beat them up if you want to and won't anybody do nothing. Our family does it all the time. We believe in suits."

At the entrance to Isaley's Maureen turned to Frieda and me, asking, "You all going to buy some ice cream?"

We looked at each other. "No," Frieda said.

Maureen disappeared into the store with Pecola.

Frieda looked placidly down the street; I opened my mouth, but quickly closed it. It was extremely important that the world not know that I fully expected Maureen to buy us some ice cream, that for the past 120 seconds I had been selecting the flavor, that I had begun to like Maureen, and that neither of us had a penny.

We supposed Maureen was being nice to Pecola because of the boys, and were embarrassed to be caught—even by each other—thinking that she would treat us, or that we deserved it as much as Pecola did.

The girls came out. Pecola with two dips of orange-pineapple, Maureen with black raspberry.

"You should have got some," she said. "They had all kinds. Don't eat down to the tip of the cone," she advised Pecola.

"Why?"

"Because there's a fly in there."

"How you know?"

"Oh, not really. A girl told me she found one in the bottom of hers once, and ever since then she throws that part away."

"Oh."

We passed the Dreamland Theater, and Betty Grable smiled down at us.

"Don't you just love her?" Maureen asked.

"Uh-huh," said Pecola.

I differed. "Hedy Lamarr is better."

Maureen agreed. "Ooooo yes. My mother told me that a girl named Audrey, she went to the beauty parlor where we lived before, and asked the lady to fix her hair like Hedy Lamarr's, and the lady said, 'Yeah, when you grow some hair like Hedy Lamarr's.' " She laughed long and sweet.

"Sounds crazy," said Frieda.

"She sure is. Do you know she doesn't even menstrate yet, and she's sixteen. Do you, yet?"

"Yes." Pecola glanced at us.

"So do I." Maureen made no attempt to disguise her pride. "Two months ago I started. My girl friend in Toledo, where we lived before, said when she started she was scared to death. Thought she had killed herself."

"Do you know what it's for?" Pecola asked the question as though hoping to provide the answer herself.

"For babies." Maureen raised two pencil-stroke eyebrows at the obviousness of the question. "Babies need blood when they are inside you, and if you are having a baby, then you don't menstrate. But when you're not having a baby, then you don't have to save the blood, so it comes out."

"How do babies get the blood?" asked Pecola.

"Through the like-line. You know. Where your belly button is. That is where the like-line grows from and pumps the blood to the baby."

"Well, if the belly buttons are to grow like-lines to give the baby blood, and only girls have babies, how come boys have belly buttons?"

Maureen hesitated. "I don't know," she admitted. "But boys have all sorts of things they don't need." Her tinkling laughter was somehow stronger than our nervous ones. She curled her tongue around the edge of the cone, scooping up a dollop of purple that made my eyes water. We were waiting for a stop light to change. Maureen kept scooping the ice cream from around the cone's edge with her tongue; she didn't bite the edge as I would have done. Her tongue circled the cone. Pecola had finished hers; Maureen evidently liked her things to last. While I was thinking about her ice cream, she must have been thinking about her last remark, for she said to Pecola, "Did you ever see a naked man?"

Pecola blinked, then looked away. "No. Where would I see a naked man?"

"I don't know. I just asked."

"I wouldn't even look at him, even if I did see him. That's dirty. Who wants to see a naked man?" Pecola was agitated. "Nobody's father would be naked in front of his own daughter. Not unless he was dirty too."

"I didn't say 'father.' I just said 'a naked man.' "

"Well . . ."

"How come you said 'father'?" Maureen wanted to know.

"Who else would she see, dog tooth?" I was glad to have a chance to show anger. Not only because of the ice cream, but because we had seen our own father naked and didn't care to be reminded of it and feel the shame brought on by the absence of shame. He had been walking down the hall from the bathroom into his bedroom and passed the open door of our room. We had lain there wide-eyed. He stopped and looked in, trying to see in the dark room whether we were really asleep—or was it his imagination that opened eyes were looking at him? Apparently he convinced himself that we were sleeping. He moved away, confident that his little girls would not lie open-eyed like that, staring, staring. When he had moved on, the dark took only him away, not his nakedness. That stayed in the room with us. Friendly-like.

"I'm not talking to you," said Maureen. "Besides, I don't care if she sees her father naked. She can look at him all day if she wants to. Who cares?"

"You do," said Frieda. "That's all you talk about."

"It is not."

"It is so. Boys, babies, and somebody's naked daddy. You must be boy-crazy."

"You better be quiet."

"Who's gonna make me?" Frieda put her hand on her hip and jutted her face toward Maureen.

"You all ready made. Mammy made."

"You stop talking about my mama."

"Well, you stop talking about my daddy."

"Who said anything about your old daddy?"

"You did."

"Well, you started it."

"I wasn't even talking to you. I was talking to Pecola."

"Yeah. About seeing her naked daddy."

"So what if she did see him?"

Pecola shouted, "I never saw my daddy naked. Never."

"You did too," Maureen snapped. "Bay Boy said so."

"I did not."

"You did."

"I did not."

"Did. Your own daddy, too!"

Pecola tucked her head in—a funny, sad, helpless movement. A kind of hunching of the shoulders, pulling in of the neck, as though she wanted to cover her ears.

"You stop talking about her daddy," I said.

"What do I care about her old black daddy?" asked Maureen.

"Black? Who you calling black?"

"You!"

"You think you so cute!" I swung at her and missed, hitting Pecola in the face. Furious at my clumsiness, I threw my notebook at her, but it caught her in the small of her velvet back, for she had turned and was flying across the street against traffic.

Safe on the other side, she screamed at us, "I *am* cute! And you ugly! Black and ugly black e mos. I *am* cute!"

She ran down the street, the green knee socks making her legs look like wild dandelion stems that had somehow lost their heads. The weight of her remark stunned us, and it was a second or two before Frieda and I collected ourselves enough to shout, "Six-finger-dog-tooth-meringue-pie!" We chanted this most powerful of our arsenal of insults as long as we could see the green stems and rabbit fur.

Grown people frowned at the three girls on the curbside, two with their coats draped over their heads, the collars framing the eyebrows like nuns' habits, black garters showing where they bit the tops of brown stockings that barely covered the knees, angry faces knotted like dark cauliflowers.

Pecola stood a little apart from us, her eyes hinged in the direction in which Maureen had fled. She seemed to fold into herself, like a pleated wing. Her pain antagonized me. I wanted to open her up, crisp her edges, ram a stick down that hunched and curving spine, force her to stand erect and spit the misery out on the streets. But she held it in where it could lap up into her eyes.

Frieda snatched her coat from her head. "Come on, Claudia. 'Bye, Pecola."

We walked quickly at first, and then slower, pausing every now and then to fasten garters, tie shoelaces, scratch, or examine old scars. We were sinking under the wisdom, accuracy, and relevance of Maureen's last words. If she was cute—and if anything could be believed, she *was*—then we were not. And what did that mean? We were lesser. Nicer, brighter, but still lesser.

Dolls we could destroy, but we could not destroy the honey voices of parents and aunts, the obedience in the eyes of our peers, the slippery light in the eyes of our teachers when they encountered the Maureen Peals of the world. What was the secret? What did we lack? Why was it important? And so what? Guileless and without vanity, we were still in love with ourselves then. We felt comfortable in our skins, enjoyed the news that our senses released to us, admired our dirt, cultivated our scars, and could not comprehend this unworthiness. Jealousy we understood and thought natural—a desire to have what somebody else had; but envy was a strange, new feeling for us. And all the time we knew that Maureen Peal was not the Enemy and not worthy of such intense hatred. The *Thing* to fear was the *Thing* that made *her* beautiful, and not us.

Mine and Beautiful

Ayii, Ayii, Ayii,
I am good looking.
My face is beautiful.
I have long shining hair.
My lips and cheeks are red.
And my nose between my eyes
is flat and well formed.
Ayii, Ayii.

Traditional Song
Translated by J.A. Houston
Eastern Eskimo, Canada

"All but Jade Snow"

Jade Snow Wong
San Francisco, 1940s

At home, Jade Precious Stone was growing up with Jade Snow. Younger Sister had always been considered the beauty of the family. From the time her looks had been barely defined at babyhood, visitors had proclaimed her adorable, and had always rushed to pick her up and play with her. She was sweet, cherubic, delicate, and had not a shred of temper.

Whenever the family took snapshots, they found Jade Precious Stone more photogenic than Jade Snow. Younger Sister was fair-skinned, round-faced, and posed gracefully. Fifth Uncle on Daddy's side, who was Cousin Kee's father, said that Jade Precious Stone had the eyebrows of the swan and the eyes of the phoenix, at which Mama beamed with pleasure, for everyone also said that this daughter looked most like her.

On the other hand, Jade Snow was said to resemble her father. Like Daddy, she developed angular features, became dark-complexioned, serious, skinny, sensitive, independent, and not at all adorable. When callers came, Daddy might have this daughter show them how many words she could correctly identify in the Chinese newspaper, and the callers would politely acknowledge her cleverness, but they would be impatient to turn back to Younger Sister.

As a child Younger Sister spent many weeks and sometimes months as an invalid. Three times she was critically ill with pneumonia. But even when she was well, she never had a great deal of energy. Her lack of physical vitality freed Jade Precious Stone from most home responsibilities, which fell therefore on the shoulders of Jade Snow. And because Jade Precious Stone needed rest, she was allowed to discontinue Chinese school at an early age. Their personal differences, which were unimportant to Jade Snow as a child, irritated her increasingly as she approached young womanhood, until finally she began to adopt an attitude of apparent indifference toward her younger sister.

At eleven, Jade Precious Stone was concerned with hairdos, manicures, and make-up, while Jade Snow rejected them as frivolous. As the Wong sisters outgrew their children's Dutch bobs, Mama bought them a Marcel curling iron which had to be heated on a gas burner. The curling iron was Chinatown's latest fad. With its help, straight and coarse black Chinese hair suddenly was transformed into round sausage curls, or done in other fluffy styles, the like of which Jade Snow's ancestors never had seen.

With the curling iron, Jade Precious Stone and Jade Snow made due experiments on one another. To Mama's and Jade Precious Stone's disgust, Jade Snow decided that she preferred to have no further connection with the Marcel process, but Jade Precious Stone used it often.

This decision had caused an explosion when all the Wongs had gathered to have a family picture taken before the departure of the two older sisters for China. Daddy was very fond of family portraits. Before he came to America he had had large portrait photographs made of his father and mother—an unusual proceeding for that place and time.

For this occasion, every female had her hair smartly marcelled; that is, all but Jade Snow, whose hair hung neatly straight to her shoulders. By turns, the family coaxed and ridiculed the recalcitrant member, but Jade Snow grew more grimly stubborn as their pressure became greater. Thus in the one Wong family picture complete with its in-laws, the camera recorded Jade Snow, defiant and tense, with the only head of straight feminine hair in the group of curly-topped, relaxed, smiling faces.

Song of Lawino

Ask me what beauty is
To the Acholi
And I will tell you;
I will show it to you
If you give me a chance!

You saw me once,
You saw my hair style
And you admired it,
And the boys loved it.
At the arena
Boys surrounded me
And fought for me.

My mother taught me
Acholi hair fashions;
Which fit the kind

Of hair of the Acholi,
And the occasion.

Listen,
Ostrich plumes differ
From chicken feathers,
A monkey's tail
Is different from that of the giraffe,
The crocodile's skin
Is not like the guinea fowl's,
And the hippo's is naked and hairless.

The hair of the Acholi
Is different from that of the Arabs;
The Indians' hair
Resembles the tail of the horse;
It is like sisal strings
And needs to be cut

With scissors.
It is black
And is different from that of white women.

A white woman's hair
Is soft like silk;
It is light
And brownish, like
That of the brown monkey,
And is very different from mine.
A black woman's hair
Is thick and curly. . . .

I am proud of the hair
With which I was born
And as no white woman
Wishes to do her hair
Like mine,
Because she is proud
Of the hair with which she was born,
I have no wish
To look like a white woman.

             Okot p'Bitek
             Acholi People, Uganda, 1960s

I Came Home Today

I came home today.
I came home and I pulled off my Revlon Wonder lashes
long long longer. I removed my blonde-streaked wig,
designed for the real me. I washed the pearly dye off
of my teeth, the Yardley pot-o-gloss from my lips, the
pink from my new fingernails (only a $1.18 at
Woolworth's). I climbed out of my Ever-Stretch girdle
and my Cross-Your-Heart Bra.
   And I stood before the mirror.
I stood before the mirror and saw the lines of my body
for the first time, how they curled and twisted, forever
flowing from all directions, to all directions.
   And I saw that this was me.
That my body was unlike any other woman's body. That
it was mine and beautiful. JUST THE WAY IT WAS.
   I came home today.
I came home to see that I was not a store mannequin, but
a human being.

Julie Lieberman
Montclair, New Jersey, 1970s

"Am I Pretty?"

Gunilla Norris
New England, 1970s

The girls came to a standstill by the brook. It was a
shaded place where sunlight only fell in patches and the
trees grew thick and leafy.

"I reckon it's cold," said Sue-Ellen staring down at
the dark brook and stirring the water idly with her bare
feet. She began to unbutton her shirt.

Lia nodded. She suddenly felt embarrassed realizing
they'd go skinny dipping. Lia looked down at her blue
organdy dress and frowned. She shifted uncomfortably
on her feet.

Sue-Ellen looked her full in the face. She sensed Lia's
hesitancy.

"You needn't swim," she said hurriedly. "It might be
too cold for you."

Lia swallowed. "No, it won't be," she said, setting
her lips firmly. She reached for her buttons. Quickly she
had crawled out of the scratchy organdy, flung her shoes
and underwear to one side and splashed into the dark,
slow moving water. It *was* cold.

Lia shrieked and splashed. In a moment Sue-Ellen
raced in. The white sprays flew up with their giggles as
they tried not to look at each other's nakedness.

But soon it grew too cold for them. Lia headed for a
sunny flat rock that stood out of the water. She crawled
up on it, hunching her shoulders around her knees. Sue-
Ellen came and sat with her.

"It sure is cold," muttered Lia and shivered.

Sue-Ellen didn't say anything. She looked at Lia. She
saw that Lia like herself had breasts forming, that she
looked white and soft under her clothes though still
speckled with a myriad of freckles like a fine cinnamon
dusting all over her.

Lia felt Sue-Ellen's eyes and swallowed. Swiftly she looked back. She saw Sue-Ellen's strong free legs dangling in the water, saw the fine pubic hair just forming and the bands of white skin next to the suntanned places.

"You're sure pretty," said Sue-Ellen. "Your hair seems like it was on fire."

Lia smiled. "Thank you," she murmured.

"What're them silver things on your teeth?" asked Sue-Ellen pointing. She'd been wanting to ask a long time and now she felt full of questions and curiosity. She wanted to know all the things about Lia she'd never dared to ask before.

"Oh them. They're for straightening my teeth." Lia swallowed and looked down. Suddenly she felt sad. She frowned and thought about home.

"My family don't think I'm pretty," she said at last.

"Certain, they're wrong," said Sue-Ellen hotly.

"You tell them," said Lia in a weary voice. "They're always trying to stuff me into uncomfortable clothes or make me over like I was some kind of thing."

Sue-Ellen didn't answer. She frowned into the water and looked at Lia from the corner of her eye. Suddenly she had to know.

"Lia," she said. "Lia, you think I'm pretty?"

There was silence. It seemed as if the light shifted a little around them, as if time slid out of focus and stood still for a moment, as if they were set apart in something old, a ritual, a first knowing.

Lia looked up because she felt the urgency in Sue-Ellen's voice. She gazed at Sue-Ellen long and hard. Lia saw the other's breasts, pushing forward, round and firm almost like a woman's. Her eyes slid away. She felt they both must turn now, run each a separate way. But they didn't. Lia swallowed. She looked down, but she could still feel Sue-Ellen's wide and urgent eyes.

"Yes, Sue-Ellen, you're pretty. You're, well, awful grown up."

And somehow her friend did seem beyond reach, clothed in that mature nakedness.

But Sue-Ellen's face broke into a grin of relief. "I ain't that grown up," she said. "Have you started yet? I mean bleeding and such as Granny told me of."

Lia shook her head.

"Neither have I," said Sue-Ellen and suddenly their lips quivered. They giggled in embarrassment. Then they both laughed, heads back, somehow free now. Lia gave Sue-Ellen a big push into the slow dark water. She jumped in after. They scuffled playfully, bare arms and legs warm as they touched. They plunged and splashed in the brook until both had ducked the other. Then they bounded out of the dark water into the light and softness of the woods, snorting and sniffing with life.

CHAPTER FOUR

Sing Daughter Sing: Mothers and Daughters

sing daughter sing
make a song
and sing
beat out your own rhythms
the rhythms of your life
but make the song soulful
and make life
sing

Micere Mugo
Zimbabwe, 1970s

In many cultures the most important relationship for women is that of mother and daughter, because it is usually from her mother that a young girl first learns what it means to be a woman. When she reaches puberty, her mother reminds her how she must look and carry herself, and what she must do to fulfill the expectations of those around her.

This chapter reflects the special nature of the mother-daughter relationship in the years when a girl comes of age. The writings are divided into two sections, "Dear Daughter" and "Dear Mother." In the first part, mothers from various cultures communicate their expectations and concerns to their coming-of-age daughters. Several of the early selections are from pre-industrial societies in which expectations were clear because a young woman was destined to fulfill exactly the same role as her mother. At puberty a mother paid special attention to her daughter to ensure that the budding young woman became adept at the skills she would need as a married woman. One important lesson the daughter learned was proper decorum. In speech, dress, manners, ideas, and above all in sexual behavior, a woman was not to bring dishonor to her family or her husband. At the same time, in those societies where women were restricted to female company the daughter filled a unique place in her mother's life. Boys were allowed to leave the family walls to mingle with the men in community life, but girls were trained young to help with household chores, and they stayed at home with the other female members of the family. Mother often became the girl's companion and even confidante, as in the pieces "She Is My Good Fortune," "The Words Would Not Come," and "Sent from the Capital to Her Elder Daughter." When it came time for marriage, the mother was often reluctant to see the young woman leave home.

Unlike traditional cultures, modern western societies encourage girls to grow as individuals separate from their mothers, to interact with men, and to achieve a measure of independence. Some contemporary mothers, however, like Mrs. Bridge in "Advanced Training," continue to give their daughters "the guidance of another era." Others, like Margaret Mead in "To Cathy" and Janice Mirikitani in "Sing with Your Body," acknowledge that coming of age means that their daughters are moving on to a life their mothers cannot define.

In the second section, "Dear Mother," daughters react to their mothers' expectations. In the first selections they speak out against what they perceive as unnecessarily restrictive guidelines and admonitions. As Anne Frank reveals in her diary, they long for the "ideal" mother, one who will treat them as equals and accept them as they are. Even daughters of modern liberated women may find points of conflict with their mothers. In the short story from India entitled "Trishanku," Tanu is shocked when her "liberated" mother reveals her true feelings about Tanu's growing friendship with boys. "Look, if you wanted to keep me in chains, why didn't you do it from the start? Why this false show of freedom!"

Whether she acknowledges it or not, at this age much of a daughter's life is in fact patterned after her mother's. In the next selection, "We Dressed for the Dance Together," Helen's adolescence is characterized by a "cocoonlike quality" as her mother grooms her to take her proper place in the social order of white South Africa. Other girls question not only their mothers' advice, but their entire way of life. In "To Grind on the Same Stone," from tribal Kenya, Kalimonje begins to resent her mother when she realizes that she must inevitably lead the same kind of life as that of her mother.

Girls come to terms with their mothers in the concluding pieces, such as "I'm Truly Your Child," accepting their mothers' imperfections as well as their own. As a result, they are less likely to blame their mothers for their own shortcomings. "A Thorny Cactus" and "A Woman's Character" speak of mutual trust and affection as the daughters mature and a healthy separation occurs.

Dear Daughter

Pay heed to the word of your Mother
as though it were the word of a god.

> Mesopotamia, 3000 B.C.

Never move your knees when sitting, nor when
    standing shake your dress;
Laugh not loud when pleased; when angry never
    talk with over-stress;
Let the sexes ne'er commingle, whether they
    be rich or poor;
Never go beyond the gateway, nor stand gazing
    from the door.

> *Book of Odes*
> China, 500 B.C.

My daughter, if you do not learn to do well the things women must do and abide by the teachings of the elders, you shall stop at a stranger's house and your place will be near the kettle pole and without being told to go you shall go for water and when you have brought the water you shall look wistfully into the door of the lodge and they will tell you to open a pack so they may do their cooking. On opening the pack you will take a bit of the dried meat, thrust it slyly into your belt and take it with you and eat it stealthily but it shall not satisfy you. Food eaten in fear satisfies not the hunger.

Traditional saying
Omaha tribe, Nebraska

"Thou'rt a Budding Flower"

In this excerpt from the epic poem Leili and Medjnun, *Leili's mother is concerned that the gossip about her daughter's youthful love for Geis will bring disgrace to the family.*

. . . Thou'rt a budding flower
Not yet in bloom, but 'tis within their power
To put a blemish on thy purity.
Persist not in this folly, guided be
By modesty and reason, and beware
Lest thou who art a precious thing and rare
Be grasped by idle hands. A vagrant stream
May stray at random, but a maid, so deem
The worldly wise, may not. Remember: wine
That gives such pleasure, is, without design,
But evil does because 'twill often flow too free,
By many treated lightly, carelessly.
Do not be like a broken looking-glass
Distorting all it mirrors, and, my lass,
Dance not as if thou wert a candle flame,
For candles gasp and flicker, and a tame
Wind snuffs them out at will. Show not thy face
But hide it from all men; know that thy place
Is in the home, and there perforce remain,
Nor ever in the street appear. Restrain
Thy youthful fancies, pray, and do not wear
Apparel that attracts the eye; take care
That none suspect thy conduct. Be discreet,
Efface thyself. Believe me, it is meet
For maidens to be shy. Be as a song
That carries not abroad for fear the throng
Make sport of it. Keep always in the shade,
But be a shadow not that doth invade
A spot where 'tis perceived. Keep thou apart
From this vain youth who thinks to steal thy heart.
What's love, what's passion?—Nothing that a chaste,
Well brought-up maid will dwell upon or waste

Her time on even. Let me tell thee plain:
If thou obeyest not, thou'lt put a stain
Upon our honour. We whom all, 'twould seem,
Regard as worthy, and in high esteem
Have ever held, will be abused and scorned. . . .
By these my words, dear child, I beg, be warned.
Thou'rt silent. Dost thou think that no great hurt
Thou'rt threatened by? . . . O dear one, to avert
Thy father's wrath I strive; if he should hear
Of thee and Geis, thou'lt fare not well, I fear.
I think it best for thee not to attend
Thy lessons more. Thou mayest with profit spend
Thy time on toys and needle-work. Away
With pencils, books and such!. . . Thou'lt have to stay
Indoors and take up household tasks that none
Dare to reproach thee or to look upon
Thy person with contempt. A maid may not
Be seen in public; such is e'er the lot
Of her who would command respect. Be meek,
To hide from strangers' eyes, obedient, seek.

Fisul Muhammed Suleiman-Ogly
Translated by Irena Zheleznova
Azerbaijan, Ottoman Empire, 16th century

I've thirty-two daughters to marry!
I've filled my whole attic with them.
Good Lord, I don't know how
I'll marry off all my children.

My daughter, my daughter,
I'm speaking to you.
My mother, my mother,
What is it you're saying?
I say that if you're good,
You'll make a happy marriage.

I say that if you're good,
You'll make a happy marriage.
You'll be dressed up fit to kill;
Now turn around the circle.

Now go on with the dance.
Hop three times and bow,
And finally you kiss
The one that you will love.

Traditional song
France

"Let Us Thank God
for Such a Find"

Sainte Mère Jeanne-Françoise
Fréymot, *Letter*
France, 1622

Well, my dear daughter, here is M. de Toulongeon who,
having eight or ten free days at his disposal, is going to
travel to you by post in order, he says, to find out
whether you will think him too swarthy, for, as regards
his temper, he hopes not to displease you. For my part, I
tell you truly, not only do I find no fault with this match
but I find in it everything one could wish. Our Lord has
afforded me thereby a satisfaction such as I do not recall
ever finding before now in the things of this world. His
birth and wealth are not what impress me most but
rather his wit, his character, his wisdom, his probity, his
reputation: in short, Françoise, let us thank God for such
a find. My child, prepare yourself to love and serve God
in your gratitude better than you have ever done and let
nothing keep you from frequently partaking in the sacraments . . . do not be beguiled by the petty vanities of
clothes and rings: you are going to be rich; but, my dear
daughter, remember always that one must use the rich-
es that God gives us without becoming attached to
them. . . . Truly I am glad that it was your relatives and
myself who arranged this match without you: for this is
how wise people act. . . .

Your brother, whose judgment is reliable, is delighted
with the match. It is true that M. de Toulongeon is some
fifteen years older than you, but, my dear child, you will
be far happier with him than you would with some
crazy, irresponsible debauchee like the young men of today. You are going to marry a man who is not at all like
that, who is not a gambler, who has spent his life honor-

ably at court and at the wars and has been granted considerable emoluments by the king. You would be lacking in the good judgment which I know you to have if you did not receive him with warmth and simplicity. Do so, my dear, with a good grace, and be assured that God has thought for you and will continue to do so if you fling yourself into his arms; for he tenderly guides all those who trust in him.

She is my good fortune, she is my good fortune.
Sing for her and keep the Evil Eye from her.
Suitors already are coming to court her,
But we won't let her go.
All Tunis should be hers.
All the oil of the coast should gloss her braided hair
And the wheat of Africa fill all the corners of her house.

My daughter, your suitors stand in line,
Their heads humbly bowed.
Your father asks for thousands,
But your mother says it's not enough.

We won't give you up, my daughter,
Not till the son of the bey comes,
Who has ruled since his youth,
Who wears a robe of silk.
He'll bring you anklets
That will jingle and move when you move.
He will offer 130 camels,
But in the eyes of a mother
That's not enough for a beloved daughter.

Traditional song
Translated by Sabra Webber
Tunisia

"The Words Would
Not Come"

Karmala Markandaya
India, 20th century

I kept Ira as long as I could but when she was past fourteen her marriage could be delayed no longer, for it is
well known with what speed eligible young men are
snapped up; as it was, most girls of her age were already
married or at least betrothed. The choice of go-between
was not easy to make: Kali was the nearest to hand and
the obvious one, but she was garrulous and self-opinion-
ated: rejection of the young man she selected would in-
volve a tedious squabble. Besides, she had sons of her
own and might well consider them suitable husbands,
which I certainly could not, for they owned no land. Old
Granny, on the other hand, would be the ideal go-
between: she was old and experienced, knew very well
what to look for and never lacked patience; but for some
years now I had not traded with her and she might with
every justification refuse to act for me. But in the end it
was to her I went.

"A dowry of one hundred rupees," I said. "A maiden
like a flower. Do your best for me and I shall be ever in
your debt. This I ask you," I said, looking straight at her,
"although Biswas takes my produce and for you there
has been nothing."

"I bear you no grudge, Rukmani," she replied.
"Times are hard and we must do what we can for ourselves and our children. I will do my best."

Thereafter never a week went by but she brought
news of this boy or that, and she and I and Nathan spent
long hours trying to assess their relative merits. At last
we found one who seemed to fulfill our requirements:
he was young and well favoured, the only son of his fa-

ther from whom he would one day inherit a good portion of land.

"They will expect a large dowry," I said regretfully. "One hundred rupees will not win such a husband, we have no more."

"She is endowed with beauty," Old Granny said. "It will make up for a small dowry—in this case."

She was right. Within a month the preliminaries were completed, the day was fixed. Ira accepted our choice with her usual docility; if she fretted at the thought of leaving us and her brothers she showed no sign. Only once she asked a little wistfully how frequently I would be able to visit her, and, although I knew such trips would have to be very rare since her future home lay some ten villages away, I assured her not a year would pass without my going to see her two or three times.

"Besides, you will not want me so often," I said. "This home, your brothers, are all you have known so far, but when you have your own home and your own children you will not miss these. . . ."

She nodded slightly, making no comment, yet I knew how bruised she must be by the imminent parting. My spirit ached with pity for her, I longed to be able to comfort her, to convince her that in a few months' time her new home would be the most significant part of her life, the rest only a preparation . . . but before this joy must come the stress of parting, the loneliness of beginning a new life among strangers, the strain of the early days of marriage; and because I knew this the words would not come. . . .

Wedding day. Women from the village came to assist. Janaki, Kali, many I hardly knew. We went with Ira to the river and, when she was freshly bathed, put on her the red sari I had worn at my own wedding. Its rich heavy folds made her look more slender than she was, made her look a child. . . . I darkened her eyes with kohl and the years fell away more; she was so pitifully young I could hardly believe she was to be married, today.

The bridegroom arrived; his parents, his relatives, our friends, the priests. The drummer arrived and squatted outside awaiting permission to begin; the fiddler joined him. There should have been other musicians—a flautist, a harmonium player, but we could not afford these. Nathan would have nothing we could not pay for. No debts, he insisted, no debts. But I grudged Ira nothing: had I not saved from the day of her birth so that she should marry well? Now I brought out the stores I had put by month after month—rice and dhal and ghee, jars of oil, betel leaf, areca nuts, chewing tobacco and copra.

"I didn't know you had so much," said Nathan in amazement.

"And if you had there would be little enough," I said with a wink at the women, "for men are like children and must grab what they see." . . .

"What a good match," everybody said. "Such a fine boy, such a beautiful girl, too good to be true." It was indeed. Old Granny went about beaming: it was she who had brought the two parties together; her reputation as a matchmaker would be higher than ever. We none of us could look into the future.

So they were married. As the light faded two youths appeared bearing a palanquin for the newly married couple, lowered it at the entrance to the hut for them to step into. Now that it was time to go, Ira looked scared, she hesitated a little before entering: but already a dozen willing hands had lifted her in. The crowd, full of good feeling, replete with food and drunk with the music, vicariously excited, pressed round, eagerly thrusting over their heads garland after garland of flowers, the earth was spattered with petals. In the midst of the crush Nathan and I, Nathan holding out his hands to Ira in blessing, she with dark head bent low to receive it. Then the palanquin was lifted up, the torchbearers closed in, the musicians took their places. We followed on foot behind, relatives, friends, well-wishers and hangers-on. Several children had added themselves to the company; they came after, jigging about in high glee, noisy and excited: a long, ragged tail-end to the procession.

Past the fields, through the winding streets of the village we went, the bobbing palanquin ahead of us. Until we came at last to where, at a decorous distance, the bullock cart waited to take them away.

Then it was all over, the bustle, the laughter, the

noise. The wedding guests departed. The throng melted. After a while we walked back together to our hut. Our sons, tired out, were humped together asleep, the youngest clutching a sugary confection in one sticky fist. Bits of food lay everywhere. I swept the floor clean and strewed it with leaves. The walls showed cracks, and clods of mud had fallen where people had bumped against them, but these I left for patching in the morning. The used plaintain leaves I stacked in one heap— they would do for the bullocks. The stars were pale in the greying night before I lay down beside my husband. Not to sleep but to think. For the first time since her birth, Ira no longer slept under our roof.

Sent from the Capital to Her Elder Daughter

More than the gems
Locked away and treasured
In his comb-box
By the God of the Sea,
I prize you, my daughter.
But we are of this world
And such is its way!
Summoned by your man,
Obedient, you journeyed
To the far-off land of Koshi.
Since we parted,
Like a spreading vine,
Your eyebrows, pencil-arched,
Like waves about to break,
Have flitted before my eyes,
Bobbing like tiny boats.
Such is my yearning for you
That this body, time-riddled,
May well not bear the strain.

> Lady Ōtomo of Sakanoue
> Translated by Geoffrey Bownas and
> Anthony Thwaite
> Japan, 8th century

Advanced Training

Evan S. Connell, Jr.
Kansas City, 1930s

Appearances were an abiding concern of Mrs. Bridge, which was the reason that one evening as she saw Ruth preparing to go out she inquired, "Aren't you taking a purse, dear?"

Ruth answered in a husky voice that whatever she needed she could carry in her pockets.

Said Mrs. Bridge, "Carolyn always takes a purse."

Ruth was standing in front of the hall mirror, standing in a way that disturbed Mrs. Bridge, though she did not know precisely why, unless it could be that Ruth's feet were too far apart and her hips a little too forward. Mrs. Bridge had been trying to cure her of this habit by making her walk around the house with a book balanced on her head, but as soon as the book was removed Ruth resumed sauntering and standing in that unseemly posture.

"And you're older than Corky," Mrs. Bridge went on with a frown; and yet, looking at her elder daughter, she could not continue frowning. Ruth really was quite lovely, just as Gladys Schmidt's husband had said; if only she were not so conscious of it, not so aware of people turning to look at her, for they did stop to look—men and women both—so deliberately sometimes that Mrs. Bridge grew uneasy, and could not get over the idea that Ruth, by her posture and her challenging walk, was encouraging people to stare.

"Is somebody coming by for you?"

"I'm only going to the drugstore."

"What on earth do you do in the drugstore?" asked Mrs. Bridge after a pause. "Madge Arlen told me she saw you there one evening sitting all by yourself in a booth. She said she supposed you were waiting for someone."

At this Ruth stiffened noticeably, and Mrs. Bridge wanted to ask, "Were you?"

"I really don't approve of you sitting around in drugstores," she went on, for she was afraid to ask directly if Ruth was going there to meet a boy—not afraid of asking the question, but of the answer. "And I don't believe your father would approve of it either," she continued, feeling helpless and querulous in the knowledge that her daughter was hardly listening. "Goodness, I should think you could find something else to do. What about playing with Carolyn and her friends?"

Ruth didn't bother to answer.

"I'll lend you my blue suede purse, if you like," said Mrs. Bridge hopefully, but again there was no response. Ruth was still admiring herself in the mirror.

"I shouldn't think you could carry much in those pockets."

Ruth stepped backward, narrowed her eyes, and unfastened the top button of her blouse.

"Really, you *need* some things," Mrs. Bridge remarked a trifle sharply. "And button yourself up, for goodness' sake. You look like a chorus girl."

"Good night," said Ruth flatly and started for the door.

"But, dear, a lady always carries a purse!" Mrs. Bridge was saying when the door closed. . . .

Mademoiselle from Kansas City

It was to Carolyn, though she was younger, that Mrs. Bridge was in the habit of confiding her hopes for them all. The two were apt to sit on the edge of Carolyn's bed until quite late at night, their arms half-entwined, talking and giggling, while across the room Ruth slept her strangely restless sleep—mumbling and rolling and burying her face in her wild black hair.

Mrs. Bridge could never learn what Ruth did in the evenings, or where she went; she entered the house quietly, sometimes not long before dawn. Mrs. Bridge had always lain awake until both girls were home, and one evening during the Christmas holidays she was still downstairs reading when Carolyn returned, bringing Jay Duchesne, who was now considerably over six feet tall and was doing his best to grow a mustache. In certain lights the mustache was visible, and he was quite proud of it and stroked it constantly and feverishly, as if all it needed in order to flourish was a little affection. Mrs. Bridge liked Jay. She trusted him. There were moments when she thought she knew him better than she knew Douglas.

"What's new, Mrs. B.?" he inquired, twirling his hat on one finger. And to Carolyn, "How's for chow, kid?" So they went out to the kitchen to cook bacon and eggs while Mrs. Bridge remained in the front room with the book turned over in her lap and her eyes closed, dozing and dreaming happily, because it seemed to her that despite the difficulties of adolescence she had gotten her children through it in reasonably good condition. Later, when Duchesne roared out of the driveway—he still drove as recklessly as ever and she was still not resigned to it—she climbed the stairs, arm in arm, with Carolyn.

"Jay's voice has certainly changed," she smiled.

"He's a man now, Mother," Carolyn explained a bit impatiently.

Mrs. Bridge smiled again. She sat on the bed and watched as Carolyn pulled off the baggy sweater and skirt and seated herself at the dressing table with a box of bobby pins.

"Funny—it's so quiet," said Carolyn.

Mrs. Bridge looked out the window. "Why, it's snowing again. Isn't that nice! I just love snowy winter nights."

Large wet flakes were floating down and clasping the outside of the window, and the street light shone on the evergreen tree in the back yard.

"There goes a rabbit!" she cried, but by the time Carolyn reached the window only the tracks were visible.

"Is Daddy asleep?" Carolyn asked.

"Yes, poor man. He didn't get away from the office until after seven and insists he has to get up at five-thirty tomorrow morning."

"That's silly."

"I know, but you can't tell him anything. I've tried, goodness knows, but it never does any good."

"Why does he do it?"

"Oh," said Mrs. Bridge irritably, for the thought of it never failed to irritate her, "he insists we'll all starve to death if he doesn't."

"That'll be the day!"

Both of them were silent for a while, watching the snow descend.

"I do hope Ruth gets home soon."

"She can drop dead for all I care."

"You know I don't like you to use that expression."

Carolyn split a bobby pin on her teeth and jammed it into her curly blond hair. "Well, what's the matter with her then? Who does she think she is, anyway?" She leaned to one side and opened the cupboard that belonged to Ruth. "Look at that! Black lace bras. Mademoiselle from Kansas City."

Presently the grandfather clock in the hall chimed twice, and Mrs. Bridge, after brushing Carolyn's cheek with her lips, went downstairs and into the kitchen, where she made herself some cocoa and moodily watched the snow building up on the sill. After a while she went upstairs again, changed into her nightgown, and got into bed beside her husband. There she lay with her hands folded on the blanket while she waited for the faint noise of the front door opening and closing.

She believed she was awake but all at once, without having heard a sound, she realized someone was downstairs. She heard a gasp and then what sounded like a man groaning. The luminous hands of the bedside clock showed four-fifteen. Mrs. Bridge got out of bed, pulled on her robe, and hurried along the hall to the top of the stairs, where she took hold of the banister and leaned over, calling just loud enough to be heard by anyone in the living room, "Ruth?"

No one answered.

"Ruth, is that you?" she asked, more loudly, and there was authority in her tone. She listened and she thought some delicate noise had stopped. The dark house was silent.

"I'm coming down," said Mrs. Bridge.

"It's me," said Ruth.

"Is there anyone with you?"

"He's leaving."

And then Ruth coughed in a prolonged, unnatural way, and Mrs. Bridge knew she was coughing to conceal another noise.

"Who's there?" she demanded, unaware that she was trembling from anger and fright, but there was only the sound of the great front door opening and shutting and seconds later the crunch of auto tires on the crust of yesterday's frozen snow and whoever it was released the brake and coasted away.

A cold draft swept up the spiral staircase. Mrs. Bridge, peering down into the gloom, saw her daughter ascending. She snapped on the hall light and they met at the top step. Ruth was taking the last of the pins out of her hair. She reeked of whisky and her dress was unbuttoned. Idly she pushed by her mother and wandered along the hall. Mrs. Bridge was too shocked to do anything until Ruth was at the door of her room; there they confronted each other again, for Ruth had felt herself pursued and turned swiftly with a sibilant ominous cry. Her green eyes were glittering and she lifted one hand to strike. Mrs. Bridge, untouched by her daughter's hand, staggered backward.

Ruth Goes to New York

That was the year Ruth finally managed to graduate from high school. She was there five years and for a while they were afraid it would be six, though she had taken the easiest courses possible. Her electives were music, drawing, athletics, and whatever else sounded easy. She seldom studied, and even when she did study she did poorly. She had been a member of the swimming team and this was the only activity listed after her name in the yearbook: "member of the girls' swimming team"—that and the desperate phrase "interested in dramatics." She had once tried out for a play, but gave a rather hysterical reading and failed to get the part. When she finished high school Carolyn was only one semester behind her, although they had started two years apart.

A few days after the graduation she said she was going to New York to get a job. She did not like Kansas City; she never had. She had not made many friends. She had never seemed happy or even much at ease in Kansas City.

Mrs. Bridge tried to become indignant when Ruth announced she was going to New York, but after all it was useless to argue.

"What on earth would you do in New York?" she asked, because Ruth had been unable to learn shorthand, nor could she operate a typewriter as efficiently as Douglas, who tapped out his English themes with one finger.

"Don't worry about me," Ruth said. She had grown tall and beautiful, and somehow—in the powerful arch of her nose and in her somber, barbaric eyes—she looked biblical, swarthy and violent.

"I'm putting a thousand dollars in the bank for you," said Mr. Bridge, "on one condition." This condition was that if she could not support herself by the time the money ran out she would agree to return to Kansas City. She laughed and put her arms around him, and no one in the family had seen her do this since she was a child.

Mrs. Bridge was disturbed that she did not want to go to college, being of the opinion that although one might never actually need a college degree it was always nice to have; and yet, thinking the matter over, she realized Ruth would only be wasting four years—obviously she was no student. But why New York? Why not some place closer to home?

Soon she was ready to leave. The entire family went to the station.

"You didn't forget your ticket, did you?" asked Mrs. Bridge.

"Not quite," said Ruth drily.

"Be sure to look up the Wenzells when you get there. I've already written them you're coming to New York, but of course they won't know where to find you." The Wenzells were people they had met one summer in Colorado and with whom they exchanged Christmas greetings.

"I will," said Ruth, who had no intention of getting in touch with them.

"Have a good trip," her mother said as they were embracing at the gate. "Don't forget to write. Let us know as soon as you arrive."

"Here are your traveling expenses," her father said, handing her some folded bills. "For God's sake, don't lose it. And behave yourself. If you don't, I'm coming after you."

"I can look out for myself," said Ruth.

He laughed, and his laughter rang out odd and bold, the laughter of a different man, a free and happy man, who was not so old after all. "That isn't what I said," he told her lightly, and Mrs. Bridge, glancing from one to the other, was struck by their easy companionship, as though they had gotten to know each other quite well when she was not around.

Once on the train Ruth kicked off her shoes and curled up in the seat. She unsnapped the catch of her traveling bag and reached in for a copy of *Theatre Arts* but felt a strange envelope. She knew immediately what it was—it was called a "train letter," and a generation or so ago they were given to young people who were leaving home for the first time. She withdrew her hand and sat motionless for quite a while. Tears gathered in her eyes and presently she was shaken with dry sobs, although she did not know whether she was laughing or weeping. Before long she dried her face and lighted a cigarette.

Much later Ruth took out the envelope, read the letter of advice, and seemed to see her mother seated at the Chippendale highboy with some stationery and a fountain pen, seeking to recall the guidance of another era.

To Cathy

That I be not a restless ghost
Who haunts your footsteps as they pass
Beyond the point where you have left
me standing in the newsprung grass,

You must be free to take a path
Whose end I feel no need to know,
No irking fever to be sure
You went where I would have you go.

Those who would fence the future in
Between two walls of well-laid stones
But lay a ghost walk for themselves,
a dreary walk for dusty bones.

So you can go without regret
Away from this familiar land
Leaving your kiss upon my hair
And all the future in your hands.

Margaret Mead
New York City, 1947

217

Sing with Your Body

To my daughter, Tianne Tsukiko

We love with great difficulty
spinning in one place
afraid to create
       spaces
          new/rhythm

the beat of a child
dangled by her own inner ear
takes Aretha with her
       upstairs, somewhere.

go quickly, Tsukiko,
       into your circled dance
go quickly
       before your steps are
       halted by who you are not

go quickly
       to learn the mixed
       rhythm of your tongue,

go quickly
       to who you are

       before

          your mother swallows
          what she has lost.

          Janice Mirikitani
          San Francisco, 1970s

Little Girl, My Stringbean,
My Lovely Woman

My daughter, at eleven
(almost twelve), is like a garden.

Oh, darling! Born in that sweet birthday suit
and having owned it and known it for so long,
now you must watch high noon enter—
noon, that ghost hour.
Oh, funny little girl—this one under a blueberry sky,
this one! How can I say that I've known
just what you know and just where you are?

It's not a strange place, this odd home
where your face sits in my hand
so full of distance,
so full of its immediate fever.
The summer has seized you,
as when, last month in Amalfi, I saw
lemons as large as your desk-side globe—
that miniature map of the world—
and I could mention, too,
the market stalls of mushrooms
and garlic buds all engorged.
Or I think even of the orchard next door,
where the berries are done
and the apples are beginning to swell.
And once, with our first backyard,
I remember I planted an acre of yellow beans
we couldn't eat.

Oh, little girl,
my stringbean,
how do you grow?
You grow this way.
You are too many to eat.

I hear
as in a dream
the conversation of the old wives
speaking of *womanhood*.
I remember that I heard nothing myself.
I was alone.
I waited like a target.

Let high noon enter—
the hour of the ghosts.
Once the Romans believed
that noon was the ghost hour,
and I can believe it, too,
under that startling sun,
and someday they will come to you,
someday, men bare to the waist, young Romans
at noon where they belong,
with ladders and hammers
while no one sleeps.

But before they enter
I will have said,
Your bones are lovely,
and before their strange hands
there was always this hand that formed.

Oh, darling, let your body in,
let it tie you in,
in comfort.
What I want to say, Linda,
is that women are born twice.
If I could have watched you grow
as a magical mother might,
if I could have seen through my magical transparent
    belly,
there would have been such ripening within:
your embryo,
the seed taking on its own,
life clapping the bedpost,
bones from the pond,
thumbs and two mysterious eyes,
the awfully human head,

the heart jumping like a puppy,
the important lungs,
the becoming—
while it becomes!
as it does now,
a world of its own,
a delicate place.

I say hello
to such shakes and knockings and high jinks,
such music, such sprouts,
such dancing-mad-bears of music,
such necessary sugar,
such goings-on!

Oh, little girl
my stringbean,
how do you grow?
You grow this way.
You are too many to eat.

What I want to say, Linda,
is that there is nothing in your body that lies.
All that is new is telling the truth.
I'm here, that somebody else,
an old tree in the background.

Darling,
stand still at your door,
sure of yourself, a white stone, a good stone—
as exceptional as laughter
you will strike fire,
that new thing!

                    Anne Sexton
                    Newton, Massachusetts, 1964

Dear Mother

The Fish

I had about as much chance, Mother,
as the carp who thrashed
in your bathtub on Friday,
swimming helplessly back and forth
in the small hard pool you made for me,
unaware how soon you would
pull me from my element
sever my head just below the gills
scrape away the iridescence
chop me into bits and pieces and
reshape me with your strong hands
to simmer in your special broth.
You bustled about the house
confident in your design,
while I waited at the edge
imploring you with glossy eyes
to keep me and love me
just as I was.

L.L. Zeiger
United States, 1970s

A Letter to Her Mother

I am a king's daughter, you a king's wife.
I am furious!
Those tablets you and your husband used
to order me into this cloister,
let's forget them.
But remember this:
even warriors seized as booty in war
are treated humanely.
At least, treat me like them!

> Eristi-Aya
> Translated by Willis Barnstone
> Akkadia, ca. 1790–1745 B.C.

"Exact Opposites"

Anne Frank
Amsterdam, 1942–1944

November 7, 1942

Dear Kitty,
Mummy and her failings are something I find harder to bear than anything else. I don't know how to keep it all to myself. I can't always be drawing attention to her untidiness, her sarcasm, and her lack of sweetness, neither can I believe that I'm always in the wrong.

We are exact opposites in everything; so naturally we are bound to run up against each other. I don't pronounce judgment on Mummy's character, for that is something I can't judge. I only look at her as a mother, and she just doesn't succeed in being that to me; I have to be my own mother. I've drawn myself apart from them all; I am my own skipper and later on I shall see where I come to land. All this comes about particularly because I have in my mind's eye an image of what a perfect mother and wife should be; and in her whom I must call "Mother" I find no trace of that image.

I am always making resolutions not to notice Mummy's bad example. I want to see only the good side of her and to seek in myself what I cannot find in her. But it doesn't work; and the worst of it is neither Daddy nor Mummy understands this gap in my life, and I blame them for it. I wonder if anyone can ever succeed in making their children absolutely content. . . .

Yours, Anne

April 2, 1943

Dear Kitty,
Oh dear: I've got another terrible black mark against my name. I was lying in bed yesterday evening waiting

for Daddy to come and say my prayers with me, and wish me good night, when Mummy came into my room, sat on my bed, and asked very nicely, "Anne, Daddy can't come yet, shall I say your prayers with you to-night?" "No, Mummy," I answered.

Mummy got up, paused by my bed for a moment, and walked slowly towards the door. Suddenly she turned around, and with a distorted look on her face said, "I don't want to be cross, love cannot be forced." There were tears in her eyes as she left the room.

I lay still in bed, feeling at once that I had been horrible to push her away so rudely. But I knew too that I couldn't have answered differently. It simply wouldn't work. I felt sorry for Mummy; very, very sorry, because I had seen for the first time in my life that she minds my coldness. I saw the look of sorrow on her face when she spoke of love not being forced. It is hard to speak the truth, and yet it is the truth: she herself has pushed me away, her tactless remarks and her crude jokes, which I don't find at all funny, have now made me insensitive to any love from her side. Just as I shrink at her hard words, so did her heart when she realized that the love between us was gone. She cried half the night and hardly slept at all. Daddy doesn't look at me and if he does for a second, then I read in his eyes the words: "How can you be so unkind, how can you bring yourself to cause your mother such sorrow?"

They expect me to apologize; but this is something I can't apologize for because I spoke the truth and Mummy will have to know it sooner or later anyway. I seem, and indeed am, indifferent both to Mummy's tears and Daddy's looks, because for the first time they are both aware of something which I have always felt. I can only feel sorry for Mummy, who has now had to discover that I have adopted her own attitude. For myself, I remain silent and aloof; and I shall not shrink from the truth any longer, because the longer it is put off, the more difficult it will be for them when they do hear it.

Yours, Anne

January 2, 1944

Dear Kitty,

This morning when I had nothing to do I turned over some of the pages of my diary and several times I came across letters dealing with the subject "Mummy" in such a hotheaded way that I was quite shocked, and asked myself: "Anne, is it really you who mentioned hate? Oh, Anne, how could you!" I remained sitting with the open page in my hand, and thought about it and how it came about that I should have been so brimful of rage and really so filled with such a thing as hate that I had to confide it all in you. I have been trying to understand the Anne of a year ago and to excuse her, because my conscience isn't clear as long as I leave you with these accusations, without being able to explain, on looking back, how it happened.

I suffer now—and suffered then—from moods which kept my head under water (so to speak) and only allowed me to see the things subjectively without enabling me to consider quietly the words of the other side, and to answer them as the words of one whom I, with my hotheaded temperament, had offended or made unhappy.

I hid myself within myself, I only considered myself and quietly wrote down all my joys, sorrows, and contempt in my diary. This diary is of great value to me, because it has become a book of memoirs in many places, but on a good many pages I could certainly put "past and done with."

I used to be furious with Mummy, and still am sometimes. It's true that she doesn't understand me, but I don't understand her either. She did love me very much and she was tender, but as she landed in so many unpleasant situations through me, and was nervous and irritable because of other worries and difficulties, it is certainly understandable that she snapped at me.

I took it much too seriously, was offended, and was rude and aggravating to Mummy, which, in turn, made her unhappy. So it was really a matter of unpleasantness and misery rebounding all the time. It wasn't nice for either of us, but it is passing.

I just didn't want to see all this, and pitied myself very

much; but that, too, is understandable. Those violent outbursts on paper were only giving vent to anger which in a normal life could have been worked off by stamping my feet a couple of times in a locked room, or calling Mummy names behind her back.

The period when I caused Mummy to shed tears is over. I have grown wiser and Mummy's nerves are not so much on edge. I usually keep my mouth shut if I get annoyed, and so does she, so we appear to get on much better together. I can't really love Mummy in a dependent childlike way—I just don't have that feeling.

I soothe my conscience now with the thought that it is better for hard words to be on paper than that Mummy should carry them in her heart.

Yours, Anne

January 5, 1944

Dear Kitty,

. . . You know that I've grumbled a lot about Mummy, yet still tried to be nice to her again. Now it is suddenly clear to me what she lacks. Mummy herself has told us that she looked upon us more as her friends than her daughters. Now that is all very fine, but still, a friend can't take a mother's place. I need my mother as an example which I can follow, I want to be able to respect her. I have the feeling that Margot thinks differently about these things and would never be able to understand what I've just told you. And Daddy avoids all arguments about Mummy.

I imagine a mother as a woman who, in the first place, shows great tact, especially towards her children when they reach our age, and who does not laugh at me if I cry about something—not pain, but other things—like "Mums" does.

One thing, which perhaps may seem rather fatuous, I have never forgiven her. It was on a day that I had to go to the dentist. Mummy and Margot were going to come with me, and agreed that I should take my bicycle. When we had finished at the dentist, and were outside again, Margot and Mummy told me that they were going into the town to look at something or buy something—I don't remember exactly what. I wanted to go, too, but was not allowed to, as I had my bicycle with me. Tears of rage sprang into my eyes, and Mummy and Margot began laughing at me. Then I became so furious that I stuck my tongue out at them in the street just as an old woman happened to pass by, who looked very shocked! I rode home on my bicycle, and I know I cried for a long time.

It is queer that the wound that Mummy made then still burns, when I think of how angry I was that afternoon. . . .

Yours, Anne

A Dutiful Daughter

Simone de Beauvoir
Paris, 1920s

I had lost the sense of security childhood gives, and nothing had come to take its place. My parents' authority remained inflexible, but as my critical sense developed I began to rebel against it more and more. I couldn't see the point of visits, family dinners, and all those tiresome social duties which my parents considered obligatory. Their replies, "It's your duty" or "That just isn't done," didn't satisfy me at all. My mother's eternal solicitude began to weigh me down. She had her own "ideas" which she did not attempt to justify, and her decisions often seemed to be quite arbitrary. We had a violent argument about a missal which I wanted to give my sister for her First Communion; I wanted to choose one bound in pale fawn leather, like those which the majority of my schoolmates had; Mama thought that one with a blue cloth cover would do just as well; I protested that the money in my money box was for me to do what I liked with; she replied that one should not pay out twenty francs for a thing that could be bought for fourteen. While we were buying bread at the baker's and all the way up the stairs and in the house itself I held my own against her. But in the end I had to give in, with rage in my heart, vowing never to forgive her for what I considered to be an abuse of her power over me. If she had often stood in my way, I think she would have provoked me to open rebellion. But in the really important things—my studies and the choice of my friends—she very rarely meddled; she respected my work and my leisure too, only asking me to do little odd jobs for her like grinding the coffee or carrying the trash bin downstairs. I had the habit of obedience, and I believed that, on the whole, God expected me to be dutiful: the conflict that threatened to set me against my mother did not break out; but I was uneasily aware of its underlying presence. My mother's whole education and upbringing had convinced her that for a woman the greatest thing was to become the mother of a family; she couldn't play this part unless I played the dutiful daughter, but I refused to take part in grown-up pretense just as much as I did when I was five years old. At the Cours Désir, on the eve of our First Communion, we were exhorted to go and cast ourselves down at our mothers' feet and ask them to forgive our faults; not only had I not done this, but when my sister's turn came I persuaded her not to do so either. My mother was vexed about it. She was aware of a certain reticence in me which made her bad-tempered, and she often rebuked me. I held it against her for keeping me so dependent upon her and continuing to impose her will upon me. In addition, I was jealous of the place she held in my father's affections because my own passion for him had continued to grow. . . .

As long as he approved of me, I could be sure of myself. For years he had done nothing but heap praises on my head. But when I reached the awkward age, he was disappointed in me: he appreciated elegance and beauty in women. Not only did he fail to conceal his disillusionment from me, but he began showing more interest than before in my sister, who was still a pretty girl. He glowed with pride when she paraded up and down dressed as "The Queen of the Night." He sometimes took part in productions which his friend Monsieur Jeannot—a great advocate of religious drama—organized in the local church clubs; Poupette often played with him. Her face framed in her long fair hair, she played the part of the little girl in Max Maurey's *Le Pharmicien*. He taught her to recite fables, putting in gestures and expression. Though I would not admit it to myself, I was hurt by the understanding between them, and felt a vague resentment against my sister.

But my real rival was my mother. I dreamed of having a more intimate relationship with my father; but even on the rare occasions when we found ourselves alone together we talked as if she were there with us. When there was an argument, if I had appealed to my father,

he would have said: "Do what your mother tells you!" I
only once tried to get him on my side. He had taken us to
the races at Auteuil; the course was black with people, it
was hot, there was nothing happening, and I was bored;
finally the horses were off: the people rushed toward the
barriers, and their backs hid the track from my view. My
father had hired folding chairs for us and I wanted to
stand on mine to get a better view. "No!" said my
mother, who detested crowds and had been irritated by
all the pushing and shoving. I insisted that I should be
allowed to stand on my folding chair. "When I say no, I
mean no!" my mother declared. As she was looking after
my sister, I turned to my father and cried furiously:
"Mama is being ridiculous! Why can't I stand on my
folding chair?" He simply lifted his shoulder in an embarrassed silence, and refused to take part in the argument.

At least this ambiguous gesture allowed me to assume
that as far as he was concerned my father sometimes
found my mother too domineering; I persuaded myself
that there was a silent conspiracy between us. But I soon
lost this illusion. One lunchtime there was talk of a wild-
living cousin who considered his mother to be an idiot:
on my father's own admission she actually was one. Yet
he declared vehemently: "A child who sets himself up
as a judge of his mother is an imbecile." I went scarlet
and left the table, pretending I was feeling sick. I was
judging my mother, and my father had struck a double
blow at me by affirming their solidarity and by referring
to me indirectly as an imbecile. What upset me even
more is that I couldn't help passing judgment on the
very sentence my father had just uttered: since my
aunt's stupidity was plain to everyone, why shouldn't
her son acknowledge it? It is no sin to tell oneself the
truth, and besides, quite often, one tells oneself the truth
unintentionally; at that very moment, for example, I
couldn't help thinking what I thought: was that wrong
of me? In one sense it was not, and yet my father's
words made such a deep impression on me that I felt at
once irreproachable and a monster of imbecility. After
that, and perhaps partly because of that incident, I no
longer believed in my father's absolute infallibility. Yet

my parents still had the power to make me feel guilty; I accepted their verdicts while at the same time I looked upon myself with different eyes than theirs. My essential self still belonged to them as much as to me: but paradoxically the self they knew could only be a decoy now; it could be false. There was only one way of preventing this strange confusion: I would have to cover up superficial appearances, which were deceptive. I was used to guarding my tongue; I redoubled my vigilance. I took a further step. As I was not now admitting everything I thought, why not venture unmentionable acts? I was learning how to be secretive.

Trishanku

Mannu Bhandari
Translated by Ruth Vanita
India, 1970s

*Trishanku is a character from Hindu mythology who tried to
reach heaven but was sent back by the gods and now remains
suspended between heaven and earth. In this excerpt from a
short story, Tanu, a fifteen-year-old Hindu girl of high caste,
feels that like Trishanku she is in limbo, frustrated by her
western-educated mother in making her own choices. She had
always believed that hers was a truly liberated household and
that she was more like a sister to her mother than a daughter.
Tanu was unprepared when one day her mother reveals her
ambivalent feelings.*

"Tanu darling, these friends of yours seem to be here
all day. And your studies are going to the dogs. After
all, you have to study too. Things can't go on like
this. . . ."

"I study at night, Ma."

"My happy nonchalance! 'You study at night.' Don't
give me that nonsense. And in any case, I don't like this
racket every day. If they come over now and again, to
have a chat, that's fine, but these days, they seem to
have made this a regular den."

I noticed the growing irritation in her tone, but did not
make any answer.

"You are so intimate with them—why don't you tell
them they ought to sit and study and allow you also to
study. If you don't know how to tell them so, I will."

But somehow the occasion to "tell them" did not
arise. The hostelers began to come less frequently, partly
because of their studies, and partly because of the other
attractions of Delhi. But Shekhar, one of the two occupying the room across the road, continued to come every

233

day, sometimes in the afternoon, sometimes in the evening. I had always met him with a crowd of friends and therefore not noticed that quality of his which now drew us close to each other. He said so little and yet tried to say so much without words. Suddenly I had begun to understand this unspoken language of his . . . not only to understand but to respond . . . it did not take me long to realize that—what can I call it but "love"—was growing between Shekhar and me.

It did not take Mummy long finding out that something was afoot . . . no matter how quietly Shekhar came stealing in, Mummy would suddenly pop up from nowhere or call from some corner of the house, "Anyone in your room, Tanu?" Mum was certainly upset by all this, and yet how could she possibly be upset by it? Our house echoing, day and night, with discussions of Love—marital love, extramarital love, love for two or three people at the same time. . . .

Anyhow, seeing Mum upset, I could not help being disturbed. Mum's not just my mother—she is a pal as well, a sort of comrade-in-arms. We have real heart-to-heart talks about everything and anything—we laugh together, we have our private jokes. If only she would say something about this too, but she did not; only when Shekhar came she would shed her customary nonchalance and keep hovering round my room like a hostel warden. . . .

However, I saw to it that out of every three hours spent with Shekhar, I studied for one hour. He enjoyed teaching me and I enjoyed learning from him. While studying, he would, off and on, write me little notes which sent such thrills racing through me! And after he would leave, those sentences, those words, those emotions would still shoot strange sensations into every fibre of my being.

The fascinating and colourful world being created within me! I felt as if I didn't need anyone—I was complete in myself. Even Mummy, who is so close to me, was being pushed out—we exchanged commonplaces but nothing more than that. Days were passing by, and I, lost in myself, living more and more in my own world, was hardly bothered about the external world at all! One day I came home from school, changed my clothes, demanded and devoured my lunch, then was going off to my room, when Mummy, who was lying down, called out: "Come here, Tanu." I went, and Mummy's face . . . ! I stood there, slightly dazed. She picked up a book from the side table and took out five or six notes. Oh God! I had given her that novel to read and forgotten that Shekhar's notes were in it!

"So this is what your great friendship with Shekhar is all about! This is what you sit and study together! This is all he comes here for!" I didn't say a word. Nothing could be more foolish than to answer back to Mummy when she's in a temper. I know that only too well. "You've been given liberty but that does not mean you should take undue advantage of it . . . ." I remained silent. "A chit of a girl carrying on in this fashion. Just because you've been given some leeway, you think you're too smart. What you need is a good spanking to knock all this romance out of you." Her saying that made me tingle from head to foot.

I looked up at her in amazement—but—this was not Mummy at all—that was not the way she looked or spoke. And yet everything she said sounded so familiar. I kept thinking I had heard it all before and suddenly—it all fell into place—my grandfather! Grandfather rising out of his grave? And in my mother who had been in combat with him ever since she could remember, who had always opposed all that he stood for! Well, Mummy's "Grandfatherish" speech went on for some time but I'd stopped listening . . . all that shook me up was—how did Grandfather get to be within Mummy?

A strange tense silence hung over the house, especially between Mummy and me! I can communicate with Mummy, make her understand, but Grandfather? Grandfather had taken complete possession of Mummy. . . .

I had shown Shekhar the red flag so he was keeping away but what was I to do all evening? It came to my mind so many times: why should I not go to Mummy and ask her straight out why she was so angry? After all, she knew of my friendship with Shekhar; I had never tried to hide it. But then I would remember that Mummy wasn't there to be talked to. I hadn't seen Shekhar for four days. . . .

But when I came back from school, I was left agape. There was Shekhar, sitting with his head in his hands, and Mummy perched on the arm of his chair, gently stroking his brow. When she saw me, she said in a perfectly natural tone, "Look at this idiot. Four days this gentleman has missed his classes, and has not been eating. Now, just make him sit down with you and have lunch." And then she sat down with us, made a great fuss of Shekhar, and saw that he ate properly. He went home, overwhelmed with gratitude to Mummy, while as for me, the flood of joy inside me literally swept away all my unasked questions. Shekhar began to come again, but once in two or three days. And we spent most of the time talking about our work. He had apologized to Mummy for his behavior and promised never again to do anything to which she might object.

But I did notice that whenever Shekhar stayed on a little later in the evening or came a little earlier in the afternoon, Grandfather would start perking up somewhere inside Mummy—one could see the symptoms on her face. She would try very hard not to let him have his way but she couldn't quite get rid of him either. Yet Mummy and I no longer maintained a silence on the subject. She would joke with me about it. "What a lovelorn fellow this Shekhar of yours is! Instead of enjoying himself and going out into the world like others of his age, there he is, always mooning on the terrace, gazing this way like a regular Majnu." I'd just laugh. Sometimes she'd get emotional about it. "Darling, you have no idea what great things I have in mind for you, what dreams of your future . . ." I'd laugh and reply, "Really Mummy, you want to dream about your own life and about mine as well! Let me do a little of the dreaming too." And sometimes she'd be all tolerant understanding, trying to "explain" things to me: "Tanu darling, you're so young: you ought to be studying right now and not occupying yourself with all this foolery. Of course you should fall in love, when you are old enough, and get married too. I have no intention of finding you a husband. I'll leave it entirely to you. But why don't you wait till you are old enough to choose properly?'' ''Well, Mummy, when you chose Papa, did Grandfather approve?'' ''When I chose! Madam, I was twenty-five years old and had finished my studies. I made my choice very carefully after a great deal of thought.'' Studies! Age! I was good enough at my studies, and as for age, I felt like saying, ''Look Mum, what your generation did at twenty-five, ours will do at fifteen—why don't you realize that?'' But I didn't say it. After all, we had already started talking of Grandfather; what if he suddenly popped up again? . . .

Exams over, and heavenly weather! My friendship was going strong and Mummy seemed not to mind. But then again a sudden shock. I'd just come home with a girl friend when Mummy called, ''Come here, Tanu.'' That tone was danger signal enough! I went and the same set expression on her face. ''Do you go over to Shekhar's room?'' She fired the question at me, point-blank range. I wanted to say, ''Well, whoever gave you that information must have given you the rest too and added a few fancy trimmings.'' But the way Mummy was simmering, I thought it best not to reply. What was all the fuss about anyway? So what if I had been to Shekhar's room a couple of times? It was hardly a criminal offense. ''Don't you remember I had forbidden you ever to go to his room? He spends hours and hours here—isn't that enough for you?''

Sorrow, anger and fear written all over her face, and I not knowing how to reach out, how to make her understand. ''The people living over the way called me and told me. Do you realize that I've never bowed my head before anyone? I've always maintained my self-respect. But now we are a laughing stock for the whole neighbourhood. We have to hide our heads in shame.'' Amazing! Now it's the whole locality speaking within Mummy. How strange that Mummy who has always been so ''different'' from her surroundings, who has always considered these people beneath contempt, should now be singing to their tune. Mummy's lecture was in full spate but I'd switched off. When she cooled down a bit I would explain to her that she was getting unnecessarily het up over nothing.

But this time it did not happen that way. Her anger remained and was beginning to make me angry too. Two
months ago, when a similar incident had occurred, I had
withdrawn into my shell but this time I've decided that if
Mummy wants to act like Grandfather, I shall have to
take up cudgels with her as she did with him—and I will.

Oh, I had hosts of arguments stored up—one day I
would systematically thrash it out with her. I'd say,
"Look, if you wanted to keep me in chains, why didn't
you do it from the start? Why this false show of freedom?" But the immediate effect of this confrontation
was the draining of all of my energy. I just stayed in my
room, in a sort of stupor. I—always the clown of the
family—had retreated totally into myself. But I kept repeating: "Don't worry, Mummy, I shall do just what I
want." Even though I have not the foggiest notion of
what I do want. I don't know what happened during
these three or four days. I remained cut off from everyone in my own room, planning my long-term strategy
for my battle against Mummy.

But today in the afternoon, I could hardly believe my
ears when I heard Mummy call from our verandah,
"Shekhar, tomorrow you all will be going home for the
vacations . . . why don't you come over and have dinner with us tonight? Bring everyone along."

At dinner time, Shekhar, Dipak and Ravi were at the
table, Mummy was serving everyone affectionately and
Papa joking away as usual. A few faces were pressed
against neighbouring windows. Everything seemed simple and natural as it was before . . . only, I was absolutely detached from the whole situation, pursuing my
own thoughts. Well, Grandfather was Grandfather—he
was just himself—it must have been easy for Mummy to
fight him. But how does one combat this mother of mine
who is, one moment, herself, and the next, her father?

"We Dressed for the Dance Together"

Nadine Gordimer
South Africa, 1940s

My adolescence and the first years of the war were concurrent; both have a haziness in my mind that comes, I suppose, from the indefinite, cocoonlike quality of the one, and the distant remove from my life of the other.

During that time my life was so much my mother's that it seemed that the only difference between us was the insignificance of age. The significance of emotional experience that separates the woman, mated, her life balanced against the life of a man, that life again balanced against the life a child begotten and born, from the girl-child, was as unrealized by my mother as by me. My mother, with her slightly raw-featured still-young face—the blood flowed very near the surface of the thin skin—accepted marriage and motherhood as a social rather than a mysterious personal relationship. Wives and husbands and children and the comfortable small plan of duties they owed to one another—for her, this was what living was. I accepted the outward everyday semblance of adult life, the men father-familiar yet creatures respected and allowed ununderstandable tastes of their own; ministered to because they were the providers and entitled to affection from their own families; women the friends, the co-workers, the companions, busy with one another in the conduct of every hour of every day. My mother's weeks were pegged out to street collections and galas and dances and cake sales and meetings of this committee and that—remote from battlefields or air raids, with my father's stomach ulcer excluding him from offering his services to South Africa's volunteer forces, this was what the war meant in our lives. Outside school, I too belonged to the busy to-and-fro that went

on above the tunnelling of black men and white in the
Mine. I too had my place, the place of the Secretary's
daughter (my father had been promoted at last), in the
hierarchy that divided the Mine Manager and his wife
(tall in a clinging skirt, an exiled Mrs. Dalloway), giving
the prizes, in a certain order of rigid gradations from the
busy small woman in the flowered apron stationed at the
tea urn—wife of a burly shift boss called Mackie.

I read the books my mother brought home on her
adult's ticket at the library; gentle novels of English family life and, now and then, stray examples of the prole-
tarian novel to which the dole in England in the thirties
had given rise. "It's about the life of the poor in England—but it won't do her any harm if she wants to read
it." —My mother was sometimes a little uncertain about
these books. "I don't believe a girl should grow up not
knowing what life is like."

A young man and a girl went up on a refuse heap
above an ugly city and kissed. There was a drunken father who was horrible in an indefinable way—but all
drunk people were horrible, I should have died of fear if
. . . but it could not even be imagined that my father
could dribble at the mouth, vomit without knowing. At
the same time I read Captain Marryat, Jane Austen, and
to Omar Khayyám in its soft skin-feel cover I had added
Rupert Brooke. "She's like us," said my mother, "we're
both great readers. Of course, George likes his heavy
stuff, medical books and so on—and detective stories! I
don't know how he can read them, but I've got to bring
them home for him every week-end." A book of Chur-
chill's speeches and another of Smuts's found a place on
top of the special little bookcase which contained the en-
cyclopaedia; my father had bought them. The clean-cut
shiny dust covers slowly softened at the edges as Anna
dusted them along with the other ornaments every day.

There was a dance, I remember, when I was about
sixteen—to raise money for a special comforts-fund that
the Mine had inaugurated for ex-employees now in the
forces. My mother said, blushing with pleasure, the almost tearful moisture that came to her eyes when she
was proud: "Daddy, this'll mean a long dress for your
daughter . . ."

My mother was completely absorbed in the making of that dress; we were up together late every night before the dance, while she sewed and fitted, and I stood on the table with my head near the heat of the light in its beaded shade, turning slowly to show how the hem fell. Then before we went to bed we sat on the kitchen table, drinking tea and talking. I had taken over the care of my mother's fine wiry hair, red, like my own: "You can have it set at the hairdresser's on the Thursday before—then it'll be nice and soft for me to do up for you on Saturday." My mother thought a moment. "But on Thursday afternoon I've promised to bake four dozen sausage rolls. I don't want to get all steamy in the kitchen after it's been done." "Tie it up! Why can't you tie it up!" I stacked the cups in the sink for Anna in the morning.

Up and down the passage, in the bathroom, snatches of our talk continued until the lights went out.

We dressed for the dance together. My mother had surprised me with a real florist's corsage—they called it a "spray"—pink carnations and pale blue delphinium, and it was pinned to the shoulder of my dress with its silver paper holder just showing. Every time I turned my head I could feel it brush my neck.

I danced with Raymond Dufalette in a blue suit with his hair so oiled that it looked as if he had just come out of the sea, dripping wet. He went to boarding school and had learned to dance the previous term; he brought me thankfully back to where my mother and father sat, ready with kindly questions about how he liked school and what he was going to do when he was finished. Then I sat, my back very stiff, looking straight before me. I was afraid I was perspiring the little organdy balloon that encased the top of each arm. I was still more afraid that my father might ask me to dance to save me.

I remember that just as I was getting desperate, a fair boy astonishingly came right across the splintered boards to ask me to dance, and the dance was a Paul Jones, so that I found myself with a succession of partners, snatched away when the music broke into a march and I walked sheepishly round with the other girls—there was Olwen, but Olwen had come with a partner, and he kept her, swaying at the side—then replaced by the young man or somebody's father who found himself opposite me when the march ended. The evening passed in the stiff hands of thin fair boys whose necks were too free of stiff collars. Their knees bumped me, hard as table legs. Their black evening suits and the crackle of shirt front encased nothingness, like the thin glossy shells, the fine glass wings of beetles which crunch to a puff of dead leaf-powder if you crush them. When the ice cream was served I ran hand in hand with my mother; we had promised to help. Over in the corner at the bar, the two Cluff boys in uniform leaned with one or two other soldiers home for the week-end. They drank beer, and laughter spurted up in their talk, backs to the dancers. "Ice cream?" I held out the tray of saucers, smiling with impartial polite reserve, not knowing whether or not I should recognize them as Alan and Francis Cluff.

"Here boys, ice cream, why not—" Alan began passing the saucers over my head. Francis said in an aside, his eyes lowered for a moment as if to screen him, "Hello, Helen." The smell of war, of young men taken in war, a disturbing mixture and contradiction of the schoolboy smell of soap in khaki, and the smooth scent of shaven skin, the warmth of body that brought out the smell of khaki as the warmth of the iron brings up the odor of a fabric, came from them.

I danced again and again that year at parties with the fair young boys in their formal dress clothes who, like myself, were in their last year at school. Once or twice in the winter holidays, one of them took me to the cinema on a Saturday night; but I was only sixteen, I was busy studying for my matriculation, there was plenty of time. "Time enough when you're working and independent, and school's behind you," said my mother.—Olwen had left school a year ago; she attended what was called a business college, upstairs in a building in the town; the chakker-chakker of typewriters sailed out of the wide-open windows and at lunchtime the girls came down to stroll about the town, not in gym frocks, but their own choice of dresses.

What was the stiffness that congealed in me and in the bodies of the young boys with the spiky-smooth hair beside me in the sinking dark of the cinema; made me sit up straight, my arms arranged along the rests helplessly when the lights went up and the music rose and the colored advertisements flipped one by one on and off the screen, and I waited? Back came the young boy with two little cardboard buckets of ice cream, edging bent, apologetic, along the row. We sat and ate with wooden spoons; the boy kept asking questions: Shall I put that down for you? Can you manage? Is it melted? Did it get on your dress? It seemed that I did nothing but smile, shake my head, assure, no. We spoke of films we had seen, veered back to school, fell back on anecdotes that began: "Well I know, I have an Uncle who told us once . . ." or "—Like my little brother; the other day he was . . ." Sudden bursts of sympathy ignited, like matches struck by mistake, between us; were batted out with the astonishment that instinctively deals with such fires. He had not read the books I had read; I knew that. He talked a great deal about the different models of motorcars. My jaws felt tight and I wanted to yawn.

We sat seriously through the film. Sometimes the young boy's foot would touch mine by mistake—they had such big feet in shoes with thick rubber soles—and there was a ruffle of apologies. The one—the nicer one, actually—had a crenelation of incipient pimples perpetually lying in anger beneath the tender shaven skin along his jaw, to which, in the imagined privacy of the dark, I always saw, out of the corner of my eye, his fingers return feeling along as if reading the bumps in the tender, disgusting language of adolescence, curt, monosyllabic as obscenity, and as searching.

At this time, too, my father was teaching me to play golf. When the hooter went at half-past four I left my books open on the dining-room table and went into my room to put on rubber-soled shoes. My father came home with the air of expectancy of someone who is waiting to go out again immediately, and we were at the first tee just as the sun shifted its day-long gaze and glanced obliquely off the grass. Afterward I sat on the veranda full of Mine officials at the clubhouse, drinking my orange squash at a rickety wicker table, with my father sipping his beer. Our heads were continually turned to talk to people; often two or three men screeched chairs over the cement to sit with us, others would swing a leg against the table while they paused to talk in passing. Even if their talk veered to channels that slowly excluded me, leaving me at some point gently washed upon the limit of my comprehension or interest, I rested there comfortably, hearing their voices rather than what they said, lulled by the warm throbbing coming up in my scarlet, blistered palms. I lolled my head back, put my dusty feet up on the bar of the table; the sky, swept clear of the day, held only radiance, far up above the shade that rose like water steeping the trees and the drop of the grass. Over at the water hole, the whole world was repeated, upside down. It all seemed simple, as if a puzzle had dissolved in my hands. The half-questions would never be asked, dark fins of feeling that could not be verified in the face of my father, my mother, the Mine officials, would not show through the surface that every minute of every day polished. I rested, my foot dancing a little tune; the way the unborn rest between one stage of labor and the next, thinking, perhaps, that they have arrived.

"To Grind on the Same Stone"

Miriam Khamadi Were
Kenya, 20th century

In the novel The Eighth Wife, *Kalimonje lives in a large compound with her mother, Khadushi, her father, Malungu, and his other three wives and all their children. Along with her age mates, she is now expected to take an interest in men and prepare herself for early marriage and motherhood. "Granny," one of the village elders, instructs the girls about the world of women.*

"When you shake hands with a young man and he scratches your palm, do not look too pleased, nor should you abuse him."

"Then what do you do, Granny?" they asked in unison.

"When I was a girl we looked at such young men for a while and then passed on."

"And if he does it again?"

"Oh, well, you'll soon discover for yourself and then you'll know which ones to encourage and which to discourage. But of course you don't say anything."

"But how can you express your feelings unless you talk?" They didn't seem to understand Granny's techniques.

"You are women, and a woman must learn to say things without using her tongue. Watch the adults about you and see how they do it." The whole thing seemed so mysterious now, especially when Granny added that a taciturn woman gives the impression of being sulky and that there was nothing worse than a girl being known to be sulky. Granny advised the girls to start their techniques of secret communication by watching their mothers or adult women around them.

It was while doing this type of homework that the girls experienced most of the frustration of having a father shared by many houses. They had little chance to watch. Kalimonje tried to watch each of the wives of her father, but she did not have much of a chance with the other mothers, who never seemed to communicate with Malungu. In spite of the rivalry between her mother and the second wife, Kalimonje could not help sympathizing with the poor woman. She spent day after day telling of her misfortunes till her mouth dried up before she stopped talking. Kalimonje was aware that her father could pass for a full year before going to the house of that poor woman. Now that she was beginning to have feelings about men, she wondered what she would do if the man she married acted towards her in the same manner.

Kalimonje now realized that she could no longer seek answers for all her questions from her mother. For the first time she felt a wall between them. There was a time when the wall was so high that Kalimonje felt completely isolated. But luckily for her the wall became lower—or was it because the house leaned over its edges? She still did not tell her mother anything, but a form of communication that did not need words developed between them. Kalimonje was relieved to realize that even as she crossed from the world where every thought was verbalized to a world where she could not possibly talk about all her thoughts and feelings, concerned spirits still found a meeting-place.

Perhaps it was fortunate for Kalimonje that the first picking of dry beans came. Occupied in picking and carrying the beans home, then drying them and beating them to separate the beans from the pods, she found little time for distracting speculation. After the beans came the harvesting of millet. This was the part of the harvesting process she hated most. It lasted forever, picking up each tiny finger of the millet and cutting it singly. Then came the fermenting time, when the millet would stay in a heap to gain flavour. When they spread it out after a week or two, the heap emitted so much heat and such a strange smell that few could bear the work. But this was the work of women, and a woman must learn to enjoy it. The men helped with the cutting and then the beating to separate the grain from the chaff. The rest of the processing, including the winnowing, was reserved for the womenfolk.

Kalimonje began to resent the kind of life a woman led. Look at her mother. She could hardly remember seeing her just sitting and taking it easy. Drawing water, carrying wood, bringing food home, cooking it. All the preparations, the digging, the children. Everything rested on mother. All that the men did was to sit under a tree and talk, waiting for an invasion so that they might guard the clan's boundaries. In Kalimonje's life there had been no such invasion. It seemed to her a rather lazy way of getting out of work.

"Mama," she once demanded, "why do you slave so?" Her mother looked at her in great surprise.

"Slave? What do you mean?"

"You never have a moment of rest."

"We have to live."

"Why don't the men help?"

Mama shrugged her shoulders and went on winnowing the millet on her straw tray. Kalimonje wasn't going to give up so easily.

"I wish I wasn't born a woman," she said with a sigh.

"Change yourself, dear," her mother suggested with an edge to her voice. To show her disgust, Kalimonje was no longer a keen helper of mother. Why didn't mama complain to the men so that they could help? But as days passed, she went back to her routine of doing almost half the daily chores. She sympathized with her mother, seeing herself soon grinding on that same stone.

"A woman has no life but for her family," her mother once told her through her half-full mouth as she munched beans. "What a person does for her family cannot be slavery." She went on to say that it was the women whose husbands did not appreciate their efforts that she felt sorry for. "But your father is not like that," she finished. But as she said so, Kalimonje thought of Asenwa's mother and how she was not appreciated.

"It's up to a woman to make her husband appreciate her," Khadushi finished. Had this been somebody other than her own mother, Kalimonje would have really objected to her implying that she was the favourite wife through her own doing. But how could she dismiss it? What other reason was there? Some people must be born luckier than others, she decided—and wondered to which group she belonged.

"I'm Truly Your Child"

Paule Marshall
Brooklyn, 1930s

Selina, in the novel Brown Girl, Brownstones, *lives in a West Indian ghetto in Brooklyn in the 1930s. Her mother, Silla, personifies the spirit of this upwardly mobile community which has gathered together in self-help associations to buy property. In contrast, Selina and her father, always at war with Silla, had sought a life different from the practical aspirations of their "prim, pious, pretentious pack" of middle-class peers. In the following excerpt Selina, at seventeen, has won the first scholarship award offered by her mother's Barbadian Association. Although she had planned to betray the Association by using the money to run away with her boyfriend to Barbados, Selina has a change of heart and turns the award down at the public presentation. In her speech she tells the members, "I can't accept it because I don't deserve it. And the reasons are despicable. . . ." Afterward the shocked mother confronts her daughter.*

"Yuh lie!"

Selina unpinned the order of the Association, placed it on a shelf and said evenly, her back to her mother, "I was not lying."

"Yuh lie!" Silla slammed the door of the coatroom underneath the main hall and the explosion, reverberating through the cavernous silence, gave violent emphasis to her accusation.

Selina turned, and her body instinctively braced. She was confronting, she felt, not only the mother but all the others. They had charged downstairs to crowd the room behind her; she sensed them wedged into the corners and secreted among the coats on the racks. Not only the mother's pitched anger, but their collective abuse, swelled the air.

"Lies! Getting up in front people talking a lot of who-struck-John about how much you like them and then throwing their money back at them. Talking in parables! Using a lot of big words and still not saying why you refuse good money. Disgracing me before the world! Oh Jesus-God, an ungrateful, conniving, wuthless whelp! If I had the will of you . . .''

Silla's rage lit the air like a dazzling pyrotechnic display, and heightened the dark handsomeness of her face, and her fine eyes. Selina felt the old admiration, but none of the old weakening—she was no longer the child who used to succumb, without will, to that powerful onslaught.

"Poor-great!" Silla hurled at her. "Poor-great—that's why you refused the money. Poor-great like the father before you."

Finally, breathing the angered air which sparked her anger, Selina silenced her with a single vehement gesture. "All right, Mother, I'll tell you even though I shouldn't." Her voice was in sober counterpoint to Silla's. "Last week I intended to take the money. But not for what you thought. Not to save for any exalted plan you had for me. I wanted it for one reason: to go away with Clive. Yes," she nodded as the mother lurched back as though shoved. "I never stopped seeing him even though I promised. That's why I became so devoted to the Association . . . Why did I change my mind? I just couldn't . . . Something happened and I couldn't any more . . .''

Silla stared at her as she would at a stranger who had accosted her on the street with some improbable story. Once, her hand tried to fend her off, to make her vanish. Once, she glanced at the coats as if seeking their help. Her incredulity, her helplessness was that of a child almost and, as the light ebbed in her eyes and the strong dark flush drained from her skin, she seemed to be quietly dying inside.

"Oh Christ-God," she cried weakly, and a dull light stirred in her eyes like the last vestige of life. "All along I did feel something was wrong. All of a sudden acting so interested in everything . . . But I din think. I din think . . .'' A strangled word stained the air. "Spitework! Spitework, that's what it tis. Because of what I did to yuh father. All these years you been waiting to get at me. Ever since the night you did call me Hitler you been waiting. You did always think I killed him. Yes. But I din do it out of hate . . ."

For a time she pursued her tortured thoughts, unable to stop, or to wake into the world again until she had confessed. "I . . . I din mean to send him to his death— it's just that I cun bear to see him suffering . . ."

Remembering his ignominious death, an uncontrollable cruelty seized Selina. "You did it because you knew he was never coming back to you."

Silla's eyes passed over her face to search the room, as though this were her invisible presence speaking and not Selina. After a silence filled with her guilt, she whispered, "Yes—and that's why you did all this—lying so and licking 'bout with the crazy boy, disgracing me tonight. Spitework, 'cause you never had no uses for me, but did think the sun rose and set 'pon yuh father alone."

"Yes, I blamed you," Selina said quietly. "Maybe you're even right about why I did all this. I don't know . . . But it's no use talking or thinking about him any more."

The mother sprang forward at her irreverence. "Not think about him? How, when he was like Christ to you?"

"He's dead!" The piercing cry was an admission long withheld and now finally wrenched from its secret place. "And I want to forget him, so that when I go away . . ."

"Going 'way?" And before Silla could recover Selina added with finality, "Yes, even though I didn't take the money. I'll find a way. And I'll be going alone."

Silla—her body thrust forward as though it, as well as her mind, sought to understand this—stared at Selina's set face. Then, groping past her, Silla found a chair, and sat numb, silent, the life shattered in her eyes and the hanging coats gathered behind her like sympathetic spectators. Finally she said, but her eyes did not clear, "Going 'way. One call sheself getting married and the other going 'way. Gone so! They ain got no more uses for me and they gone. Oh God, is this what you does get for the nine months and the pain and the long years putting bread in their mouth . . . ?"

And although Selina listened and felt all the mother's anguish she remained sure.

Silla was saying numbly, "Here it tis just when I start making plans to buy a house in Crown Heights she . . ."

"I'm not interested in houses!" Her scream burst the room and soared up to the main hall.

The mother nodded bitterly. "Yes, you did always scorn me for trying to get little property."

"I don't scorn you. Oh, I used to. But not any more. That's what I tried to say tonight. It's just not what I want."

"What it tis you want?"

"I don't know." Her reply was a frail lost sound and, strangely, it seemed to assuage Silla. She scrutinized Selina's pensive face, beginning dimly, it appeared, to understand. Her arms half lifted in a protective gesture, and her warning sounded. "Girl, do you know what it tis out there? How those white people does do yuh?"

At her solemn nod, at the sad knowing in her eyes, Silla's head slowly bowed.

Quickly Selina found her coat and, putting it on, stared at the mother's bowed face, seeing there the finely creased flesh around her eyes, the hair graying at her temples and, on her brow, the final frightening loneliness that was to be her penance. "Mother," she said gently, "I have to disappoint you. Maybe it's as you once said: that in making your way you always hurt someone. I don't know . . ." Then remembering something Clive had said, she added with a thin smile, "Everybody used to call me Deighton's Selina but they were wrong. Because you see I'm truly your child. Remember how you used to talk about how you left home and came here alone as a girl of eighteen and was your own woman? I used to love hearing that. And that's what I want. I want it!"

Silla's pained eyes searched her adamant face, and after a long time a wistfulness softened her mouth. It was as if she somehow glimpsed in Selina the girl she had once been. For that moment, as the softness pervaded her and her hands lay open like a girl's on her lap, she became the girl who had stood, alone and innocent, at the ship's rail, watching the city rise glittering with promise from the sea.

"G'long," she said finally with a brusque motion. "G'long! You was always too much woman for me anyway, soul. And my own mother did say two head-bulls can't reign in a flock. G'long!" Her hand sketched a sign that was both a dismissal and a benediction. "If I din dead yet, you and your foolishness can't kill muh now!"

"A Woman's Character"

Box-Car Bertha, as told to Dr. Ben Reitman
Seattle, 1930s

My mother wasn't what the world would call a good woman. She never said she was. And many people, including the police, said she was a bad woman. But she never agreed with them, and she had a way of lifting up her head when she talked back to them that made me know she was right. I loved her deeply from the first day I can remember until she died. I love to think of her. Her example and influence and sacrifice (she always denied that she ever made sacrifices for her children) proved that she loved us and that she was a woman of rare courage and of fine principles all her own. . . .

Mother was always busy cooking and serving meals and cleaning, and she taught me and the other girls how to cook and clean and to wash men's clothes.

"Bertha," she would say, "as long as you can keep men clean and well fed and love them a little, they'll be perfectly satisfied. They're all babies. They need to be looked after. Teach them to depend upon you. But never let them make a slave of you."

Mother was a handsome blonde, straight-shouldered, deep-breasted, with penetrating steel-grey eyes, and with a sort of glow about her that attracted everyone, especially when she talked. She was the kind of woman who looks after everyone, and everybody called her "Mother Thompson" even when she was so young that all the tramps (as well as all the others) tried to make love to her. . . .

Mother soon had a job cooking in a short order restaurant. She registered as a special student at the University of Washington and put us four children in school. We had all been irregular, and lacked proper credits, but upon examination we were placed. I started work in Seattle High School.

We managed pretty well during the next two years. Mother was a good provider. Her work at the restaurant was hard and of long hours, but she came from it as if it had not touched her and entered upon our own life with gaiety and enthusiasm. In addition to everything else she made our clothes for us, designing them to suit our hair and coloring as well as our figures, and did it so well that I had the feminine satisfaction of seeing the other girls in high school envying me for my clothes. But most of the girls of my own age seemed rather silly to me then. School did not matter a great deal, anyway. It seemed ridiculous to study Latin grammar when the whole exciting world was waiting outside. . . .

Seattle became monotonous to me. It was late spring. I was nearly seventeen, weighed about a hundred and sixty pounds, was built, E. A. O. said, "like a truck horse," and I was restless. I walked along the waterfront and the freight yards. I read the ads of the excursions to the east and the south and the north. I remembered women I had seen getting off freight cars, women hitch-hiking. Over at I. W. W. hall I met a number of women hoboes who had been tramping about the country, and listened eagerly to their stories. Ena was restless, too, and bit by bit we decided that we wanted to take a look at the world and see for ourselves what it was like. Ena was fourteen, blonde, and dainty, with small wrists and ankles, childlike still, yet showing clearly the attractive woman she was about to become. After a few days of planning, I spoke up for both of us.

"Ena and I want to go out on the road," I told mother. "Ena wants to go to school in the east. She has some talent to write and draw. I think the east has more opportunities. . . ."

Mother put her arms around both of us, saying, "I knew you were getting ready to leave me," she said gently. "I want to tell you something before you go. I've always been a rough-neck. I never had any morals, nor did I ever teach you any. But I've been a happy mother. I'm proud of both of you. Remember that I never made any sacrifice for you, nor did I give up any pleasure or good times for you. I never did anything different because I had children. And so don't either of you ever do anything for me that isn't easy and natural for you to do. I haven't any advice to give you. You both know plenty now. Just remember one thing, however—a woman's character, her value to the world, and her love for man is not in her hips, but in her heart and head.''

E. A. O. bought us tickets on the boat from Seattle to San Francisco. A gay little crowd came down to see us off and sang I. W. W. songs and a parody on "We'll never say good-bye in heaven." Ena and I had light woolen dresses, new coats. Mother had packed our grip, and had given us an extra dress apiece, extra shoes, underwear, stockings, and a few toilet necessities.

"That's all you'll need," she said, "and baggage is a nuisance."

We moved into San Francisco bay next morning while the sun was coming up deep red on the water's edge. I was up and dressed and on deck. My heart throbbed as deeply as the ship's engines. I was wildly happy with life and in anticipation of the future.

A Thorny Cactus

Martha Marenof
Jerusalem, 1940

*Miriam, a young Jewish woman living in Jerusalem at the out-
break of World War II, must make an important decision. She is
torn between entering a marriage arranged by her father in the
traditional manner or leaving home for a less restricted life on a
kibbutz. Miriam looks to her mother for support, as she has always regarded her mother as a modest symbol of rebellion
against her father's orthodox ways. Born in the United States
and an avid reader of English books, Esther has continued her
reading through the years in spite of her husband's objections.
Now, however, Esther seems willing to see Miriam married.*

Miriam awoke with an uneasy feeling that something
was about to happen, something that would shake the
foundations of her existence. Yet she couldn't think, for
the moment, what it was.

Beyond her window the Jerusalem sky was faultless
blue. It had not begun to gather clouds for winter rain.
Folk from other lands said the sky was closer to earth in
Jerusalem.

The earth!

That was it. The earth had changed since yesterday.
Miriam drew her blanket about her though it was warm.
The earth on which she had been walking these seventeen years of her life might not hold her this day. If she
stepped off the bed an abyss would open and she would
fall down . . . down . . .

She slipped her hand under her pillow. Yes, the letter
was there. It had not been a dream. It was up to her now
to make the fateful decision. If she tore it to bits without
rereading it she would still belong to her family—to her
father and her mother and her seven brothers. If not she
might find herself suspended in mid-air, no longer part

257

of all that was familiar to her. No, she couldn't do it, not so soon.

She took hold of the letter, then lay still and listened. No one was near. She drew it out noiselessly and reread the words, already deeply inscribed in her consciousness:

> We have a place for you if you wish to join a kibbutz. But consider the matter well. This life is difficult and dangerous, especially in our state of war. If you decide to come, report at headquarters and you will be assigned to a training school.

Consider the matter! But time was so short. A great change had come to Miriam's piece of Jerusalem earth. War! To the world it meant fighting, dying. To the girls of Miriam's sphere it meant hasty marriage to protect them from soldiers who already filled the sacred city.

Hasty marriage! Yes, a generation before, her mother had been caught and held fast by a set of circumstances such as were now weaving themselves round her. Since war had come Batya had been married off and Sarah and Naomi and even Leah who was only fifteen but large for her age. They had all had their braids cut off and traditional head garbs put on. Hanna and herself alone were left of all their group.

And last Tuesday night, when she came in from a walk with Hanna, Reb Eliyahu the Matchmaker was sitting at the table talking with her father. He had looked at her with that knowing smile that made him the most feared figure among the girls of the quarter known as Abraham's Vineyard.

Familiar sounds came through the door, yet they seemed far distant this day. Her mother was pouring her father's breakfast tea as she always did on the Sabbath morning, and her brothers were putting on their Sabbath robes for the synagogue.

The door opened. Swiftly Miriam thrust the letter beneath the blanket. Her mother was dressed for the synagogue with her black satin dress and her black lace headdress.

Miriam looked into her mother's still youthful, calm

face. Something of her quiet resignation seemed disturbed. "Is anything wrong, Miriam? Are you well?"

"Oh, I'm . . . I'm fine. I'll get dressed and walk to Hanna."

"I want you to do an errand for me, Miriam. Father has his Talmud Fest tonight. Some time today go to Freda and ask her to bring her wine glasses as soon as it is dark."

"Yes, Mother."

Her mother stood looking at Miriam for a moment, then said, "Miriam, you are grown up." She turned and left.

That was strange. Her mother so seldom paused to indulge in intimate moments with her children. What had made her say that?

Miriam heard the front door open and shut, then open and shut again. They had all gone, then, gone to the synagogue—her mother and her father and her brothers. Good that unmarried girls were not required to attend.

She was alone now. She should get up and dress and go to Hanna with the letter. Hanna too had hungered for that strange and fascinating life that had come into their land with the pioneers from the outer world. They had talked about it and dreamed about it during their intimate walks. She wondered. If Hanna agreed to walk out of their limited existence with her, would she, could she take the step?

The sun bright sky was not hazy this day. "So clear," thought Miriam. "I wish my mind were half as clear."

Then it seemed as if a shadow fell. Mother! it happened to you. I can't let it happen to me! . . .

Ever since she could remember Miriam had had the urge to learn things out of books. She had pleaded to go to school. Her father said, "No, for the boys there is the Talmud. A girl need but to learn to read a prayer and write a letter."

"The schools are filled with girls," she pleaded.

"Daughters of pioneers, unbelievers; they are not of us."

Then on the day she turned twelve something happened inside her. She forgot the respect she should have felt for her father. She shouted, "I must go to school."

"My daughter to school?" thundered Nehemiah.

"Yes, father, I must go," weeping bitterly.

"Sit down, my child," said Reb Nehemiah, his voice soft, "and I will tell you why it is not possible for a child of mine. . . ."

She said, "But mother reads English books."

"Hush! I forbid you to show disrespect to your mother. And never mention school to me again. Tell mother that I will fast tomorrow to expiate your sin."

That night Miriam overheard her father pleading with her mother. "Esther, who can tell what it may lead to! Miriam has become inquisitive of foreign learning. Suppose it happens to one of the boys?"

Her mother said, "I must read."

"Esther, a child is quickening within you. God may punish us. The child may be born unwhole, or worse— without capacity for learning."

Esther said, "I must read."

"You are my wife and it is forbidden me to grieve you. I shall not talk of this again, but I shall fast a day every week until you realize your duty."

"Nehemiah," said Esther, "I have respected your every wish, but this I cannot do. I must read."

Next morning her mother came to Miriam's room. She sat on the bed and stroked her head, silent tears in her eyes.

"Mother," Miriam whispered, "what can I do?"

"You should have been born a boy, like the others. For them there is something."

"Mother, teach me to read your books."

"Your father forbids it."

"But I must . . ."

"He is your father and you must obey." Then abruptly she got up and went through the door.

Miriam always thought of her twelfth birthday as "that day." She sealed her lips and never again spoke of her urge to learn. But the fire within her did not extinguish itself. She began to tread a path of knowledge alone and lonely. She was always at the corner of the Street of the Prophets when school was out and picked up the papers those fortunate girls threw away. She

cherished every scrap until every mark on it was inscribed in her consciousness.

One day she was marketing on King David Avenue and Eliezer, the grocer's clerk, wrapped her package in a Hebrew newspaper. It was sacrilege to read it for the sacred language was here used for secular writing. She read it. The next time she marketed she asked him again to wrap her things in a newspaper. After that she found several sheets round her groceries. She learned what they were thinking in those tall buildings that had grown up in new Jerusalem, in the pioneer colonies miles away, and even beyond the shores of the little land.

Miriam learned to read English, too, from her mother's books when no one was at home. Her mother did not lack books. In some curious way it had become known that in the quarter called Abraham's Vineyard there lived an American born woman who was hungry for books and folk from those tall houses brought them to her. One English lady was her mother's special friend and often came to visit.

Esther sent Miriam on an errand to this lady's house one day. She was asked to come again at any time. There was always a book to pick up and read. Miriam found herself going often to this house, sitting in a large chair, reading.

A knock startled Miriam from her thoughts. She went to the door. It was Hanna. Miriam was surprised. "I was coming to your house." Her hand went to her pocket and there was the faint rustle of paper.

"Miriam," said Hanna nervously.

"What is it? Has anything happened?"

"Come with me this afternoon!"

"Where to?"

"Shneller's Grove. I am to meet a man!"

Stunned, Miriam asked, "When did it happen?"

"Last Wednesday. His family came to see me. Mother made me come and answer questions. Then they went to see him. Father is disappointed because he does not wear the caftan and has cut off his sidelocks. But he agreed to the match because of the war. O Miriam!"

"Why didn't you tell me sooner?"

"I couldn't after . . . after what we had planned."

"Yes! We thought otherwise."

"I know; but what is the use? When they talk to you there is nothing you can say, nothing." She paused, then added, "What if I don't agree? What if later I am forced to marry a man who does wear a caftan and sidelocks?"

"I'll come," said Miriam, and Hanna walked away without another word. Miriam had not told her about the letter. She walked over to the window. She watched Hanna walk up the narrow lane between the two rows of low dwellings that was their quarter of Jerusalem. It had come to Hanna, suddenly, and she submitted without a struggle. What would she, Miriam, do? What if her father came home that evening and said to her what she had often heard him say to fathers of marriageable daughters, "It is the sacred duty of a father to give his daughter to a man." What would she do if her father came in and said, "Miriam, your time has come."

Miriam did not realize how long she had stood at the window. They were coming from the synagogue. Reuben, her ten-year-old brother, came in first. "Miriam, I heard a secret."

"A secret?"

"Yes. Reb Eliyahu was talking to father about you."

"Hush, child."

"Reb Eliyahu said you are not so young any more, and there are soldiers in the city."

"What did father say?"

"That's the secret!"

Dinner was over. The usual Sabbath afternoon descended upon Miriam and the household. Esther, her black headdress framing her pale, patient face, sat down near the window to read. Reb Nehemiah retired for his nap. The boys went out to play. Miriam went to her room to change her dress. Her mother looked up when she came out.

"Where are you going, daughter?"

That was strange. Usually when her mother sat down to read on Saturday afternoon she became oblivious to the world. Miriam answered, "To Hanna's."

"She is meeting someone in the Grove, I heard."

"Yes," answered Miriam, and looked at her mother.

"You know, child, I had a dream last night. I wanted to talk to you, but a thorny cactus stood between us. I thought of it this moment. Go ahead. Give Hanna my greetings."

On the way to the Grove Miriam stopped at Freda's to deliver her mother's message.

Miriam's mother was still sitting at the window when she returned home. It was dark. Esther was no longer reading, but she could not light a lamp until the Sabbath was ushered out. She always sat at the window in the dark this way when the Sabbath light was spent.

Reb Nehemiah and the boys came in from evening prayer. He lit the braided candle to usher out the Sabbath and called to Miriam, "Come, daughter, and hold the candle high while I pronounce the blessings. God will send you a tall husband."

Miriam winced. She came and held the candle. They lit the lamp when the prayer was over and set the table for the Talmud Fest. Reb Nehemiah was happy.

"Think of it, Esther, again I have completed the Talmud study in three years and the allotted time is seven."

"I am happy for you," said Esther.

"You are happy for me? No, you are happy with me. If you were not my breadwinner I could not devote all my days to the Talmud. You will share my life to come. I shall sit with Abraham, Isaac, and Jacob, and you will sit at my feet."

Suddenly he was silent. Miriam knew why. A dark cloud marred the vision of his life to come . . . the English books his wife read.

Freda came with the wine glasses. Miriam took them from her and set them on the table. Guests arrived. Reb Shlomo, Hanna's father, came in and announced, "Wish me good luck. Today I promised my daughter Hanna to a man!"

Then the men were at the table. Miriam's seven brothers were all there, the married ones seated, the younger boys standing. Miriam, her mother, and a few women who came to watch and to help serve stood near the door.

The glasses were filled. The great moment came. Reb Nehemiah lifted his cup and happily chanted the closing verses of the Talmud:

My God, you have created me in your image. You have created me to imbibe the sacred words and not while away my time in idleness. Blessed be the name of God.

Then, as was the custom, he turned to the first page and began the study of the Talmud anew. They sipped the wine and partook of the refreshments with blessings. They chanted psalms of joy.

Miriam, at the door, looked on. She had looked on at her father's Talmud Fest when she was thirteen, and when she was ten, and when she was seven. It suddenly came to her that this might be the last time. She was struck by a sense of loss. How can one give up everything that is familiar? Perhaps Hanna was right after all.

The door opened.

Reb Eliyahu the Matchmaker filled it and stood for a moment taking in the scene of joy before him.

"Come in, come in, Reb Eliyahu," Reb Nehemiah rose to greet him.

Reb Eliyahu flounced in. He was followed by a youth in a long caftan; red sidelocks under his traditional fur hat.

Miriam stepped back and slipped into her room. She hastily packed a few things, together with the letter that she had guarded through the day. She would go to her mother's English friend for the night and then follow the instructions in the letter.

She was at the back door. She paused for a moment. Her father's great day would end in mourning. Never again would he have a Talmud Fest so complete in happiness.

Her hand was on the door knob when she heard, "Miriam!" That was all Esther said. She gathered her daughter into her arms and held her tight. She kissed her. Miriam felt a hot tear on her cheek. Her mother whispered, "God bless you!"

Esther pushed Miriam out and closed the door behind her.

Miriam had expected a thorny cactus to rise up and block her way. But none was there. The path was clear.

Where Are Those Songs?

Women in traditional Africa usually work and play together, farming their fields, pounding their grain, trading their goods, and rearing their children. Every child has many "mothers." Songs are part of the very fabric of their lives. They are sung when people gather together to work, to tell stories, to proclaim a person's worth, and to celebrate important events. Chants and songs are used to pass on the secrets of womanhood and the rites of female initiation. Through these rites, the daughters of the tribe learn their domestic duties. The collective singing of these songs bonds women, one to another.

Where are those songs
my mother and yours
always sang
fitting rhythms
to the whole
vast span of life?

What was it again
they sang
   harvesting maize, threshing millet, storing the
   grain . . .

What did they sing
bathing us, rocking us to sleep . . .
and the one they sang
stirring the pot
(swallowed in parts by choking smoke)?

What was it
the woods echoed
as in long file
my mother and yours and all the women on our ridge
beat out the rhythms
   trudging gaily
   as they carried

piles of wood
through those forests
miles from home

What song was it?

And the row of bending women
hoeing our fields
to what beat
did they
break the stubborn ground
as they weeded
our *shambas*?

What did they sing
at the ceremonies
    child-birth
    child-naming
    second birth
    initiation. . . ?
how did they trill the *ngemi*
what was
the warriors' song?
how did the wedding song go?
sing me
the funeral song.

What do you remember?

Sing
    I have forgotten
    my mother's song
    my children
    will never know.

This I remember:
Mother always said
    sing child sing
    make a song
    and sing
    beat out your own rhythms
    the rhythms of your life

but make the song soulful
and make life
sing

Sing daughter sing
around you are
uncountable tunes
some sung
others unsung
sing them
to your rhythms
observe
listen
absorb
soak yourself
bathe
in the stream of life
   and then sing
   sing
   simple songs
   for the people
   for all to hear
   and learn
   and sing
   with you

      Micere Mugo,
      Zimbabwe, 1970s

CHAPTER FIVE

The Great Adventure: Taking Risks

Let her
Swim, climb mountain peaks, pilot airplanes,
battle against the elements, take risks,
go out for adventure, and

     she will not

feel before the world . . . . timidity

          Simone de Beauvoir,
          France, 1953

Excitement, risk-taking, adventure, quest for the unknown—these words historically have described the lives of men. It is the young male who has been expected to explore the world, while the young woman waits at home. Even in areas of the world where girls and boys are both encouraged to follow their dreams, in practice there are frequently greater restraints on young women, and they may learn to avoid the unknown. The history and literature of most cultures, however, reveal women who have succeeded in living adventurously, although they often did so in secrecy or in male attire. This chapter highlights those girls who, at puberty, are the seekers of adventure, though for some the search may be confined to yearnings before assuming the traditional role of womanhood.

The first section, "I Dream of Action," reveals the depth of feeling of girls who yearn for unique lives filled with action. In "Breaking Tradition," young women move beyond expressions of longing and into acts of defiance, sometimes subtle, sometimes bold. To those whose future is regulated by an early arranged marriage and by subservience to their family, adventure may not mean sailing the high seas, conquering new lands, or seeking a fortune. It may mean, rather, escaping to a new place, forming new relationships, or choosing whom to marry, or whether to marry at all. For others, adventure means developing new skills and performing in areas once reserved for males.

In "Leaving Home," young women find the constraints of family life intolerable and feel the need to make decisions on their own. Leaving home may be an act of rebellion by the young woman or the realization that her dreams can be fulfilled only out in the world beyond the family. In the concluding section, "Finding Courage," young women face their moment of truth, whether it be in testing survival skills or in standing by their convictions. In the process, they discover courage and new sources of strength.

I Dream of Action

My Brilliant Career

Miles Franklin
Possum Gulley, Australia, 1890

Stella Maria Sarah Miles Franklin was sixteen when she wrote
My Brilliant Career, *the story of a young girl in the Australian bush country in 1895. The heroine, Sybylla, lives on a dairy farm where, in the midst of unrelenting drought and bankruptcy, she longs for a new life.*

"Sybylla, what are you doing? Where is your mother?"

"I'm ironing. Mother's down at the fowl-house seeing after some chickens. What do you want?"

It was my father who addressed me. Time, 2 o'clock P.M. Thermometer hung in the shade of the veranda registering 105½ degrees.

"I see Blackshaw coming across the flat. Call your mother. You bring the leg-ropes—I've got the dog-leg. Come at once; we'll give the cows another lift. Poor devils—might as well knock 'em on the head at once, but there might be rain next moon. This drought can't last for ever."

I called mother, got the leg-ropes, and set off, pulling my sunbonnet closely over my face to protect my eyes from the dust which was driving from the west in blinding clouds. The dog-leg to which father had referred was three poles about eight or ten feet long, strapped together so they could be stood up. It was an arrangement father had devised to facilitate our labour in lifting the cows. A fourth and longer pole was placed across the fork formed by the three, and to one end of this were tied a couple of leg-ropes, after being placed round the beast, one beneath the flank and one around the girth. On the other end of this pole we would put our weight while one man would lift with the tail and another with the horns. New-chum cows would sulk, and we would have great work with them; but those used to the performance would help themselves, and up they'd go as nice as a daisy. The only art needed was to draw the pole back quickly before the cows could move, or the legropes would pull them over again.

On this afternoon we had six cows to lift. We struggled manfully, and got five on their feet, and then proceeded to where the last one was lying, back downwards, on a shadeless stony spot on the side of a hill. The men slewed her round by the tail, while mother and I fixed the dog-leg and adjusted the ropes. We got the cow up, but the poor beast was so weak and knocked about that she immediately fell down again. We resolved to let her have a few minutes' spell before making another attempt at lifting. There was not a blade of grass to be seen, and the ground was too dusty to sit on. We were too overdone to make more than one-worded utterances, so waited silently in the blazing sun, closing our eyes against the dust.

Weariness! Weariness!

A few light wind-smitten clouds made wan streaks across the white sky, haggard with the fierce relentless glare of the afternoon sun. Weariness was written across my mother's delicate careworn features, and found expression in my father's knitted brows and dusty face. Blackshaw was weary, and said so, as he wiped the dust, made mud with perspiration, off his cheeks. I was weary—my limbs ached with the heat and work. The poor beast stretched at our feet was weary. All nature was weary, and seemed to sing a dirge to that effect in the furnace-breath wind which roared among the trees on the low ranges at our back and smote the parched and thirsty ground. All were weary, all but the sun. He seemed to glory in his power, relentless and untiring, as he swung boldly in the sky, triumphantly leering down upon his helpless victims.

Weariness! Weariness!

This was life—my life—my career, my brilliant career! I was fifteen—fifteen! A few fleeting hours and I would be old as those around me. I looked at them as they stood there, weary, and turning down the other side of the hill of life. When young, no doubt they had hoped for, and dreamed of, better things—had even known them. But here they were. This had been their life; this was their career. It was, and in all probability would be, mine too. My life—my career—my brilliant career! . . .

I say naught against the lower life. The peasantry are the bulwarks of every nation. The life of a peasant is, to a peasant who is a peasant with a peasant's soul, when times are good and when seasons smile, a grand life. It is honest, clean, and wholesome. But the life of a peasant to me is purgatory. Those around me worked from morning till night and then enjoyed their well-earned sleep. They had but two states of existence—work and sleep.

There was a third part in me which cried out to be fed. I longed for the arts. Music was a passion with me. I borrowed every book in the neighbourhood and stole hours from rest to read them. This told upon me and made my physical burdens harder for me than for other children of my years around me. That third was the strongest part of me. In it I lived a dream-life with writers, artists, and musicians. Hope, sweet, cruel, delusive Hope, whispered in my ear that life was long with much by and by, and in that by and by my dream-life would be real. So on I went with that gleaming lake in the distance beckoning me to come and sail on its silver waters, and Inexperience, conceited, blind Inexperience, failing to show the impassable pit between it and me.

"The Great Invention"

Selma Lagerlöf
Translated by Velma Swanston Howard
Stockholm, 1873

Selma Lagerlöf spent the winter of her fourteenth year with her aunt and uncle to receive treatments for her lame leg. In her diary she revealed her plans to transcend what she felt were her dull looks, shy personality, and physical disability.

Monday, February 24, 1873

In the parlour

Cousin Allan has a toy that I never tire of looking at. It is a small, inexpensive toy; in fact, it is only a stick of wood about the length of my hand. But the remarkable thing about it is that it can fly.

At one end of the stick is a small wheel with eight tiny wings made of stiff paper. At the other end is a little "winch" of steel wire, and between the wheel and the winch runs an elastic band.

When Allan wants the stick to fly he turns the winch round and round until the rubber band is stretched to its utmost. He twists the winch until it can't turn, and puts the toy down. The rubber band begins to lose its tautness, thereby setting the paper wheel in motion. It turns very fast and, after two or three revolutions, it shoots upward, drawing the stick along. If the band has been drawn tight enough, the stick goes up all the way to the ceiling, flying back and forth up there, knocking against the plaster, as if it would bore its way out to the open.

The stick is green, and the wings on the wheel are red and white. When the little machine flies round the room, it looks exactly as if it were a witch flying on a broomstick.

Yesterday afternoon, as I sat studying my lesson, Al-

lan wound up his toy and let it fly. I shut my grammar
and followed it with my eyes. As the toy rose toward the
ceiling it flashed upon me that one ought to be able to
make a real flying machine—one that could be used by
man, with the little flying stick as a pattern.

At first I thought that this was just nonsense; but now
I'm beginning to wonder if it wouldn't be a good idea. It
would be a great pleasure for us human beings to be able
to travel by air. But I don't believe the big gas-filled bal-
loons have any future. They are forever bursting, and
even if they do not burst they move with the wind and
are carried hither and thither, no one knows where.

But if one had a large enough wheel with steady wings
and a connecting rod, like the wheel on a spindle, at
which one could sit and work with the feet to make the
wheel revolve, I think that would be a good flying machine.

Tuesday, February 25, 1873

I lay thinking of the flying machine all the morning.
Since such big birds as cranes and geese can fly, it ought
to be possible for men to fly also. But it all depends, of
course, upon whether one can make the wheel turn fast
enough.

Wednesday, February 26, 1873

I have stopped thinking of the student, and I don't try to
write stories. It is far more important that I figure out
how my flying machine should be constructed. Of
course I know it can't be finished before I am grown, but
there's no harm in having everything well thought out.

Thursday, February 27, 1873

When my machine is ready I'm going to fly to Stock-
holm. How the Stockholmers will stare and how they
will wonder what kind of bird that is! Centralplan will be
black with people gazing, spellbound, at the sky. And
when Aunt Georgina, sitting at the bedroom window
sewing, sees all the people, she calls to Uncle Oriel and
Ulla to come and look out.

And when the airship comes near, it flies back and forth a couple of times over Centralplan that the people may behold it; then, to the amazement of everyone, it descends in the yard of Klara Strandgata Number 7.

I wonder what Uncle Oriel will say then.

But I shall tell him, at once, that it was here at Number 7, with Aunt and Uncle, that I caught the idea for the great invention, and because of that I have made my first journey by air to their home.

"An Ever Growing Longing"

Raden Adjeng Kartini
Translated by Agnes Louise Symmers
Indonesia, 1899

*At the end of the nineteenth century Javanese culture was un-
dergoing social change as a result of western colonialism when
Kartini began a long-distance correspondence with the Dutch
feminist Stella Zeehandelaar. Although the two never met,
their letters were extremely important to the young Javanese
woman, who felt estranged from her family and her culture.*

To Stella Zeehandelaar,
   I am the eldest of the three unmarried daughters of the
Regent of Japara, and have six brothers and sisters. What
a world, eh? My grandfather, Pangeran Ario Tjondrone-
goro of Demak, was a great leader in the progressive
movement of his day, and the first regent of middle Java
to unlatch his door to that guest from over the Sea—
Western civilization. All of his children had European
educations; all of them have, or had (several of them are
now dead), a love of progress inherited from their father; and these gave to their children the same upbringing which they themselves had received. Many of my
cousins and all my older brothers have gone through the
Hoogere-Burger School—the highest institution of learning that we have here in India; and the youngest of my
three older brothers has been studying for three years in
the Netherlands, and two others are in the service of that
country. We girls, so far as education goes, fettered by
our ancient traditions and conventions, have profited
but little by these advantages. It was a great crime
against the customs of our land that we should be taught
at all, and especially that we should leave the house
every day to go to school. For the custom of our country
forbade girls in the strongest manner ever to go outside

of the house. We were never allowed to go anywhere, however, save to the school, and the only place of instruction of which our city could boast, which was open to us, was a free grammar school for Europeans.

When I reached the age of twelve, I was kept at home—I had to go into the "box." I was locked up, and cut off from all communication with the outside world, toward which I might never turn again save at the side of a bridegroom, a stranger, an unknown man whom my parents would choose for me, and to whom I should be betrothed without my own knowledge. European friends—this I heard later—had tried in every possible way to dissuade my parents from this cruel course toward me, a young and life-loving child; but they were able to do nothing. My parents were inexorable; I went into my prison. Four long years I spent between thick walls, without once seeing the outside world.

How I passed through that time, I do not know. I only know that it was terrible. But there was one great happiness left me: the reading of Dutch books and correspondence with Dutch friends was not forbidden. This—the only gleam of light in that empty, somber time, was my all, without which, I should have fallen, perhaps, into a still more pitiable state. My life, my soul even, would have been starved. But then came my friend and my deliverer—the Spirit of the Age; his footsteps echoed everywhere. Proud, solid ancient structures tottered to their foundation at his approach. Strongly barricaded doors sprang open, some as of themselves, others only painfully halfway, but nevertheless they opened, and let in the unwelcome guest.

At last in my sixteenth year, I saw the outside world again. Thank God! Thank God! I could leave my prison as a free human being and not chained to an unwelcome bridegroom. Then events followed quickly that gave back to us girls more and more of our lost freedom.

In the following year, at the time of the investiture of our young Princess [Queen Wilhelmina of the Netherlands], our parents presented us "officially" with our freedom. For the first time in our lives we were allowed to leave our native town, and to go to the city where the festivities were held in honor of the occasion. What a great and priceless victory it was! That young girls of our position should show themselves in public was here an unheard-of occurrence. The "world" stood aghast; tongues were set wagging at the unprecedented crime. Our European friends rejoiced, and as for ourselves, no queen was so rich as we. But I am far from satisfied. I would go still further, always further. I do not desire to go out to feasts, and little frivolous amusements. That has never been the cause of my longing for freedom. I long to be free, to be able to stand alone, to study, not to be subject to any one, and, above all, *never, never* to be obliged to marry.

a song in the front yard

I've stayed in the front yard all my life.
I want a peek at the back
Where it's rough and untended and hungry weed
   grows.
A girl gets sick of a rose.

I want to go in the back yard now
And maybe down the alley,
To where the charity children play
I want a good time today.

They do some wonderful things.
They have some wonderful fun.
My mother sneers, but I say it's fine
How they don't have to go in at quarter to nine.
My mother, she tells me that Johnnie Mae
Will grow up to be a bad woman.
That George'll be taken to Jail soon or late
(On account of last winter he sold our back gate).

But I say it's fine. Honest, I do.
And I'd like to be a bad woman, too,
And wear the brave stockings of night-black lace
And strut down the streets with paint on my face.

Gwendolyn Brooks
Chicago, 1940s

Breaking Tradition

"Her Feet Will Grow the Size of an Elephant's"

Madame Wei Tao-Ming
China, 1909

Madame Wei Tao-Ming was born in 1896 into a wealthy family in the southern China province of Canton. Her family, in the feudal tradition, was ruled over by her father's mother. This paternal grandmother held complete authority over matters within the household and only when absolutely necessary would her son interfere. Even in so important a matter as bound feet, however, the little girl at the age of five successfully defied her grandmother. She created such bedlam within the household by her screams and tantrums that her grandmother relented. "Very well, then. Take the bandages off. Her feet will grow the size of an elephant's. No one will ever marry her, but so be it. I wash my hands of the whole business."

Astonished and amused by this unusual assertiveness, her father took his daughter, dressed in boy's clothing and a short haircut, with him on his rounds of coffee houses and clubs. By the age of twelve, fascinated by talk of unrest and revolution in China and bored by her mother's ceremonial visits to friends, the young girl centered her life around her studies and her talks with her father.

Early in the winter of my thirteenth year . . . (in spite of my normal-sized feet), various offers were made to my father for my hand in marriage. The whole thing, of course, was to be arranged between the parents—neither I nor the young man in question would have very much to say about it.

Paternal Grandmother was delighted by these possibilities and immediately took over. Prompted by her, my father allowed his choice to light upon a certain young man whose father was the Governor of Canton. My grandmother, of course, had already satisfied herself that his family and fortune were sufficiently important.

I had never thought of marriage one way or the other. It had always seemed a remote and unreal idea, but when Grandmother began to get excited about the prospect, I acquiesced with the vague idea in my mind that this would keep peace in the family. Anyway, I reasoned, I did not have to do anything about it for a long time. Shortly, as was customary, my engagement to a young man I had never seen was celebrated by an enormous party at which neither of us appeared.

But, hidden behind a curtain, I watched the proceedings. It was definitely Paternal Grandmother's "show." She was enthroned on a small platform, surrounded by friends. Suddenly there rang out a trumpet blast and the "delegates"—representatives of my fiancé's family—fell into line and advanced towards Grandmother in solemn procession. Next I heard the high, wistful notes of a flute, and then four white horses appeared, harnessed in gold-studded scarlet leather, with crimson scarves across their chests. They were led by valets in livery, wearing plumed caps, and slung between each pair of steeds were huge baskets filled with fruits and gifts; these were for me—heavy gold bracelets, jade brooches and ear pendants, pearl hairpins, and bolts of vivid silks. As each person reached the dais, he prostrated himself before Paternal Grandmother and touched his forehead to the floor in front of her. She sat beaming with pleasure at the adulation.

After this, months went by and my grandmother was absolutely in her element; I ignored the whole situation as best I could. Then, one day I was told that my fiancé was eager to have our marriage take place sometime in the following year, and his parents had written for the date to be set. I was panic-stricken. The idea of marrying someone who was a total stranger frightened me. Moreover, reports of the young man from my brothers and various friends had not painted him as a prepossessing character. He was about eighteen and was said to be a spoiled child. He had already some nominal official post, and gossip had it that his father secured it for him by making the necessary arrangements.

My brother dug up other little tidbits about him which did not sound very encouraging—that he was not particularly industrious, but was, in fact, such a playboy that he had to have a servant especially designated to follow him around to give him assistance whenever needed. In addition, in spite of these tendencies, he had shown himself to be a stickler for old-fashioned conventions.

For example, we had a telephone in our house on which I used to call my father at his office. My brother told me that my fiancé's family, on hearing that we had a telephone, had announced that they considered such things an improper Western importation, and that they would never permit one in his house. Minor detail that the telephone incident was, it was an indication of my betrothed's family's attitude towards everything. Furthermore, I found that my father-in-law-to-be did not approve of "modern, educated women," and had said of me, "She knows too much already. She spends too much of her time outside her parents' house, and a woman of our society should not run after learning."

When this remark was repeated to my father, it did not go very well with him either; and I could see that he already was worried about the coming marriage. But my father, for all his intelligence and good character, was essentially a conservative man. He could never bear to do anything radical or drastic.

However, in response to my pleadings, he did begin to try to find some way in which the engagement could be broken off without either family's losing face. He spent weeks trying to locate an intermediary who would handle these difficult negotiations. I became very impatient and persuaded my brother, who was completely sympathetic, to write my fiancé and tell him in tactful phrases exactly how I felt. The gist of what he wrote was that I could not be happy in marriage unless my husband had been either to Europe or America to finish his education; if this long journey was impossible, he should at least attend the University of Peking, which was run entirely on new standards. My brother said I felt that my future husband should know something of the modern world, and that I would be unhappy with one who did not share my ideas.

I thought, of course, that this would be the end of the matter, and that the young man would have an excuse to break off the engagement himself. However, he was more stubborn than I thought. He did not take me seriously. At any rate, he replied to my brother, "Your dear sister's ideas are most excellent, but, unfortunately, it is impossible for me to do as she wishes." Then came a beautifully hypocritical phrase: "You have forgotten that I occupy an official position. I could scarcely permit myself to abandon the responsibilities I have assumed, which are heavy indeed."

We were making no progress in this fashion. My father, upset by the whole scandalous business, was no help at all.

Finally, I took the bull by the horns. As a matter of fact, I did not realize what an extraordinary thing it was that I did. I not only thought of myself as quite grown up, but in my determination to be emancipated, my plan seemed a very minor detail. So I wrote my fiancé a letter which stated in effect: "Why don't you marry someone more to your taste? I intend to go to America or Europe to finish my studies and this does not seem to fit into your picture of marriage." Then I put in some conciliatory phrases, suggesting that he marry some young girl, "beautiful and worthy of bearing your name, who will be a help to you in your devotion to your duty."

The hubbub which ensued was unbelievable. To the best of my knowledge no Chinese girl of good family had ever done such a thing before. Both families, especially mine, lost an enormous amount of face. My father was shocked beyond words, and, needless to say, my grandmother took to her bed and gave every appearance of dying of shock. My only support was Mother, who, though miserable at the disgrace which had been brought on the family, was still secretly happy that I had not been forced into the marriage. She cried a great deal, but she cried more from affection for me and general emotion than because of the end of the engagement. I had won the battle at a terrific emotional cost to the whole family.

"The Other End of the String"

Maxine Hong Kingston
Stockton, California, 1950s

Maxine Hong Kingston's parents, born in a small peasant village in China, came to America in the 1930s bringing with them age-old Chinese marriage traditions. Entering her early teens in the 1950s, Americanized Maxine strives to make herself "unsellable."

I learned that young men were placing ads in the *Gold Mountain News* to find wives when my mother and father started answering them. Suddenly a series of new workers showed up at the laundry; they each worked for a week before they disappeared. They ate with us. They talked Chinese with my parents. They did not talk to us. We were to call them "Elder Brother," although they were not related to us. They were all funny-looking FOB's, Fresh-off-the-Boat's, as the Chinese-American kids at school called the young immigrants. FOB's wear high-riding gray slacks and white shirts with the sleeves rolled up. Their eyes do not focus correctly—shifty-eyed—and they hold their mouths slack, not tight-jawed masculine. They shave off their sideburns. The girls said *they'd* never date an FOB. My mother took one home from the laundry, and I saw him looking over our photographs. "This one," he said, picking up my sister's picture.

"No. No," said my mother. "This one," my picture. "The oldest first," she said. Good. I was an obstacle. I would protect my sister and myself at the same time. As my parents and the FOB sat talking at the kitchen table, I dropped two dishes. I found my walking stick and limped across the floor. I twisted my mouth and caught my hand in the knots of my hair. I spilled soup on the FOB when I handed him his bowl. "She can sew,

287

though," I heard my mother say, "and sweep." I raised
dust swirls sweeping around and under the FOB's
chair—very bad luck because spirits live inside the
broom. I put on my shoes with the open flaps and
flapped about like a Wino Ghost. From then on, I wore
those shoes to parties, whenever the mothers gathered
to talk about marriages. The FOB and my parents paid
me no attention, half ghosts half invisible, but when he
left, my mother yelled at me about the dried-duck voice,
the bad temper, the laziness, the clumsiness, the stupidity that comes from reading too much. The young men
stopped visiting; not one came back. "Couldn't you just
stop rubbing your nose?" she scolded. "All the village
ladies are talking about your nose. They're afraid to
eat our pastries because you might have kneaded the
dough." But I couldn't stop at will anymore, and a
crease developed across the bridge. My parents would
not give up, though. "Though you can't see it," my
mother said, "a red string around your ankle ties you to
the person you'll marry. He's already been born, and
he's on the other end of the string."

"Escape!"

Nuruddin Farah
Somalia, 20th century

Nuruddin Farah used a Somali proverb he had heard since childhood to title his book, From A Crooked Rib: *"God created Woman from a crooked rib, and anyone who trieth to straighten it, breaketh it!" In this excerpt his heroine, Ebla, has been promised to Giumaleh, a man old enough to be her father.*

A dwelling. It was a dwelling like any other dwelling in the neighbourhood. Not in the least different. The number of human beings in the encampment was ten times less than that of the cattle. It was the dwelling of a certain *Jes* (a unit of several families living together). It seemed to be unique and, in a way, it was. Every place has its unique features. And this place had more than one.

In the dark, the huts looked more or less like ant-hills, maybe of an exaggerated size. The huts were made of wattle, weaved into a mat-like thing with a cover on top. They were supported by sticks, acting as pillars. Each had one door—all of four feet high. It was a portable home, to be put on the hump-back of a camel when the time came for moving to a pastoral area farther up or down, to the east or the west. It was the portable hut, unlike the stone house or mud hut in a town.

The lives of these people depended upon that of their herds. The lives of the herds also depended upon the plentiness or the scarcity of green grass. But would one be justified in saying that their existence depended upon green pasture—directly or indirectly? Yes: life did depend on green pastures.

Ebla was a member of this *Jes*. She had been on the move with them from the time she was born. Her father and mother had died when she was very young. In fact, she couldn't remember vividly anything about them. She had always been entrusted to the care of her grandfather, who was himself an invalid, though not such a bad one as all that. He always got through to the people, and was very much respected. And his word was very much listened to.

For a woman, she was very tall, but this was not exceptional here. She stood six feet high. She would have been very beautiful, had it not been for the disproportion of her body. She could not read nor write her name. She only knew the Suras, which she read when saying her prayers. She learnt these by heart, hearing them repeated many times by various people. She thought about things and people in her own way, but always respected the old and the dead. Her mother and father meant more to her than anybody else, except her grandfather, who was responsible for her upbringing.

Ebla became disappointed with life many times—in people more than a dozen times. But these occasions were not grave: the circumstances were minor, at least in the way she approached them. To her, a refusal did not matter. Neither would a positive answer make her pleased. But acceptance of her opinions, both by her relations and her would-be husbands, did make her pleased. She thought of many things a woman of her background would never think of. Translated, Ebla roughly means ''Graceful'' and she always wanted her actions to correspond with her name.

Ebla had been toying with the idea of leaving home for quite some time. However, she did not know whether this was to be a temporary change of air—in a town—or a permanent departure. She loved her grandfather, but maybe she mistook pity for love. Anyway, it was only when she thought of her grandfather that she felt the wringing of her heart and a quick impulse not to leave him.

Problems are created by people, Ebla thought, still lying on her mat in the hut. But there is no problem without a solution. Maybe it is good that I should stay to take care of my grandfather, to see to it that he dies peacefully and is buried peacefully. But should I think of someone who does not think of me? It is he who has given my hand to the old man, exchanging me for camels.

She let her hand touch the mat on which she had been lying awake the whole night. It was the same mat on which she sat to talk to many of her suitors, in the dark. In this same hut—or in another one: maybe in a different area, twenty or thirty miles farther up or down, in one direction or another. She sniggered at what some had said to her. She enjoyed talking to others. But none of them was an old man like Giumaleh, the one to whom fate had handed her over. It was yesterday morning that her grandfather had accepted Giumaleh's proposal. He was an old man of forty-eight: fit to be her father. Two of his sons had alternately courted her. But only the younger one was very keen on her. Probably he did not propose because his elder brother had not yet got married. At least, that was the hint that he gave—not to Ebla in person, but to friends. Gossip goes around swiftly: women hear a lot and talk a lot, and tell many lies. But Ebla did not believe a word of it. Obstinate, they would say, maybe hammering the word on her had made her that way. Maybe in a way she was obstinate.

She closed her eyes and imagined herself in the same bed with Giumaleh. Horrible. She just could not imagine it without going absolutely berserk. It was madly terrifying. The way things were, nobody seemed to care whether they harmed one another. Everybody for himself. No one gave a damn if something he did was inconvenient to others. One came out of one's mother's womb alone. One tried to solve one's problems alone. One died alone, isolated. One was put in a grave, and left behind under the ground. As soon as the corpse had been put in the grave and everyone had headed for his home to mourn, it was said that the dead heard the sound of people. Even the sound which was made by their feet. That is what the prophet and great saints had said.

Soft warm air blew the door to and fro: very comforting. "It makes one pleased," she thought, "the wind blowing things like that." Actually what served as the door was a piece of cloth hanging from above the ceiling just to hide those inside. It would be inconvenient to be inside those huts with nothing to hide you.

Ebla stood up and dusted her robe, a very big robe wrapped around her body. A piece of it hung on her back, to serve as a baby-carrier or even as a vessel, or a shoulder-cover—or for countless other purposes.

She was very much worried, not for herself, but for her grandfather. She could not dismiss the thought just by shrugging her shoulders. She was not that type. She was a woman, a responsible woman of eighteen, going on nineteen.

Ordinarily, she was not a weak-minded girl. Not once in her life had she stopped doing anything because it would harm others. But this time, it was different. It was too much for her, far too much. She could not bear to think of waiting to get married to Giumaleh. To be in the doldrums—or to disappoint everyone, especially her grandfather? If she stayed, she thought, she would always be in low spirits. And if she went what would happen?

Yes. What if she went?

Something rang in her mind. But where would she go to? And to whom? And with whom?

Next to her, her friend, a girl of her own age, was snoring in her sleep. But she looked absolutely dead. Ebla stood up. Her left arm was asleep. She massaged it with her right hand. The edge of her robe lay underneath her friend's knee. Ebla tried to give it a tug without waking up her friend. At first she appeared to have woken up. Ebla stopped, motionless for a while. But the friend had put more of Ebla's robe underneath her body. Decidedly (and come what may, she thought) she pulled her robe. Thank God! The robe pulled out. And the friend still lay asleep, as if undisturbed.

Many hours of the night still remained. Ebla dreaded the long hours ahead of her, awaiting her as if in an ambush: an enemy, an unidentified enemy, who fixed his eyes on you when he felt like it. But she walked out into the warm night to think over the situation.

She wished she were not a woman. But would being a man make her situation any better? She wondered.

"But let me sort out my ideas; and see what I can do about them," she told herself.

Escape! To get free from all restraints, from being the

wife of Giumaleh. To get away from unpleasantries. To break the ropes society had wrapped around her and to be free and be herself. Ebla thought of all this, and much else.

"But why is a woman, a woman? To give companionship to man? To beget him children? To do a woman's duty? But that is only in the house. What else?" she asked herself. "Surely a woman is indispensable to man, but do men realize it?

"A man needs a woman. A woman needs a man. Not to the same degree? A man needs a woman to cheat, to tell lies to, to sleep with. In this way a baby is born, weak and forlorn. He decides to belittle his mother immediately he is old enough to walk. He slides away, becomes a heavy burden until he is independent, gets his basic education, like talking, walking, eating, under the care of his mother. When a child, he fidgets about like a lid on top of a boiler. He is infuriating at this stage—he should be put in a cage. After a while, he walks, he talks—only his mother's language at first. He smiles at his mother. . . . But Giumaleh is the wrong match," she suddenly told herself. "I definitely can't marry him."

But who or what should she escape from? This was the real question which needed to be answered. Inside her, she knew why she wanted to escape. Actually it was more than a want: it was a desire, a desire stronger than anything, a thing to long for. Her escape meant her freedom. Her escape meant her new life. Her escape meant her parting with the country and its harsh life. Her escape meant the divine emancipation of the body and soul of a human being.

She desired, more than anything, to fly away; like a cock, which has unknotted itself from the string tying its leg to the wall. She wanted to fly away from the dependence on the seasons, the seasons which determine the life or death of the nomads. And she wanted to fly away from the squabbles over water, squabbles caused by the lack of water, which meant that the season was bad. She wanted to go away from the duty of women. Not that she was intending to feel idle and do nothing, nor did she feel irresponsible, but a woman's duty meant loading and unloading camels and donkeys after the destina-

tion had been reached, and that life was routine: goats
for girls and camels for boys got on her nerves more than
she could stand. To her, this allotment of assignments
denoted the status of a woman, that she was lower in
status than a man, and that she was weak. "But it is only
because camels are stupid beasts that boys can manage
to handle them," she always consoled herself. She
loathed this discrimination between the sexes: the idea
that boys lift up the prestige of the family and keep the
family's name alive. Even a moron-male cost twice as
much as two women in terms of blood-compensation.
As many as twenty or thirty camels are allotted to each
son. The women, however, have to wait until their fates
give them a new status in life: the status of marriage. A
she-camel is given to the son, as people say "tied to his
navel" as soon as he is born. "Maybe God prefers men
to women," she told herself.

But Ebla had no answers to the questions how to escape, where should she escape to, whom should she go
to, and when she should escape. . . .

The clock would strike four in the morning. It was
Tuesday—to her like any other day, for even Friday was
not different. To men perhaps it was, as they all went to
a praying-place, or to a mosque. To women Friday only
meant more work, more washing and more cooking to
be done.

She had nothing to carry along with her. She never
owned much, only a spare sheet to wear when the one
she had on got dirty—and it was old. The muezzin had
not announced the nearing of the morning prayers: the
first wailing had not been heard. The sound of watering
camels had not yet started. She stopped as if to take
something, but it was only to ease up the hang-over. She
touched her toes and heard the sound her joints made.
The hut was very dark. There were no matches to light,
no maps to take. The only fire which provided a dim
light had been blown out before Ebla and her friend had
fallen asleep. Ebla's colleague was still snoring her head
off. Ebla stretched her long arms down to pick up her
shoes and the sheet. She had placed them somewhere in
the evening. She took both of them in her hands and
walked out of the hut. She put one foot outside and one

inside and kept standing there motionless. For a while she hesitated, not wondering whether or not she should go—she had settled that and there was nothing to make her change her mind—but should she or shouldn't she tell her colleague in the hut where she intended to go?

She lifted her foot back. Her body stood an inch away from the door. She could feel the mild wind. She turned her back on the door and headed inwards. She stopped a few inches from where her friend lay snoring. She wanted to call to her friend and say that she had decided to escape. She opened her mouth, but before she was able to say anything, she heard a bang on the outside wall. She stopped, wanting to find out what had made the noise, to see if anybody was outside, and to regain her lost self, for she did not know for a fraction of a second who she was. The noise had not been repeated and Ebla was prepared to go out and not wake up her colleague. "It is much better that way," she thought to herself.

She swayed as if she were drunk.

The whole area was silent. Not a sound was to be heard. The unmarried males slept ouside the huts and in the clearing. White sheets covered their bodies. Ebla passed near them, not making any sound. She walked bare-footed, and wrapped her sheet around her shoes, and put the bundle between her arm and ribs. She tiptoed as if she were a thief who had preyed upon somebody whom he knows. She cast her eyes downward. She finally reached the entrance to the dwelling. It was a thorn-fence, which had just been built. There was a stick put across, which served as the gate. Should she go underneath or should she lift the stick? She stopped and bent down to see if she could pass underneath. Being unable to do that she lifted the stick. The gate creaked. The prickles stood out and the stick had touched some of them as she lifted it. Her heart began pounding frightfully fast. She thought she had made a loud noise. She looked around, but there was nothing coming, nobody, not a living soul. The cock crowed, then there was silence again. She replaced the stick in a hurry and stood on the outside of the dwelling-boundary.

"My God, I am out," she said to herself.

She headed west and in the direction where the travellers to Belet Wene would pass by. She hid herself under a big tree, near the detour, which encircled the main road.

"*Alhamdulillah, Subbanallah, Istagfurullah.*" She kept on repeating these words, which did not convey much to a young woman of her background. She said them because she had heard others say them. She knew the words were Arabic and that they were God's words, and sacred. She counted on her finger-joints just as she had seen others do it. Actually, she let her thumbs run over her fingers one by one. Thus rhythmically, and sometimes inaccurately, she counted, saying each word three times, until she had said every word ninety-nine times: that was the number which represented God's names.

Fate in her faith. Ebla put her faith and her fate along with it into the hands of God. "And I am certain that God will understand my situation. And of course, He won't let me down.

"If I am asked by the caravan people where I am going, what shall I say? I suppose I must tell them the truth. But what is truth—that which corresponds to the notions we have in mind or that which corresponds to our doings? Why do we think differently from the way we behave? If I tell the truth, then it won't get me anywhere, for certain. If I say I ran away because my grandfather had decided to give my hand in (sacred?) marriage to a man—an old man, I must say to drive home the point that I had to escape. But what is wrong in getting married to a man—old or young? Age doesn't determine the genuineness of marriage, does it? Sometimes there are old men who are much more likeable husbands than young ones. People are argumentative, and surely they will bring up this question.

" 'You are allowed to tell lies if the situation makes it necessary,' said Prophet Mohammed. That is what our Prophet has said, and everything he said ought to be obeyed. But is this a necessity—I mean telling lies under the present circumstances? Every situation has its serious side—is this the most serious situation or are there many more to follow it?"

Ebla had not been able to reach a decision when she

heard the caravans approaching her. Things appeared to crowd in upon her instantly.

The travellers could see her tall figure—and it gave more charm to the light caused by the dawn. Ebla was nature, nature had become personified in her. The trees, the earth, the noise, the talking of the caravan people were also part of nature. The dawn-wind caressed her cheeks. The birds chirped their songs. The stars withdrew into their tiny holes in the sky—maybe to rest and at the same time to get charged for the night which would await them. The moon faded into the blue colour of the sky—and lost its conspicuousness. Silence. Death of voices. Feet-shufflings. The still unused energy in the peasants of whom the caravan was made up was shown in their powerful strides—each of them a separate individual. The milk which they had drunk before they started their trip shook inside their bellies. The camels walked haughtily as if whatever they carried on their backs was their own and as if the peasants who walked behind them, with sticks in their hands, were there to guard the property. The master mistook himself for the slave. Heaps upon heaps of cow-hide, goat-hide, frankincense and other articles for sale unknowingly danced their way to their altar in the town.

As if he wasn't sure of what he had seen, the young man who led the first camel by the reins, opened his eyes a little bit more. His hesitations confirmed, he said: "What are you doing here, cousin Ebla?"

Although she wasn't his cousin, in that area people still address each other in those terms—that is their polite form of saying hello even to a stranger.

"I am sick," Ebla said, thinking that would explain everything.

"What are you doing here? And especially if you are sick? Home is a long way from here," said the young man, as tall as Ebla. By now, he had forgotten that he was leading the caravan. The first camel had mischievously led the rest of the camels astray. The young man, therefore, had to stride away from her to resume his responsibility. The other people in the caravan had by then come level with her. One by one, they asked her about her mission to town.

She told them why she was there: "I am sick, I need some injections. And I want to buy some clothes."

"For your wedding?" some had asked.

"Yes," she said and nodded her head.

And she smiled ironically.

"No Noodle Board for Me"

Isaac Bashevis Singer
Yanev, Poland, 19th century

Throughout history there have been girls who have had to hide their sexual identity and disguise themselves as boys in order to fulfill their dreams. For instance, the American Revolutionary heroine Deborah Sampson joined the army dressed as a man. Similarly, the Chinese legendary heroine Hah Mu Lan fought as a man to save the honor of her family. One of the most poignant stories of such women is Isaac Bashevis Singer's Yentl the Yeshiva Boy. *After her father's death, Yentl was pressured by the marriage brokers to find a husband. A voice inside her kept saying "no."*

. . . What becomes of a girl when the wedding's over? Right away she starts bearing and rearing. And her mother-in-law lords it over her. Yentl knew she wasn't cut out for a woman's life. She couldn't sew, she couldn't knit. She let the food burn and the milk boil over; her Sabbath pudding never turned out right, and her *challah* dough didn't rise. Yentl much preferred men's activities to women's. Her father Reb Todros, may he rest in peace, during many bedridden years had studied Torah with his daughter as if she were a son. He told Yentl to lock the doors and drape the windows, then together they pored over the Pentateuch, the Mishnah, the Gemara, and the Commentaries. She had proved so apt a pupil that her father used to say:
"Yentl—you have the soul of a man."
"So why was I born a woman?"
"Even heaven makes mistakes."
There was no doubt about it, Yentl was unlike any of the girls in Yanev—tall, thin, bony, with small breasts and narrow hips. On Sabbath afternoons, when her father slept, she would dress up in his trousers, his fringed

garment, his silk coat, his skullcap, his velvet hat, and study her reflection in the mirror. She looked like a dark, handsome young man. There was even a slight down on her upper lip. Only her thick braids showed her womanhood—and if it came to that, hair could always be shorn. Yentl conceived a plan and day and night she could think of nothing else. No, she had not been created for the noodle board and the pudding dish, for chattering with silly women and pushing for a place at the butcher's block. Her father had told her so many tales of yeshivas, rabbis, men of letters! Her head was full of Talmudic disputations, questions and answers, learned phrases. Secretly, she had even smoked her father's long pipe.

Yentl told the dealers she wanted to sell the house and go to live in Kalish with an aunt. The neighborhood women tried to talk her out of it, and the marriage brokers said she was crazy, that she was more likely to make a good match right here in Yanev. But Yentl was obstinate. She was in such a rush that she sold the house to the first bidder, and let the furniture go for a song. All she realized from her inheritance was one hundred and forty rubles. Then late one night in the month of Av, while Yanev slept, Yentl cut off her braids, arranged sidelocks at her temples, and dressed herself in her father's clothes. Packing underclothes, phylacteries, and a few books into a straw suitcase, she started off on foot for Lublin.

On her way to Lublin, Yentl assumes the name Anshel and meets a young student, Avigdor. Joining him at his yeshiva, Yentl is happily absorbed in her studies until the unexpected happens—she falls in love with Avigdor. Avigdor, in turn, is lamenting the rejection by his love, Hadass, and urges Yentl (Anshel) to marry her in his place. Yentl, in order to please him, agrees and manages to deceive the innocent Hadass who knows "little of the ways of men." Yentl's anxiety about this deception grows, however, and finally she leaves Hadass to reveal herself to Avigdor as Yentl, Reb Todros' daughter, not his son!

* * *

According to the law Avigdor was now forbidden to spend another moment alone with Yentl; yet dressed in the gabardine and trousers, she was again the familiar Anshel. They resumed their conversation on the old footing:

"How could you bring yourself to violate the commandment every day: 'A woman shall not wear that which pertaineth to a man'?"

"I wasn't created for plucking feathers and chattering with females."

"Would you rather lose your share in the world to come?"

"Perhaps. . . ."

Avigdor raised his eyes. Only now did he realize that Anshel's cheeks were too smooth for a man's, the hair too abundant, the hands too small. Even so he could not believe that such a thing could have happened. At any moment he expected to wake up. He bit his lips, pinched his thigh. He was seized by shyness and could not speak without stammering. His friendship with Anshel, their intimate talk, their confidences, had been turned into a sham and delusion. The thought even occurred to him that Anshel might be a demon. He shook himself as if to cast off a nightmare; yet that power which knows the difference between dream and reality told him it was all true. He summoned up his courage. He and Anshel could never be strangers to one another, even though Anshel was in fact Yentl. . . . He ventured a comment:

"It seems to me that the witness who testifies for a deserted woman may not marry her, for the law calls him 'a party to the affair.' "

"What? That didn't occur to me!"

"We must look it up in Eben Ezer."

"I'm not even sure that the rules pertaining to a deserted woman apply in this case," said Anshel in the manner of a scholar.

"If you don't want Hadass to be a grass widow, you must reveal the secret to her directly."

"That I can't do."

"In any event, you must get another witness."

Gradually the two went back to their Talmudic conversation. It seemed strange at first to Avigdor to be disput-

ing holy writ with a woman, yet before long the Torah
had reunited them. Though their bodies were different,
their souls were of one kind. Anshel spoke in a sing-
song, gesticulated with her thumb, clutched her sidelocks, plucked at her beardless chin, made all the
customary gestures of a yeshiva student. In the heat of
argument she even seized Avigdor by the lapel and
called him stupid. A great love for Anshel took hold of
Avigdor, mixed with shame, remorse, anxiety. If I had
only known this before, he said to himself. In his
thoughts he likened Anshel (or Yentl) to Bruria, the wife
of Reb Meir, and to Yalta, the wife of Reb Nachman. For
the first time he saw clearly that this was what he had always wanted: a wife whose mind was not taken up with
material things. . . . His desire for Hadass was gone
now, and he knew he would long for Yentl, but he dared
not say so. He felt hot and knew that his face was burning. He could no longer meet Anshel's eyes. He began to
enumerate Anshel's sins and saw that he too was impli-
cated, for he had sat next to Yentl and had touched her
during her unclean days. *Nu*, and what could be said
about her marriage to Hadass? What a multitude of
transgressions there! Wilful deception, false vows, mis-
representation!—Heaven knows what else. He asked
suddenly:

"Tell the truth, are you a heretic?"

"God forbid!"

"Then how could you bring yourself to do such a
thing?"

The longer Anshel talked, the less Avigdor understood. All Anshel's explanations seemed to point to one
thing: she had the soul of a man and the body of a
woman. Anshel said she had married Hadass only in order to be near Avigdor.

"You could have married me," Avigdor said.

"I wanted to study the Gemara and Commentaries
with you, not darn your socks!"

For a long time neither spoke. Then Avigdor broke the
silence:

"I'm afraid Hadass will get sick from all this, God forbid!"

"I'm afraid of that too."

"What's going to happen now?"

Dusk fell and the two began to recite the evening prayer. In his confusion Avigdor mixed up the blessings, omitted some and repeated others. He glanced sideways at Anshel who was rocking back and forth, beating her breast, bowing her head. He saw her, eyes closed, lift her face to heaven as though beseeching: You, Father in Heaven, know the truth. . . . When their prayers were finished, they sat down on opposite chairs, facing one another yet a good distance apart. The room filled with shadows. Reflections of the sunset, like purple embroidery, shook on the wall opposite the window. Avigdor again wanted to speak but at first the words, trembling on the tip of his tongue, would not come. Suddenly they burst forth:

"Maybe it's still not too late? I can't go on living with that accursed woman. . . . You. . . ."

"No, Avigdor, it's impossible."

"Why?"

"I'll live out my time as I am. . . ."

"I'll miss you. Terribly."

"And I'll miss you."

"What's the sense of all this?"

Anshel did not answer. Night fell and the light faded. In the darkness they seemed to be listening to each other's thoughts. The law forbade Avigdor to stay in the room alone with Anshel, but he could not think of her just as a woman. What a strange power there is in clothing, he thought. But he spoke of something else:

"I would advise you simply to send Hadass a divorce."

"How can I do that?"

"Since the marriage sacraments weren't valid, what difference does it make?"

"I suppose you're right."

"There'll be time enough later for her to find out the truth."

The maidservant came in with a lamp but as soon as she had gone, Avigdor put it out. Their predicament and the words which they must speak to one another could not endure light. In the blackness Anshel related all the particulars. She answered all Avigdor's questions.

The clock struck two, and still they talked. Anshel told Avigdor that Hadass had never forgotten him. She talked of him frequently, worried about his health, was sorry—though not without a certain satisfaction—about the way things had turned out with Peshe.

"She'll be a good wife," said Anshel. "I don't even know how to bake a pudding."

"Nevertheless, if you're willing. . . ."

"No, Avigdor. It wasn't destined to be. . . ."

"Choked with Ribbons"

Frances Willard
Wisconsin Territory, 1850s

In her autobiography, Glimpses of Fifty Years, *Frances Willard, founder and leader of the Women's Christian Temperance Union, shows the beginnings of her militant spirit in this reminiscence of her adolescent years.*

No girl went through a harder experience than I, when my free, out-of-door life had to cease, and the long skirts and clubbed-up hair spiked with hair-pins had to be endured. The half of that down-heartedness has never been told and never can be. I always believed that if I had been left alone and allowed as a woman, what I had had as a girl, a free life in the country, where a human being might grow, body and soul, as a tree grows, I would have been "ten times more of a person," every way. Mine was a nature hard to tame, and I cried long and loud when I found I could never again race and range about with freedom. I had delighted in my short hair and nice round hat, or comfortable "Shaker bonnet," but now I was to be "choked with ribbons" when I went into the open air the rest of my days. Something like the following was the "state of mind" that I revealed to my journal about this time:

This is my birthday and the date of my martyrdom. Mother insists that at last I *must* have my hair "done up woman-fashion." She says she can hardly forgive herself for letting me "run wild" so long. We've had a great time over it all, and here I sit like another Samson "shorn of my strength." That figure won't do, though, for the greatest trouble with me is that I never shall be shorn again. My "back" hair is twisted up like a corkscrew; I carry eighteen hair-pins; my head aches miserably; my feet are entangled in the skirt of my hateful new gown. I can never jump over a fence again, so long as I live. As for chasing the sheep, down in the shady pasture, it's out of the question, and to climb to my "Eagle's-nest" seat in the big burr-oak would ruin this new frock beyond repair. Altogether, I recognize the fact that my "occupation's gone."

Something else that had already happened, helped to stir up my spirit into a mighty unrest. This is the story as I told it to my journal:

This is election day and my brother is twenty-one years old. How proud he seemed as he dressed up in his best Sunday clothes and drove off in the big wagon with father and the hired men to vote for John C. Frémont, like the sensible "Free-soiler" that he is. My sister and I stood at the window and looked out after them. Somehow, I felt a lump in my throat, and then I couldn't see their wagon any more, things got so blurred. I turned to Mary, and she, dear little innocent, seemed wonderfully sober, too. I said, "Wouldn't you like to vote as well as Oliver? Don't you and I love the country just as well as he, and doesn't the country need our ballots?" Then she looked scared, but answered, in a minute, " 'Course we do, and 'course we ought,— but don't you go ahead and say so, for then we would be called strong-minded.'

These two great changes in my uneventful life made me so distressed in heart that I had half a mind to run away. But the trouble was, I hadn't the faintest idea where to run to. Across the river, near Colonel Burdick's, lived Silas Hayner and several of his brothers, on their nice prairie farms. Sometimes Emily Scoville, Hannah Hayner, or some other of the active young women, would come over to help mother when there was more work than usual; and with Hannah, especially, I had fellowship, because, like myself, she was venturesome in disposition; could row a boat, or fire a gun, and liked to be always out-of-doors. She was older than I, and entered into all my plans. So we two foolish creatures planned to borrow father's revolver and go off on a wild-goose chase, crossing the river in a canoe and launching out to seek our fortunes. But the best part of the story is that we were never so silly as to take a step beyond the old home-roof, contenting ourselves with talking the matter over in girlish phrase, and very soon perceiving how mean and ungrateful such an act would be. Indeed, I told Mary and mother all about it, after a little while, and that ended the only really "wild" plan that I ever made, except another, not unlike it, in my first months at Evanston, which was also nothing but a plan.

"You must go to school, my child, and take a course of study; I wish it might be to Oberlin"—this was my mother's quiet comment on the confession. "Your mind is active; you are fond of books and thoughts, as well as of outdoors; we must provide them for you to make up for the loss of your girlish good times;" so, without any scolding, this Roman matron got her daughter's aspirations into another channel. To be busy doing something that is worthy to be done is the happiest thing in all this world for girl or boy, for old or young.

On the day I was eighteen, my mother made a birthday cake and I was in the highest possible glee. I even went so far as to write what Oliver called a "pome," which has passed into oblivion but of which these lines linger in memory's whispering-gallery:

I Am Eighteen

The last year is passed:
The last month, week, day, hour and moment.
For eighteen years, quelling all thoughts
And wishes of my own,
I've been obedient to the powers that were
Not that the yoke was heavy to be borne
And grievous,
Do I glory that 'tis removed—
For lighter ne'er did parents fond
Impose on child.

It was a *silver* chain:
But the bright adjective
Takes not away the *clanking* sound
That follows it. . . .
The clock has struck!
O! heaven and earth, I'm free!
And here, beneath the watching stars, I feel
New inspiration. Breathing from afar
And resting on my spirit as it ne'er
Could rest before, comes joy profound.
And now I feel that I'm alone and free
To worship and obey Jehovah only. . . .

Toward evening, on this "freedom day," I took my seat
quietly in mother's rocking-chair, and began to read
Scott's *Ivanhoe*. Father was opposed to story books, and
on coming in he scanned this while his brow grew
cloudy.

"I thought I told you not to read novels, Frances," he
remarked seriously.

"So you did, father, and in the main I've kept faith
with you in this; but you forget what day it is."

"What day, indeed! I should like to know if the day
has anything to do with the deed!"

"Indeed it has—I am eighteen—I am of age—I am now
to do what *I* think right, and to read this fine historical
story is, in my opinion, a right thing for me to do."

God and the Free Throw

Caryl Rivers
Maryland, 1950s

It had to be hitting 95 inside the gym, where the stench of stale air and sweat was only a shade less rancid than the Black Hole of Calcutta. But I was oblivious to it all. I had a basketball, a real basketball, and I planned to make the most of the occasion.

I heaved, and missed the basket by a good five feet. I ran to grab the ball before it could be snatched away. If that happened, I'd have to go back to the leaky volleyball that landed with a dull thud when it dropped limply from the rim of the basket. Eleven-year-old girls inevitably got stuck with the volleyball. The good basketballs were usually appropriated by the older boys at the recreation center.

Back to the foul line I trotted. I gritted my teeth, trying not to lock my braces together, and tried to remember the things my father had taught me: elbows in, deep bend at the knees, the ball gripped tightly along the seams with the fingertips. I bent and pushed. The ball arched upward, caught the rim, rolled about for a minute, and slipped through. I whooped. Not exactly a perfect swish, but I got it in.

The ball bounced from the floor into the arms of a grinning fifteen-year-old boy who galloped off with it, dribbling down to the far end of the court where his friends were waiting. I sighed and went to look for the volleyball.

Basketball was sweaty and grubby—and rife with enough opportunity for body contact to be considered faintly seedy and lower-class. A girl who played tennis could lay claim to some panache; the very name of the sport rang with echoes of chic little dresses and long tanned legs and country club living. But girls' basketball meant sweaty armpits and dirty sneakers. One of my teammates in high school was a fine player who was tall and quick and had the face of Scarlett O'Hara. She went to a formal dance at the Naval Academy when she was a senior, and she was standing with her date in Bancroft Hall when another young woman—bedecked in enough tulle to clothe the Ballet Russe—sidled over. In a voice dripping with venom and magnolia, she said loudly to my friend: "Aren't you the *mahvelous* basketball player from Silver Spring?" As the young men looked her way, my friend was certain that under the white satin gown they could all see the sneakers and the sweat.

Fortunately, I discovered basketball long before I discovered boys. I was tall, and I went to Catholic school, in a middle-class Maryland neighborhood where all basketball, even the girls' kind, was a matter of passion.

The Catholic Youth Organization ran a girls' league for both grade schools and high schools. All things considered, the CYO was the greatest advantage of being a member of the One True Faith, being more immediately visible than God's Grace or my Guardian Angel. CYO Girls basketball was, to my mind, one of the Catholic Church's finest achievements, ranking somewhere below Pope John and a few notches above the Council of Trent. In the stifling '50s, the era of Togetherness and penis envy, of momism and exploding suburbia, the CYO gave girls a chance to be aggressive, rowdy, and competitive, all under the aegis of Good Clean Fun. I suspect there were motives other than feminist ones behind all this sponsored activity. The good sisters no doubt figured that while we were on the courts or in the showers, we would not be in the back seats of cars, jeopardizing our immortal souls with open-mouthed kisses. One order of nuns that detected the ugly scent of sex in the CYO made the girls' team wear garter belts and long blue stockings under their gym suits, making them look like tall blue elves. We had to polish our sneakers before each game (after a few applications of Kiwi, the canvas started to crack), and we were not allowed to curse or slug anybody. We disregarded the last two, though we never cursed loud enough for the "ref" to hear or gave anyone an elbow in the direct line of vision of a nun.

I made the CYO team in the seventh grade, and unlike most girls, I had my own private coach. My father had played semipro basketball as a young man, and he taught me all the dirty tricks—how to elbow so the "ref" wouldn't see you, the fine art of "hipping," and how to stagger and fall after you have fouled another player to make it look like she ran into you. He also taught me a jump shot, and I think I was the only girl in the league to own one. The hook shot seemed to be the favorite of the girls, and some developed it to a fine art. But the jump shot made me the high scorer in many a game.

For a period of five years of my life I ate, drank, and breathed basketball. The gym was packed as solidly for the girls' games as it was for the boys'. In the close games with our fiercest rivals (usually bearing the name of some mild-mannered saint), the gym would fairly rock with the noise. I can remember stepping to the foul line, hearing the noise fall to a murmur, feeling the eyes on me as I made the obligatory sign of the cross. If God could see the fall of a sparrow, the chances were that he wouldn't overlook a free throw with the score tied in the last quarter.

It was a taste of glory; the basketball years were a brief and shining moment, and I never forgot them. I got headlines—O.K., they were only small ones in the *Catholic Standard*—but, dammit, headlines nonetheless, and a few small trophies and an all-star jacket that has faded with the years, but the silver cloth still gleams in my mind's eye like Galahad's armor.

To play basketball in the '50s was to step out of woman's inherited role, to cast off docility for ferocity, to control, if not your destiny, at least the arc of one particular piece of cowhide for a slice of eternity. Even as I made the sign of the cross, I knew damn well that it was my own control that would seal the fate of the foul shot, and Divine Will had precious little to do with it. If you have played basketball—really played it with pride and passion—you can never really be docile again.

I grew up and away from basketball. There wasn't any choice in those days. It was O.K. to be a jock until you got to a certain age, and then there weren't any more respectable team sports to play. There were a few semipro women's basketball or softball teams around, but to call them semipro is stretching it. I played basketball in college for a while, but no one came to the games, or cared much whether we won or lost. I switched to tennis, and tried to lose prettily to dashing young males. I could never quite bring it off, because inevitably I'd get a soft lob and the old CYO killer instinct would grab hold and I'd ram it down his throat and my "dainty-lil-ole-me" act was shot to hell.

It was no great loss. In parochial school, we were supposed to learn to emulate the Virgin Mary, to be sweet and docile and accepting of God's Will. Basketball knocked all that down the tubes. Besides, we figured it wasn't God's Will for us to lose. We prayed as hard as we played—for insurance—and if we got carried away at times, even the Virgin Mary would forgive us. How could she really be offended by a devout prayer: "Holy Mary, Mother of God, let us kick the shit out of Blessed Sacrament."

Leaving Home

Home

Home is a slipper I step into,
a bathrobe and a cup of tea.
Every floor is warm and every
crack in the ceiling is known.
Home is constant dowhatyouwantto
and feeling so big because it's My House.
After a party I Go Home and after school I
Go Home and whoever else enters is never really
as glad as if we were in Their House.
This is My Room and My Mail and My Driveway.
This is My Bed and My Name and My Dinner on the
    table.

There is a dog living here and a washing machine and
a mother, a father, a sister, and a cat. We have our own
little boxes but we are a family. We are a family because
all of our pictures are on the stairs.
I wash dishes and do laundry and walk the dog.
I am a daughter who gets clothes and food and is cul-
    tured, loved, and
encouraged. I am also a daughter who gets cranky and
    acts
no possible way I would act with a friend.
This is also a house that has rebelled, that has had
    sickness,
role changing, sexual deviance, neurosis, and fear.

This is also a house that has seen drugs, nightmares, and
  endless insomnia.
There are many different kinds of plants in My House.
  The father and
the daughter both love them. The daughter is now a
  woman. The daughter is
getting ready to climb out onto the roof and steal away.
  The daughter is sorry
but the daughter must go. The daughter is very, very
  sorry.
The daughter is ready.
This is My House and My Room and My Clock and the
  time is ripe
to peel the skin off this body and let it dance, let it dance.

Amy Smiley,
New York, 1978

An Unfinished Woman

Lillian Hellman
New Orleans, 1920s

as, they told me, turning into a handful. Mrs. Still-
n said I was wild, Mr. Stillman said that I would, of
urse, bring pain to my mother and father, and Fizzy
id I was just plain disgusting mean. It had been a bad
onth for me. I had, one night, fallen asleep in the fig
ee and, coming down in the morning, refused to tell
my mother where I had been. James Denery the Third
and I had waited

Cotton Flowers

Flowers have blossomed, red, black and white on Juma
  lake.
Now tell me, O flowers,
which one of them is he, which one is she?

Cotton flowers blossom in the garden
and illuminate the whole village.
Girls born to no purpose must shine in another man's
  house.

Flowers in hands, wither in the hands.
Flowers in the bunch, wither in the bunch.
A child kept in the lap, will wither in the lap.

Two red flowers on the silk cotton tree
look down like a pair of eyes.
Our house is well guarded.

Let's go to the river bank, sister,
that has the finest sand in the world.
We'll shine our bangles, and wet them with our tears.

Mother will toss sweets, father will toss money.
My brother has a goddess in his blood
and I will enjoy many lives.

"When did you go to the river to fetch water? It's dark
  already!"
"You know, mother, girls can't walk fast,
and the way is deep with fine sand."

Mother, mother, home can't keep me.
Mother, mother, I must go.
Mother, mother, don't call me silly.

Mother, don't utter such a thing.

Don't say I'll leave you.
Is there greater wealth than a mother, whose husband is
    alive?

Traditional women's oral poetry
Translated by Dr. Prithvindra Chakravarti and
Ulli Beier
Birbham District, India

The Empty Ho

I remember a house I have left.
Now it is empty.
The curtains stir with the wind,
boards lash obstinately
against old walls.
In the garden, where grass begins
to overflow its empire,
in drawing rooms with covered furnit
in deserted mirrors
solitude walks, glides, shod
in silent and soft velvet

I w
ma
co
sa
n
t

velvet.

porch where its foot impresses a print,
hollow, smothered corridor
girl grew, here sprouted
dy of slender, mournful cypress.
n her back stretched two braids
win guardian angels.
hands never did anything
ore than to close windows.)

Gray adolescence with vocation of shadow,
with destiny of death:
the stairway sleeps; the house
which knew not how to hold you, crumbles.

Rosario Castellanos
Mexico, 20th century

had hit me very hard in a tug-of-war and
until the next day to hit him over the head with a
lain coffee pot and then his mother complained
mother. I had also refused to go back to dancing
And I was now spending most of my time w
group from an orphanage down the block. I guess th
phan group was no more attractive than any other,
to be an orphan seemed to me desirable and a self-m
piece of independence. In any case, the orphans w
more interesting to me than my schoolmates, and if th
played rougher they complained less. Frances, a dar
beauty of my age, queened it over the others because he
father had been killed by the Mafia. Miriam, small and
wiry, regularly stole my allowance from the red purse
my aunt had given me, and the one time I protested she
beat me up. Louis Calda was religious and spoke to me
about it. Pancho was dark, sad, and, to me, a poet, because once he said, "Yo te amo." I could not sleep a full
night after this declaration, and it set up in me forever after both sympathy and irritability with the first sexual
stirrings of little girls, so masked, so complex, so foolish
as compared with the sex of little boys. It was Louis
Calda who took Pancho and me to a Catholic Mass that
could have made me a fourteen-year-old convert. But
Louis explained that he did not think me worthy, and
Pancho, to stop my tears, cut off a piece of his hair with a

knife, gave it to me as a gift from royalty, and then shoved me into the gutter. I don't know why I thought this an act of affection, but I did, and went home to open the back of a new wristwatch my father had given me for my birthday and to put the lock of hair in the back. A day later when the watch stopped, my father insisted I give it to him immediately, declaring that the jeweler was unreliable.

It was that night that I disappeared, and that night that Fizzy said I was disgusting mean, and Mr. Stillman said I would forever pain my mother and father, and my father turned on both of them and said he would handle his family affairs himself without comments from strangers. But he said it too late. He had come home very angry with me: the jeweler, after my father's complaints about his unreliability, had found the lock of hair in the back of the watch. What started out to be a mild reproof on my father's part soon turned angry when I wouldn't explain about the hair. (My father was often angry when I was most like him.) He was so angry that he forgot that he was attacking me in front of the Stillmans, my old rival Fizzy, and the delighted Mrs. Dreyfus, a new, rich boarder who only that afternoon had complained about my bad manners. My mother left the room when my father grew angry with me. Hannah, passing through, put up her hand as if to stop my father and then, frightened of the look he gave her, went out to the porch. I sat on the couch, astonished at the pain in my head. I tried to get up from the couch, but one ankle turned and I sat down again, knowing for the first time the rampage that could be caused in me by anger. The room began to have other forms, the people were no longer men and women, my head was not my own. I told myself that my head had gone somewhere and I have little memory of anything after my Aunt Jenny came into the room and said to my father, "Don't you remember?" I have never known what she meant, but I knew that soon after I was moving up the staircase, that I slipped and fell a few steps, that when I woke up hours later in my bed, I found a piece of angel cake—an old love, an old custom—left by my mother on my pillow. The headache was worse and I vomited out of the window. Then I

dressed, took my red purse, and walked a long way
down St. Charles Avenue. A St. Charles Avenue mansion had on its back lawn a famous doll's-house, an elaborate copy of the mansion itself, built years before for the
small daughter of the house. As I passed this showpiece,
I saw a policeman and moved swiftly back to the doll palace and crawled inside. If I had known about the fanta-
sies of the frightened, that ridiculous small house would
not have been so terrible for me. I was surrounded by or-
nate, carved reproductions of the mansion furniture,
scaled for children, bisque figurines in miniature, a working toilet seat of gold leaf in suitable size, small draperies of
damask with a sign that said "From the damask of Marie
Antoinette," a miniature samovar with small bronze cups,
and a tiny Madame Récamier couch on which I spent the
night, my legs on the floor. I must have slept, because I
woke from a nightmare and knocked over a bisque figu-
rine. The noise frightened me, and since it was now almost
light, in one of those lovely mist mornings of late spring
when every flower in New Orleans seems to melt and mix
with the air, I crawled out. Most of that day I spent walking, although I had a long session in the ladies' room of the
railroad station. I had four dollars and two bits, but that
wasn't much when you meant it to last forever and when
you knew it would not be easy for a fourteen-year-old girl
to find work in a city where too many people knew her.
Three times I stood in line at the railroad ticket windows to
ask where I could go for four dollars, but each time the
question seemed too dangerous and I knew no other way
of asking it.

Toward evening, I moved to the French Quarter, feeling sad and envious as people went home to dinner. I
bought a few Tootsie Rolls and a half loaf of bread and
went to the St. Louis Cathedral in Jackson Square. (It
was that night that I composed the prayer that was to become, in the next five years, an obsession, mumbled
over and over through the days and nights: "God forgive me, Papa forgive me, Mama forgive me, Sophronia,
Jenny, Hannah, and all others, through this time and
that time, in life and in death." When I was nineteen,
my father, who had made several attempts through the
years to find out what my lip movements meant as I re-

peated the prayer, said, "How much would you take to stop that? Name it and you've got it." I suppose I was sick of the nonsense by that time because I said, "A leather coat and a feather fan," and the next day he bought them for me.) After my loaf of bread, I went looking for a bottle of soda pop and discovered, for the first time, the whorehouse section around Bourbon Street. The women were ranged in the doorways of the cribs, making the first early evening offers to sailors, who were the only men in the streets. I wanted to stick around and see how things like that worked, but the second or third time I circled the block, one of the girls called out to me. I couldn't understand the words, but the voice was angry enough to make me run toward the French Market.

The Market was empty except for two old men. One of them called to me as I went past, and I turned to see that he had opened his pants and was shaking what my circle called "his thing." I flew across the street into the coffee stand, forgetting that the owner had known me since I was a small child when my Aunt Jenny would rest from her marketing tour with a cup of fine, strong coffee.

He said, in the patois, "*Que faites, ma 'fant? Je suis fermé.*"

I said, "*Rien. Ma tante attend*—Could I have a doughnut?"

He brought me two doughnuts, saying one was *lagniappe*, but I took my doughnuts outside when he said "*Mais où est vo' tante à c'heure?*"

I fell asleep with my doughnuts behind a shrub in Jackson Square. The night was damp and hot and through the sleep there were many voices and, much later, there was music from somewhere near the river. When all sounds had ended, I woke, turned my head, and knew I was being watched. Two rats were sitting a few feet from me. I urinated on my dress, crawled backwards to stand up, screamed as I ran up the steps of St. Louis Cathedral and pounded on the doors. I don't know when I stopped screaming or how I got to the railroad station, but I stood against the wall trying to tear off my dress and only knew I was doing it when two women stopped to stare at me. I began to have cramps in my stomach of a kind I had never known before. I went into the ladies' room and sat bent in a chair, whimpering with pain. After a while the cramps stopped, but I had an intimation, when I looked into the mirror, of something happening to me: my face was blotched, and there seemed to be circles and twirls I had never seen before, the straight blonde hair was damp with sweat, and a paste of green from the shrub had made lines on my jaw. I had gotten older.

Sometime during that early morning I half washed my dress, threw away my pants, put cold water on my hair. Later in the morning a cleaning woman appeared, and after a while began to ask questions that frightened me. When she put down her mop and went out of the room, I ran out of the station. I walked, I guess, for many hours, but when I saw a man on Canal Street who worked in Hannah's office, I realized that the sections of New Orleans that were known to me were dangerous for me.

Years before, when I was a small child, Sophronia and I would go to pick up, or try on, pretty embroidered dresses that were made for me by a colored dressmaker called Bibettera. A block up from Bibettera's there had been a large ruin of a house with a sign, ROOMS—CLEAN—CHEAP, and cheerful people seemed always to be moving in and out of the house. The door of the house was painted a bright pink. I liked that and would discuss with Sophronia why we didn't live in a house with a pink door.

Bibettera was long since dead, so I knew I was safe in this Negro neighborhood. I went up and down the block several times, praying that things would work and I could take my cramps to bed. I knocked on the pink door. It was answered immediately by a small young man.

I said, "Hello." He said nothing.

I said, "I would like to rent a room, please."

He closed the door but I waited, thinking he had gone to get the lady of the house. After a long time, a middle-aged woman put her head out of a second-floor window and said, "What you at?"

I said, "I would like to rent a room, please. My mama is a widow and has gone to work across the river. She gave me money and said to come here until she called for me."

"Who your mama?"

"Er. My mama."

"What you at? Speak out."

"I told you. I have money . . ." But as I tried to open my purse, the voice grew angry.

"This is a nigger house. Get you off. *Vite.*"

I said, in a whisper, "I know. I'm part nigger."

The small young man opened the front door. He was laughing. "You part mischief. Get the hell out of here."

I said, "Please"—and then, "I'm related to Sophronia Mason. She told me to come. Ask her."

Sophronia and her family were respected figures in New Orleans Negro circles, and because I had some vague memory of her stately bow to somebody as she passed this house, I believed they knew her. If they told her about me I would be in trouble, but phones were not usual then in poor neighborhoods, and I had no other place to go.

The woman opened the door. Slowly I went into the hall.

I said, "I won't stay long. I have four dollars and Sophronia will give more if . . ."

The woman pointed up the stairs. She opened the door of a small room. "Washbasin place down the hall. Toilet place behind the kitchen. Two-fifty and no fuss, no bother."

I said, "Yes ma'am, yes ma'am," but as she started to close the door, the young man appeared.

"Where your bag?"

"Bag?"

"Nobody put up here without no bag."

"Oh. You mean the bag with my clothes? It's at the station. I'll go and get it later . . ." I stopped because I knew I was about to say I'm sick, I'm in pain, I'm frightened.

He said, "I say you lie. I say you trouble. I say you get out."

I said, "And I say you shut up."

Years later, I was to understand why the command worked, and to be sorry that it did, but that day I was very happy when he turned and closed the door. I was asleep within minutes.

Toward evening, I went down the stairs, saw nobody, walked a few blocks and bought myself an oyster loaf. But the first bite made me feel sick, so I took my loaf back to the house. This time, as I climbed the steps, there were three women in the parlor, and they stopped talking when they saw me. I went back to sleep immediately, dizzy and nauseated.

I woke to a high, hot sun and my father standing at the foot of the bed staring at the oyster loaf.

He said, "Get up now and get dressed."

I was crying as I said, "Thank you, Papa, but I can't."

From the hall, Sophronia said, "Get along up now. *Vite.* The morning is late."

My father left the room. I dressed and came into the hall carrying my oyster loaf. Sophronia was standing at the head of the stairs. She pointed out, meaning my father was on the street.

I said, "He humiliated me. He did. I won't . . ."

She said, "Get you going or I will never see you whenever again."

I ran past her to the street. I stood with my father until Sophronia joined us, and then we walked slowly, without speaking, to the streetcar line. Sophronia bowed to us, but she refused my father's hand when he attempted to help her into the car. I ran to the car meaning to ask her to take me with her, but the car moved and she raised her hand as if to stop me. My father and I walked again for a long time.

He pointed to a trash can sitting in front of a house. "Please put that oyster loaf in the can."

At Vanalli's restaurant, he took my arm. "Hungry?"

I said, "No, thank you, Papa."

But we went through the door. It was, in those days, a New Orleans custom to have an early black coffee, go to the office, and after a few hours have a large breakfast at a restaurant. Vanalli's was crowded, the headwaiter was so sorry, but after my father took him aside, a very small table was put up for us—too small for my large father, who was accommodating himself to it in a manner most unlike him.

He said, "Jack, my rumpled daughter would like cold crayfish, a nice piece of pompano, a separate bowl of

Béarnaise sauce, don't ask me why, French fried potatoes . . ."

I said, "Thank you, Papa, but I am not hungry. I don't want to be here."

My father waved the waiter away and we sat in silence until the crayfish came. My hand reached out instinctively and then drew back.

My father said, "Your mother and I have had an awful time."

I said, "I'm sorry about that. But I don't want to go home, Papa."

He said, angrily, "Yes, you do. But you want me to apologize first. I do apologize but you should not have made me say it."

After a while I mumbled, "God forgive me, Papa forgive me, Mama forgive me, Sophronia, Jenny, Hannah . . ."

"Eat your crayfish."

I ate everything he had ordered and then a small steak. I suppose I had been mumbling throughout my breakfast.

My father said, "You're talking to yourself. I can't hear you. What are you saying?"

"God forgive me, Papa forgive me, Mama forgive me, Sophronia, Jenny . . ."

My father said, "Where do we start your training as the first Jewish nun on Prytania Street?"

When I finished laughing, I liked him again. I said, "Papa, I'll tell you a secret. I've had very bad cramps and I am beginning to bleed. I'm changing life."

He stared at me for a while. Then he said, "Well, it's not the way it's usually described, but it's accurate, I guess. Let's go home now to your mother."

We were never, as long as my mother and father lived, to mention that time again. But it was of great importance to them and I've thought about it all my life. From that day on I knew my power over my parents. That was not to be too important: I was ashamed of it and did not abuse it too much. But I found out something more useful and more dangerous: if you are willing to take the punishment, you are halfway through the battle. That the issue may be trivial, the battle ugly, is another point.

The First Night Was Cold

The first night was cold —
   damn cold . . .
I feel really old for 15,
   there just isn't any place to go.
Mama, I miss you —
   and I just spent my last dollar for cigarettes.

Pearl Nestor
United States, 1970s

Finding Courage

I Am Growing World

There are things I'm not frightened
To try. . . .
Let me tumble and spring, let me go
Let me be. Wait and see. . . .
I am growing, world
Water me with the wisdom of
Your tears.

Cherie Millard
United States, 1976

"In the Woods"

Sarah Brown
Massachusetts, 1970

In the summer of her fifteenth year, Sarah Brown, who often read and dreamed about survival in the woods, decided to see if she could live off the land. Taking only essentials and her dog, Nick, Sarah spent five days in an uninhabited wooded area in Massachusetts and recorded her experiences in her journal.

Monday, August 10, 1970

I am in the woods!

It's impossible for me to explain how much those words mean, and how much lies behind them. It's been a long road that's led me here—but I *am* here, and I'm going to make it!

I wasn't sure this morning that I'd be O.K., though. Yesterday afternoon, I took a last preliminary walk around, but at 8:30 this morning, it was as though I'd never seen any of this—everything seemed totally unfamiliar. It was a scary feeling!

But my camp is set up, lunch is eaten, and supper is all ready to be cooked. Already I feel sure about myself in a way I never have before! All that I have to rely on this week is myself—success or failure is dependent only on my own capabilities. I've never been in a position like this before—and that's a big part of why I'm here.

I've been raised in a comfortable, suburban setting, with white, middle-class values, and I disagree partially or totally with many of those values. But I see no sense or solution in rebelling through fads and unthinking hostility. This seems especially meaningless when you have no alternatives to those values you are protesting. I have some idea of just what it is that makes me Sarah Brown instead of someone else, and I have some idea of what Sarah Brown can do—but I need to know better before I can assert myself as an individual. These woods are my path to that knowledge of myself.

So—I've got my mosquito netting hung, my sleeping bag unrolled, a fire ring built, canteens filled—everything's neat and convenient. I'm on top of a small slope that ends in a swamp. There are several large, prominent rocks around. The trees are young and scattered. It's a pretty spot.

Setting up took such a short time that, since I was feeling ambitious, I decided to go fishing. So Nick and I walked to Weston Pond. We went by a country road and a highway and the distance was only about two miles. The worst part was walking along the highway—the cars made me really nervous. But boy, did Nick get some looks!

I am probably the world's worst fisherman. But with the aid of a grub out of a log, and a *lot* of luck, I finally pulled in a sunfish. I did a miserable job of cleaning it, and then Nick and I walked back.

Tuesday, August 11, 1970

There were no stars last night (I know because I was awake most of it!) and the sky is very gray this morning. I'm afraid it's going to rain, and I'm scared—but that's not going to stop me. I will "let it be a challenge"!

I'd better get going.

I've won! It's raining hard—and I'm warm and dry—and proud.

I was really panicked this morning, but I explored around for shelter and found a beautiful place. I'm about 25 yards away from where I was before. There's a boulder set into the side of the hill so that one side of it is buried. The boulder has split in half, forming a crack between the halves that's about eight feet long, five feet deep and three and one-half feet wide. My house.

I placed several long sticks across the top of the crack and draped my poncho and groundcloth across the boulder halves. The sides held down by stones, it makes a very secure shelter. The sleeping bag is spread on the floor, my pack is leaning against a wall, and Nick is lying at the opening. Everything is dry and comfortable and I'm really pretty proud of myself.

Oh—I also made a fast trip to the field, and I have day-lily tubers, sheep sorrel, blueberries, apples and wintergreen, as well as water. What else could I possibly want?

I've also got a lot of time to use—and a lot of thinking and writing to fill it up with.

It's amazing how much adjusting I've had to do just in a day and a half. I've changed my eating habits—I now eat whenever I find food, although I try to collect stuff for one "big meal" a day. I've changed my sight. I'm looking more carefully, and seeing more things than I ever have before. In fact, all my senses are sharpening and adjusting to quiet sounds and subtle smells and a much more sensual atmosphere than my usual one. It's a neat thing! . . .

Friday, August 14, 1970

I'm going to live in the woods someday—build a house away from roads and people. I belong with trees and animals much more than I do with apartments and big crowds.

I've discovered and learned so much that I can't put into words! I have a new reverence and feeling and *desire* for life—and I have found out what peace is. Those are pretty big things—and you can't explain or describe either of them.

"One of the Pack"

Jean Craighead George
Alaska, 1960s

The heroine of the novel Julie of the Wolves *is a thirteen-year-old Eskimo girl who runs away to escape an unhappy arranged marriage. Heading toward her pen pal in San Francisco, she finds herself lost without food in the barren wilderness of the tundra. Desperate, Miyax tries to live off the leavings of a pack of Arctic wolves. First she must be accepted by Amaroq, their leader.*

"I never dreamed I could get lost, Amaroq," she said, talking out loud to ease her fear.

"At home on Nunivak Island where I was born, the plants and birds pointed the way for wanderers. I thought they did so everywhere . . . and so, great black Amaroq, I'm without a compass."

It had been a frightening moment when two days ago she realized that the tundra was an ocean of grass on which she was circling around and around. Now as that fear overcame her again she closed her eyes. When she opened them her heart skipped excitedly. Amaroq was looking at her!

"Ee-lie," she called and scrambled to her feet. The wolf arched his neck and narrowed his eyes. He pressed his ears forward. She waved. He drew back his lips and showed his teeth. Frightened by what seemed a snarl, she lay down again. When she was flat on her stomach, Amaroq flattened his ears and wagged his tail once. Then he tossed his head and looked away.

Discouraged, she wriggled backward down the frost heave and arrived at her camp feet first. The heave was between herself and the wolf pack and so she relaxed, stood up, and took stock of her home. It was a simple affair, for she had not been able to carry much when she

331

ran away; she took just those things she would need for the journey—a backpack, food for a week or so, needles to mend clothes, matches, her sleeping skin, and ground cloth to go under it, two knives, and a pot.

She surveyed her camp. It was nice. Upon discovering the wolves, she had settled down to live near them in the hope of sharing their food, until the sun set and the stars came out to guide her. She had built a house of sod, like the summer homes of the old Eskimos. Each brick had been cut with her *ulo*, the half-moon-shaped woman's knife, so versatile it can trim a baby's hair, slice a tough bear, or chip an iceberg.

A dull pain seized her stomach. She pulled blades of grass from their sheaths and ate the sweet ends. They were not very satisfying, so she picked a handful of caribou moss, a lichen. If the deer could survive in winter on this food, why not she? She munched, decided the plant might taste better if cooked, and went to the pond for water.

As she dipped her pot in, she thought about Amaroq. Why had he bared his teeth at her? Because she was young and he knew she couldn't hurt him? No, she said to herself, it was because he was speaking to her! He had told her to lie down. She had even understood and obeyed him. He had talked to her not with his voice, but with his ears, eyes, and lips; and he had even commended her with a wag of his tail.

She dropped her pot, scrambled up the frost heave and stretched out on her stomach.

"Amaroq," she called softly. "I understand what you said. Can you understand me? I'm hungry—very, very hungry. Please bring me some meat."

The great wolf did not look her way and she began to doubt her reasoning. After all, flattened ears and a tail-wag were scarcely a conversation. She dropped her forehead against the lichens and rethought what had gone between them.

"Then why did I lie down?" she asked, lifting her head and looking at Amaroq. "Why did I?" she called to the yawning wolves. Not one turned her way.

Amaroq got to his feet, and as he slowly arose he

seemed to fill the sky and blot out the sun. He was enormous. He could swallow her without even chewing.

"But he won't," she reminded herself. "Wolves do not eat people. That's *gussak* talk. Kapugen said wolves are gentle brothers." . . .

Amaroq wailed again, stretching his neck until his head was high above the others. They gazed at him affectionately and it was plain to see that he was their great spirit, a royal leader who held his group together with love and wisdom.

Any fear Miyax had of the wolves was dispelled by their affection for each other. They were friendly animals and so devoted to Amaroq that she needed only to be accepted by him to be accepted by all. She even knew how to achieve this—bite him under the chin. But how was she going to do that? . . .

"*Ee-lie*, okay," she said. "I'll learn to roughhouse. Maybe then you'll accept me and feed me." She pranced, jumped, and whimpered; she growled, snarled, and rolled. But nobody came to roughhouse.

Sliding back to her camp, she heard the grass swish and looked up to see Amaroq and his hunters sweep around her frost heave and stop about five feet away. She could smell the sweet scent of their fur.

The hairs on her neck rose and her eyes widened. Amaroq's ears went forward aggressively and she remembered that wide eyes meant fear to him. It was not good to show him she was afraid. Animals attacked the fearful. She tried to narrow them, but remembered that was not right either. Narrowed eyes were mean. In desperation she recalled that Kapu had moved forward when challenged. She pranced right up to Amaroq. Her heart beat furiously as she grunt-whined the sound of the puppy begging adoringly for attention. Then she got down on her belly and gazed at him with fondness.

The great wolf backed up and avoided her eyes. She had said something wrong! Perhaps even offended him. Some slight gesture that meant nothing to her had apparently meant something to the wolf. His ears shot forward angrily and it seemed all was lost. She wanted to get up and run, but she gathered her courage and pranced closer to him. Swiftly she patted him under the chin.

The signal went off. It sped through his body and triggered emotions of love. Amaroq's ears flattened and his tail wagged in friendship. He could not react in any other way to the chin pat, for the roots of this signal lay deep in wolf history. It was inherited from generations and generations of leaders before him. As his eyes softened, the sweet odor of ambrosia arose from the gland on the top of his tail and she was drenched in wolf scent. Miyax was one of the pack.

"Turning Out"

Harriet Hanson Robinson
Lowell, Massachusetts, 1836

Loom and Spindle is a personal reminiscence about the early days of the Lowell textile mills. When Harriet was only eleven she took part in a strike which was organized primarily through the Factory Girls' Association. The strike was defeated when the workers ran out of money and the leaders were fired and even evicted from their boardinghouses.

One of the first strikes of cotton-factory operatives that ever took place in this country was that in Lowell, in October, 1836. When it was announced that the wages were to be cut down, great indignation was felt and it was decided to strike, *en masse*. This was done. The mills were shut down, and the girls went in procession from their several corporations to the "grove" on Chapel Hill, and listened to "incendiary" speeches from early labor reformers.

One of the girls stood on a pump, and gave vent to the feelings of her companions in a neat speech, declaring that it was their duty to resist all attempts at cutting down the wages. This was the first time a woman had spoken in public in Lowell, and the event caused surprise and consternation among her audience.

Cutting down the wages was not their only grievance, nor the only cause of this strike. Hitherto the corporations had paid twenty-five cents a week towards the board of each operative, and now it was their purpose to have the girls pay the sum; and this, in addition to the cut in wages, would make a difference of at least one dollar a week. It was estimated that as many as twelve or fifteen hundred girls turned out, and walked in procession through the streets. They had neither flags nor music, but sang songs, a favorite (but rather inappropriate) one being a parody on "I won't be a nun."

> "Oh! isn't it a pity, such a pretty girl as I—
> Should be sent to the factory to pine away and die?
> Oh! I cannot be a slave,
> I will not be a slave,
> For I'm so fond of liberty
> That I cannot be a slave."

My own recollection of this first strike (or "turn out" as it was called) is very vivid. I worked in a lower room, where I had heard the proposed strike fully, if not vehemently, discussed; I had been an ardent listener to what was said against this attempt at "oppression" on the part of the corporation, and naturally I took sides with the strikers. When the day came on which the girls were to turn out, those in the upper rooms started first, and so many of them left that our mill was at once shut down. Then, when the girls in my room stood irresolute, uncertain what to do, asking each other, "Would you?" or "Shall we turn out?" and not one of them having the courage to lead off, I, who began to think they would not go out, after all their talk, became impatient, and started on ahead, saying, with childish bravado, "I don't care what you do, *I* am going to turn out, whether any one else does or not;" and I marched out, and was followed by the others.

As I looked back at the long line that followed me, I was more proud than I have ever been since at any success I may have achieved, and more proud than I shall ever be again until my own beloved State gives to its women citizens the right of suffrage.

The agent of the corporation where I then worked took some small revenges on the supposed ringleaders; on the principle of sending the weaker to the wall, my mother was turned away from her boardinghouse, that functionary saying, "Mrs. Hanson, you could not prevent the older girls from turning out, but your daughter is a child, and *her* you could control."

"Like Joan of Arc"

Nellie L. McClung
Manitoba, 1880s

In the late 19th century, as Canadians pushed into new wilderness areas, pioneer women often found that the ideal of the Victorian "lady" contrasted sharply with the realities of the rough life women had to lead. Nellie McClung, who was to become an active fighter for women's rights, in 1880 moved with her family of seven to the Northwest country in Manitoba. This excerpt from her autobiography shows her at twelve coming of age in the man's world of the frontier.

After the Christmas dinner of turkey and plum pudding, the men sat and talked of the trouble Louis Riel was causing. He had come back from Montana, where he had been teaching school and was now in Saskatchewan, stirring up the half-breeds and Indians and inciting them to make raids on the white settlers.

"Why don't they arrest him now, and get him safely in jail before someone is killed?" Mother was greatly disturbed over the situation. "I can't sleep," she said, "thinking of the poor women there, frightened to go to sleep at night. They say he has given guns to the Indians and there will be another massacre like there was in Minnesota."

Frank Burnett was indignant that the Government had not sent an armed force, just as soon as the trouble began.

"Uniforms would settle the trouble," he said, "the red coats and the flash of steel, a few guns fired and the half-breeds and Indians would know there was law in the country. Riel should be hanged anyway for the murder of Thos. Scott."

I wanted to talk. Mr. Schultz had told us about it in school. The half-breeds and Indians had a grievance, a

337

real one. The settlers were crowding in on them, their land was being surveyed over again, and divided into squares like ours. They had long narrow lots, as they had along the Red and Assiniboine, so they could live side by side, and now a new arrangement of land was being made and they were afraid their land was going to be taken from them. When they sent letters to Ottawa, they got no replies.

I knew how they felt. I had often asked for explanations and got the prescribed 19th century dusty answer, "because I say so—that's all the reason you need." How I hated it! And how unfair I felt it to be! The Government officials were treating the Indians the same way.

I knew the government was to blame but I would not be allowed to say it, and if I did get it said, I might get Mr. Schultz into trouble. Mother would feel he was undermining our respect for authority.

But much to my delight, Hannah came forward and defended the half-breeds. Hannah was always listened to when she spoke. She had what I lacked, a quiet and dignified way of expression.

"The country belonged to the Indians and half-breeds," she said in her even voice. "We must not forget that. I know they have made little use of it and must yield it to white settlers, in time, but there's enough territory for everyone if it is handled right, and they could be easily appeased and satisfied."

She told about the new survey, about the delay in getting the patents out for the land the half-breeds had proved-up on, about the slaughter of the buffalo, the Indians' source of food, and clothing.

Hannah was fifteen then, with a fine presence, fair skin, a round face, and fine large greenish-blue eyes, and abundant bright brown hair, inclined to curl. She had been wiping dishes behind the stove and came out with a plate in one hand, and a flour-sack tea towel in the other. Her face was flushed and her eyes bright and to me she looked like Joan of Arc. I was very proud of her, but I knew there was a sudden tightening of the atmosphere. Even now, men do not like to be taught by women, but at that time for a girl of fifteen to presume to have an opinion, was against all tradition. However, Hannah had a prestige all her own.

She went on. "It is not the Catholic church, and it is not Louis Riel, who is causing the trouble—it is the stupidity of the Government at Ottawa, and if settlers are killed by the Indians theirs will be the guilt. A few words of explanation, a few concessions and peace could be restored."

"My God!" exclaimed Frank Burnett in real concern, "that's hot talk, Hannah, you've said enough to hang you in some countries. If you were in Russia, you would be shot for a Nihilist, my girl."

My mother was too much amazed to speak. If I had said half of what Hannah had, she would know what to do with me, but Hannah, quiet, dignified Hannah, the image of her own mother, Margaret Fullerton McCurdy, could not be sent upstairs in disgrace.

Hannah went on wiping the dishes with great composure. She had said what she wanted to say and now withdrew from the conversation. Her hearers had heard the truth, and they could take it or leave it. Responsibility had passed from her to them.

Mr. Burnett continued the argument. "I am afraid there is bad work going on at Northfield School," he said. "I gather that is where Hannah gets her ideas. This man Schultz is a German; he has no love for British institutions and is using his position as a teacher to undermine the children's respect for authority. We'll have to look into this. We'll have to call a meeting of the trustees."

My heart stood still. Had we involved our teacher in some trouble that might lead to his losing his job?

They all began to talk; and I could feel a hostile tide of opinion gathering and sweeping ahead of it all good sense and reason and it seemed to me I would have to speak, no matter what happened. Will would listen to me anyway. I went over and stood before him.

"Will," I said, "I want to talk, make them keep quiet."

"Nellie has something on her mind," Will called out in his good humored way. "It is not often this poor tongue-tied child wants to talk, and she should get her chance on Christmas day, of all times.''

Mother rose up to protest, but Will waved her back.

''Let the kid talk,'' he said, ''talk won't hurt anyone. It's the things we don't say that hurt us, I know.''

Then came the ordeal, when the silence fell on the room. I have faced audiences who were hostile since then and encountered unfriendly glances, but the antagonism here was more terrible, being directed, not as much against what I had to say, as against the fact that I dared to say anything.

I addressed Will, as people air their views in letters addressed to the Editor. ''The Government is like the Machine Company, Will,'' I said. ''The half-breeds are dissatisfied with the way they are treated, they are afraid they are going to be put off their farms, just as we were afraid when the tongue of the binder broke, and we saw we were going to lose our crop. The half-breeds have written letters, and sent people to see the Government and asked them to send out someone to straighten out their troubles just as you, Will, wrote letters to the Company and asked them to send an expert, who would put the binder in good shape. The Government won't answer the half-breeds, won't notice them, won't talk to them—and the only word they send them is a saucy word—'what we will send you will be an army; we'll put you in your place.' Just as the Machine Company wrote to us a saucy letter saying that it was our own fault if the binders broke, and they couldn't supply us with brains. It's the same spirit. We should understand how the half-breeds feel. That's all I want to say,'' and before anyone could say a word, I left the room, glad to get away.

Hannah came out soon after and we went upstairs and took counsel together. ''Don't worry,'' she said to me in her comforting way, ''Mr. Schultz is safely away at Pelican Lake and won't be back for two weeks. Two weeks is quite a long time—they'll cool off before that, father said there was a lot of truth in what we said, but they talked him down.''

''What did Will say?'' I asked anxiously.

''Oh, Will just laughed about us and said we had put

the case well, but mother thinks we are in the same class as Guy Fawkes who put the stick of dynamite under the House of Parliament, and she says she will go to the trustees herself, if no one else will."

Night Crossing

In the midst of the night, a sampan glides toward us.
Dark bamboos on the bank, swift current . . .
An oar shatters the star-studded firmament.
A bird wanders in the dark and disappears.
Silently the sampan glides between the palms
Whose crests are swept by a searchlight from the out-
  post.

Loaded rifles, all hands on alert,
We await the moment to dart across the river.

Tucking her black trousers up to her thigh
The boat-girl, smelling of grass and flowers, helps us
Unload our motley bundles.
In the dark, we imagine her red cheeks;
Holding her hand
We breathe her breath, sense her brisk gestures.

Loudly, the water clatters against the sampan.
Heavily loaded, it rolls and leaves the bank so slowly.
"Comrade" asks a voice, "can I help you?"
Shaking her head, she swings the bow.
In the midst of enemy outposts she lives
Keeping for herself the sorrow and joys of her heart.
The sampan emerges from the dark
Challenging the current, the onrushing wave,
Again the oar shatters the sky and the stars.
The other bank is silent, a palm greets us.
Standing still, our boat-girl is watching the guardpost
at the hamlet's entrance.
Her arms still swinging the oar.
Her slender silhouette looms over the river.
One more effort, and we will reach the bank;
A feeling of tender joy flushes our bodies.

A long burst has been fired from the outpost,
Red and white tracers thunder everywhere.

"Be quiet," she says, "don't be afraid,"
And the sampan swiftly
Darts toward the enemy, defying its bullets.
Silhouetted in the sky, what a dashing figure;
"Lie down," she whispers, "let me maneuver,
Don't be worried!" The boat moves ahead;
Emotion packs the night.
Our hearts are pinching; anger fills our eyes.
Bullets rain in the river.
In our hands, our rifles burn with anger.

In safe haven, the sampan is tied to a tree.
Slowly, we shake the girl's hand.
"Thank you," we say . . . A smile lights
her face; "I belong to the youth corps,
And I only do my duty," she answers.
We press our march across the village

Still thinking, still hearing
The light tread of her walk.

Valiant image, valiant girl
In future battles come with us.

Giang Nam
North Vietnam, 1960s

"The One Who Asks"

Doria Ramirez, as told to Sandra Weiner
California, 1969

I am Doria Ramirez and I am eighteen years old. I went to school when I was ten years and got out when I was thirteen because I had to help my parents. We used to get up at 3:30 in the morning to pick potatoes and I didn't like it. Always I didn't like it. It was very cold. Another reason I had to leave—I didn't have any shoes with me and I didn't have any sweater and it was in the winter time.

I knew we didn't have any money so I couldn't say, "Poppa I need shoes for my feet." But when I saw all the other children with shoes I knew that there had to be a way to change that life. The way I was feeling I didn't want my sisters to feel the same thing. It was then I started thinking that this was not a life for the migrant worker or any worker. Without shoes and warm clothes all these Mexican children could not go to school. My father did not feel it this way but when I used to see my younger brothers working so hard and feeling so tired at age thirteen years, I wanted to see them in a different position in their life. We are nine in our family and we were being paid piece rate. With a big family you can work a long day and think you are making some money. But in the winter time when there is no work it doesn't help to have such a large family. My father would never go to the Welfare. He always told us that he didn't like to go to the Welfare because you had to let the Governor's office know what size shoe he was wearing and what size underwear—and he didn't like it. It was too private. My mother tried to sew our clothes but when you don't have any money you have the time, but you can't buy the material to sew.

The growers give us the jobs because we are a large

344

family. I am not afraid to ask the growers for more money because I used to see families just starving. My father asked, "Why do you always have to argue with the grower?" But always in a family there has to be one member that asks. There has to be one that talks too much. And I was the one. My father would say, "Don't ask for more or they will not let us work and take all the money away." To him it always has to be the way they gave us. I said, "No, that's not enough, I don't want to live that way." He would answer, "My father lived that way and we can live the same way."

We do whatever each farm needs, either thinning, or tying, or hoeing, or picking. We have picked almost every fruit and vegetable growing, but the hardest job that I know, as a woman, is sugarbeets. Even the men say it is hard. After thinning you leave each plant five inches apart from the other. That's very hard because always you have to be bent over on your knees with a small hoe, maybe twelve hours and this makes you sick with the kidneys or back. You must thin it while it is still a young plant. If you try sitting it doesn't work and you do not get the work done.

There was this man, he was a labor contractor for the ranchers, and he hired about two hundred people and I made about thirty-three or thirty-two rows that day. You have to be a fast person. I had gone with shoes and socks into the field but I came out without the shoes or socks because the blisters on my feet they were paining me. So I went back to the car to lie down because I couldn't stand or move. I was already half with fever from tiredness. The labor contractor didn't want to pay my father and he was saying, "Well, your daughter has to come out and get the money, she knows how to sign her name." And even though I was feeling so sick I was happy because I thought we were going to have so much money for the family. And all we got was seven dollars for nine people working twelve hours.

I always had to work to help my parents because I love my parents. We just stick together. This is why it's good to have a big family because together we make our own home. A small home but it's my home and I don't need any other home because I have my family. We have two rooms, a kitchen and another room, and we sleep like hot dogs.

I get up when my mother starts preparing the lunches for the day in the field. She bakes bread and makes tacos and tortillas. At night when we return home she washes the clothes and hangs up just pants on the clothes wire, and the neighbors say, "You have only boys," and my mother said, "No, we are six girls and three boys." In the evenings parents are tired and do not talk very much.

Another time I saw my father crying. That day had been a bad day for us. We had arrived in the field at 4:30 in the morning and they had to put big lights on the tractors so we could see how to pick the potatoes. And we picked all day until 5 o'clock in the evening. There were six of us and we earned only twelve dollars. And that was when my father wanted to cry. It was then I started to think again that I must make a change. My father, he said, "Now I understand you and why you are so angry at the growers."

Once I got really mad when I was working with one of the growers and we were organizing and he fired all the people that were organizing or interested in a union. When we walked from the fields everybody walked with us. But the next day the farmer found other people to work for him and we knew it would take a long time before all the migrant workers understood about the union. It took my father a long time. Now I spend a lot of time helping to organize farm workers and we hope the dream of a union will come true. It's just like Martin Luther King when he said, "I have a dream too."

I am much happier now because I am learning so much. When I was in school I didn't learn anything. I had to rush from school to pick cotton and I would forget the English and arithmetic. I never learned to speak English but I learned English real good when I started walking on the picket lines asking people not to buy grapes in the stores that sold them. At the first boycott they wouldn't take me because I didn't speak the language. So I had to learn fast to speak English. Everybody helped me who knew how to speak it. I still don't know how to read or write but I will learn.

It is hard to believe now that I had lived the way we did for so long. I remember at home on Saturday we would all take baths and eat together and then my father would play the trumpet. My sister and my brother-in-law played the guitar and my little sister played the guitar and we would sing and dance. Even though our life is with so much work we love to have fun and have some happiness. You have to carry some happiness in your heart.

She Walked Alone

Elizabeth Eckford, as told to Daisy Bates
Little Rock, Arkansas, 1957

On September 4, 1957, by the order of the Supreme Court, Central High in Little Rock, Arkansas, was to be integrated. Fifteen-year-old Elizabeth Eckford was one of the nine black students chosen to enter the high school. There was a last-minute decision, however, to call off the entrance of the students because of increasing threats of mob violence. Governor Faubus had sent in the Arkansas National Guard with orders not to allow the blacks to enter the school. Since Elizabeth's family had no phone, she was not contacted. She arrived alone at school that day, unaware that she would have no protection.

That night I was so excited I couldn't sleep. The next morning I was about the first one up. While I was pressing my black and white dress—I had made it to wear on the first day of school—my little brother turned on the TV set. They started telling about a large crowd gathered at the school. The man on TV said he wondered if we were going to show up that morning. Mother called from the kitchen, where she was fixing breakfast, "Turn that TV off!" She was so upset and worried. I wanted to comfort her, so I said, "Mother, don't worry."

Dad was walking back and forth, from room to room, with a sad expression. He was chewing on his pipe and he had a cigar in his hand, but he didn't light either one. It would have been funny, only he was so nervous.

Before I left home Mother called us into the living-room. She said we should have a word of prayer. Then I caught the bus and got off a block from the school. I saw a large crowd of people standing across the street from the soldiers guarding Central. As I walked on, the crowd suddenly got very quiet. Superintendent Blossom had told us to enter by the front door. I looked at all the people and thought, "Maybe I will be safer if I walk down the block to the front entrance behind the guards."

At the corner I tried to pass through the long line of guards around the school so as to enter the grounds behind them. One of the guards pointed across the street. So I pointed in the same direction and asked whether he meant for me to cross the street and walk down. He nodded "yes." So, I walked across the street conscious of the crowd that stood there, but they moved away from me.

For a moment all I could hear was the shuffling of their feet. Then someone shouted, "Here she comes, get ready!" I moved away from the crowd on the sidewalk and into the street. If the mob came at me I could then cross back over so the guards could protect me.

The crowd moved in closer and then began to follow me, calling me names. I still wasn't afraid. Just a little bit nervous. Then my knees started to shake all of a sudden and I wondered whether I could make it to the center entrance a block away. It was the longest block I ever walked in my whole life.

Even so, I still wasn't too scared because all the time I kept thinking that the guards would protect me.

When I got right in front of the school, I went up to a guard again. But this time he just looked straight ahead and didn't move to let me pass him. I didn't know what to do. Then I looked and saw that the path leading to the front entrance was a little further ahead. So I walked until I was right in front of the path at the front door.

I stood looking at the school—it looked so big! Just then the guards let some white students go through.

The crowd was quiet. I guess they were waiting to see what was going to happen. When I was able to steady my knees, I walked up to the guard who had let the white students in. He too didn't move. When I tried to squeeze past him, he raised his bayonet and then the other guards closed in and they raised their bayonets.

They glared at me with a mean look and I was very frightened and didn't know what to do. I turned around and the crowd came toward me.

They moved closer and closer. Somebody started yelling, "Lynch her! Lynch her!"

I tried to see a friendly face somewhere in the mob—someone who maybe would help. I looked into the face of an old woman and it seemed a kind face, but when I looked at her again, she spat on me.

They came closer, shouting, "No nigger bitch is going to get in our school. Get out of here!"

I turned back to the guards but their faces told me I wouldn't get help from them. Then I looked down the block and saw a bench at the bus stop. I thought, "If I can only get there I will be safe." I don't know why the bench seemed a safe place to me, but I started walking toward it. I tried to close my mind to what they were shouting, and kept saying to myself, "If I can make it to the bench I will be safe."

When I finally got there, I don't think I could have gone another step. I sat down and the mob crowded up and began shouting all over again. Someone hollered, "Drag her over to this tree! Let's take care of the nigger." Just then a white man sat down beside me, put his arm around me and patted my shoulder. He raised my chin and said, "Don't let them see you cry."

Then, a white lady—she was very nice—she came over to me on the bench. She spoke to me but I don't remember now what she said. She put me on the bus and sat next to me. She asked me my name and tried to talk to me but I don't think I answered. I can't remember much about the bus ride, but the next thing I remember I was standing in front of the School for the Blind, where Mother works.

I thought, "Maybe she isn't here. But she has to be here!" So I ran upstairs, and I think some teachers tried to talk to me, but I kept running until I reached Mother's classroom.

Mother was standing at the window with her head bowed, but she must have sensed I was there because she turned around. She looked as if she had been crying, and I wanted to tell her I was all right. But I couldn't speak. She put her arms around me and I cried.

Acknowledgments

We would like to thank the following authors and publishers for permission to reprint these selections:

"I Am on My Way Running, Song for a Young Girl's Puberty Ceremony," Anonymous, translated by Frances Densmore. From *Papago Music*, Bureau of American Ethnology, Bulletin No. 90, Washington, D.C. 1929.

CHAPTER ONE: *The Circle Dance: Onset of Puberty*

Epigraph, "Coming of Age Dance," Anonymous. From *The Inland Whale*, by Theodora Kroeber. Copyright © 1959 by Indiana University Press. Reprinted by permission of Indiana University Press.

"Maiden Songs," Maria Chona. From *Papago Woman*, by Ruth M. Underhill. Copyright © 1979 by Holt, Rinehart and Winston. Reprinted by permission of Holt, Rinehart and Winston, CBS College Publishing.

"Poor Little Maiden," Anonymous. From *Singing for Power: The Song Magic of the Papago Indians of Southern Arizona*, by Ruth Underhill. Copyright © 1938 by Regents of the University of California. Reprinted by permission of University of California Press.

"Dance Mad," Anonymous. From *The Inland Whale*, by Theodora Kroeber. Copyright © 1959 by Indiana University Press. Reprinted by permission of Indiana University Press.

"Thou Art a Girl No More," Anonymous. From *The Way We Lived: California Indian Reminiscences, Stories, and Songs*, edited by Malcolm Margolin. Heydey Books, Berkeley, California. Copyright © 1981. Reprinted by permission of Malcolm Margolin.

"The Fattening," Anonymous. From "The Money-Doubler's Widow," *Old Wives' Tales: Life-Stories from*

bly Schott. Reprinted by permission of Penelope Scambly Schott.

CHAPTER TWO: *The Spring of Pleasure: Sexuality*

Epigraph, "When Maidens Are Young," Aphra Behn. From *Alone Amid All This Noise*, by Ann Reit. Four Winds Press, N.Y., 1976.

"Sweet Secret." From *The Diary of a Young Girl*, by Anne Frank. Copyright © 1952 by Otto H. Frank. Reprinted by permission of Doubleday & Company, Inc.

"The Secret Phrase," by Jessamyn West. From *Cress Delahanty*. Copyright © 1953 by Jessamyn West. Reprinted by permission of Harcourt Brace Jovanovich, Inc.

"Francina," by Marta Brunet, translated by Marilyn Bauman. From *Spanish-American Literature in Translation*, Vol. II (A Selection of Poetry, Fiction and Drama since 1888), edited by Willis Knapp Jones. Copyright © 1963 by Frederick Ungar Publishing Co., Inc. Reprinted by permission of Frederick Ungar Publishing Co., Inc.

"The Kiss." From *The Lying Days*, by Nadine Gordimer. Copyright © 1953 by Nadine Gordimer, renewed 1979. Reprinted by permission of Russell & Volkening, Inc.

"A Rush to Motherhood," by Lucille Lang Day. Copyright © 1980 by Lucille Lang Day. Originally appeared in *California Living Magazine, San Francisco Sunday Examiner and Chronicle*. Reprinted by permission of Lucille Lang Day.

"Research." From *The Prime of Miss Jean Brodie*, by Muriel Spark (J.B. Lippincott, Publishers). Copyright © 1961 by Muriel Spark. Reprinted by permission of Harper & Row, Publishers, Inc.

"How Beautiful!" From *My Home, My Prison*, by Raymonda Tawil. Copyright © 1979 by Raymonda Hawa Tawil, Peretz Kidron and Adam Publishers. Reprinted by permission of Holt, Rinehart and Winston, Publishers.

"I Dial . . . I Dial," by Debbie Hoeltzell. From *Male and Female Under 18: Frank Comments from Young People About Their Sex Roles*, edited by Nancy Larrick and Eve Merriam. Avon Books. Copyright © 1973 by Nancy Larrick and Eve Merriam. Reprinted by permission of Nancy Larrick.

"The World Her Oyster." From *Rumors of Peace*, by Ella Leffland. Copyright © 1979 by Ella Leffland. Reprinted by permission of Harper & Row, Publishers, Inc.

"The Price of a Buffalo," Anonymous. From *Women of Vietnam*, by Arlene Eisen Bergman. Copyright © 1974 by Arlene Eisen Bergman, People's Press, San Francisco.

"Ballad," Anonymous, translated by Willis Barnstone. From *A Book of Women Poets from Antiquity to Now*, edited by Aliki Barnstone and Willis Barnstone. Copyright © 1980 by Schocken Books Inc. Reprinted by permission of Schocken Books Inc.

"Sister," by Mririda N'Ait Attik, translated by Daniel Halpern and Paula Paley. Copyright © 1974 by Daniel Halpern and Paula Paley. Reprinted by permission of Unicorn Press, Inc., P.O. Box 3307, Greensboro, NC 27402.

"The Lesson." From *A Tree Grows in Brooklyn*, by Betty Smith. Copyright 1942 by Betty Smith. Reprinted by permission of Harper & Row, Publishers, Inc.

"Rejection of a Lover," Anonymous, translated by Ulli Beier. From *Luo Zaho, Indonesian Poetry*, collected by W. A. Braawem. Copyright © 1967 Papua Pocket Poets. Reprinted by permission of Unicorn Press, Inc., P.O. Box 33097, Greensboro, NC 27402.

"My Golden Horizon," by Nelly Ptaschkina. From *Diary of Nelly Ptaschkina*, translated by Pauline D. Chary, edited by M. Jacques Povolotsky. Copyright 1923 by Jonathan Cape Ltd. Reprinted by permission of Jonathan Cape Ltd.

"When I Grow Up, I Won't Marry," Nisa, !Kung Tribe, Kalahari Desert, Africa. Excerpted by permission of the publisher from *Nisa: The Life and Words of a !Kung Woman*,

CHAPTER THREE: *The Wish: Appearance*

uch. Copyright © 1979 by G.P. Putnam's Sons. Reprinted by permission of G.P. Putnam's Sons.

"The Elite European Hairdressing and Beauty Salon." From *A Mortal Flower*, by Han Suyin. Copyright © 1965 Han Suyin. Reprinted by permission of Jonathan Cape Ltd.

"Thin Fever." From *Solitaire*, by Aimee Liu. Copyright © 1979 by Aimee Liu. Reprinted by permission of Harper & Row, Publishers, Inc.

"The Complaint of a Beautiful Girl," by Nguyen Gia Thieu. From *We the Vietnamese: Voices from Vietnam*, edited by François Sully with the assistance of Marjorie Weiner Normand. Copyright © 1971 by Praeger Publishers, Inc. Reprinted by permission of Holt, Rinehart and Winston, Publishers.

"The Little Bouilloux Girl." From *My Mother's House* and *Sido*, by Colette, translated by Una Vicenzo Trowbridge and Enid McLeod. Copyright © 1953 by Farrar, Straus and Young (now Farrar, Straus & Giroux, Inc). Reprinted by permission of Farrar, Straus & Giroux, Inc.

"Why Am I So Ugly?" From *Clan of the Cave Bear* by Jean M. Auel. Copyright © 1980 by Jean M. Auel. Reprinted by permission of Crown Publishers, Inc.

"When I Was Growing Up," by Nellie Wong. From *This Bridge Called My Back: Writings by Radical Women of Color*, edited by Cherrie Moraga and Gloria Anzaldua. Copyright © 1981 by Persephone Press Inc. Reprinted by permission of Nellie Wong and Persephone Press Inc.

"The Disrupter of Seasons." From *The Bluest Eye* by Toni Morrison. Copyright © 1970 by Toni Morrison. Reprinted by permission of Holt, Rinehart and Winston.

"Ayii, Ayii, Ayii," Song. From *Songs of the Dream People*, edited by James Houston. Copyright © 1972 by James Houston. A Margaret K. McElderry book (New York: Atheneum, 1972). Reprinted by permission of Atheneum Publishers.

"All but Jade Snow." From *Fifth Chinese Daughter*, by Jade Snow Wong. Copyright 1950 by Jade Snow Wong.

First appeared in *Kamadhenu*, edited by G. S. Sharat Chandra. Reprinted by permission of G. S. Sharat Chandra.

"A Letter to Her Mother," Eristi-Aya, translated by Willis Barnstone. From *A Book of Women Poets from Antiquity to Now*, edited by Aliki Barnstone and Willis Barnstone. Copyright © 1980 by Schocken Books Inc. Reprinted by permission of Schocken Books Inc.

"Exact Opposites." From *The Diary of a Young Girl*, by Anne Frank. Copyright © 1952 by Otto H. Frank. Reprinted by permission of Doubleday & Company, Inc.

"A Dutiful Daughter." From *Memoirs of a Dutiful Daughter*, by Simone de Beauvoir, translated by James Kirkup. Copyright © 1958 by Librairie Gallimard. Translation copyright © 1959 by Harper & Row, Publishers, Inc. Reprinted by permission of Simone de Beauvoir.

"Trishanku," by Mannu Bhandari, translated by Ruth Vanita. From MANUSHI, January 1979. Akshar Prakashan Pvt. Ltd. 2/36 Ansari Road, Daryagunj, Delhi 110002 India. Reprinted by permission of Mannu Bhandari.

"We Dressed for the Dance Together." From *The Lying Days*, by Nadine Gordimer. Copyright © 1953 by Nadine Gordimer, renewed 1979. Reprinted by permission of Russell & Volkening, Inc.

"To Grind on the Same Stone." From *The Eighth Wife*, by Miriam Khamadi Were, African Secondary Readers Series, East African Publishing House, Kenya, 1972. Reprinted by permission of East African Publishing House.

"I'm Truly Your Child." From *Brown Girl, Brownstones*, by Paule Marshall. Copyright © 1959 by Paule Marshall. Reprinted by permission of The Feminist Press, Box 334, Old Westbury, NY 11568.

"A Woman's Character." From *Sister of the Road: The Autobiography of Box-Car Bertha*, as told to Dr. Ben Reitman, Harper & Row, Publishers, Inc., 1976.

"A Thorny Cactus." From *Across Time and Space, An Anthology of Literature Reflecting a Century of Change in Mod-*

CHAPTER FIVE: *The Great Adventure: Taking Risks*

Prentice-Hall, Inc., 1976. Reprinted by permission of Gisella Konopka.

"I Am Growing World," by Cherie Millard. From *Young Girls: A Portrait of Adolescence*, by Gisella Konopka. Prentice-Hall, Inc., 1976. Reprinted by permission of Gisella Konopka.

"In the Woods." From *Five Days of Living with the Land*, by Sarah Brown. Copyright © 1971 by Sarah Brown. Reprinted by permission of Addison-Wesley Publishing Company, Inc.

"One of the Pack." From *Julie of the Wolves*, by Jean Craighead George. Copyright © 1972 by Jean Craighead George. Reprinted by permission of Harper & Row, Publishers, Inc.

"Turning Out." From *Loom and Spindle*, by Harriet H. Robinson. Originally published by Thomas & Crowell, Chicago, 1898.

"Like Joan of Arc." From *Clearing in the West: My Own Story*, by Nellie McClung. Copyright 1936 by Fleming H. Revell Company. Reprinted by permission of Fleming H. Revell Company.

"Night Crossing," by Giang Nam. From *We the Vietnamese: Voices from Vietnam*, edited by François Sully with the assistance of Marjorie Weiner Normand. Copyright © 1971 by Praeger Publishers, Inc. Reprinted by permission of Holt, Rinehart and Winston, Publishers.

"The One Who Asks," by Doria Ramirez. From *Small Hands, Big Hands*, by Sandra Weiner. Copyright © 1970 by Sandra Weiner. Reprinted by permission of Random House, Inc.

"She Walked Alone," by Elizabeth Eckford. From *The Long Shadow of Little Rock*, by Daisy Bates. Copyright © 1962. Reprinted by permission of David-McKay Co., Inc.

NEW AVON ◉ DISCUS TITLES

FANTASISTS ON FANTASY
Robert H. Boyer and Kenneth J. Zahorski   86553-X/$3.95
This volume offers a glimpse into the world of eighteen
of the world's premier fantasy writers, with twenty-two
pieces—ranging from critical essays to personal letters—
in which the real experts in the field explore the theory,
the technique and the aesthetics of fantasy literature.

COUNTING THE EONS Isaac Asimov   67090-9/$3.95
From "the greatest explainer of the age" (Carl Sagan)
comes an "entertaining, witty and informative"
(*Library Journal*) collection of seventeen essays
covering the most fantastic phenomena of the universe
from robots to Einstein, black holes to anti-matter.

KRISHNAMURTI: The Years of Fulfillment
Mary Lutyens   68007-6/$4.95
This "extraordinary document" (*San Francisco Chronicle*),
is the second volume in the illuminating biography—
begun in KRISHNAMURTI: The Awakening Years—of one of
the most radiant spiritual personalities of all time.

FATAL FLOWERS: On Sin, Sex and Suicide in the Deep South
Rosemary Daniell   65946-8/$3.95
Here is a shockingly intimate, unsparing portrait
of women destroyed by a society drenched in sexual
obsession and Bible-belt repression. "One of those fine
female writers unique in her region (Eudora Welty,
Flannery O'Connor, Katherine Anne Porter, Alice Walker,
Caroline Gordon)."   *Time*

AV☉N PAPERBACKS